Essential Readings in Zen

ROY MELVYN

Copyright © 2000 Roy Melvyn

All rights reserved.

ISBN-13:978-1467944489
ISBN-10:1467944483

CONTENTS

FORWARD	7
THE TEACHINGS OF BODHIDHARMA	9
INTRODUCTION	10
OUTLINE OF PRACTICE	12
BLOODSTREAM SERMON	14
WAKE-UP SERMON	24
BREAKTHROUGH SERMON	32
THE ZEN TEACHING OF INSTANTANEOUS AWAKENING BY BAIZHANG HUAHAI	42
INTRODUCTION	43
A TREATISE ON ENTERING THE TAO OF SUDDEN ENLIGHTENMENT	44
HSIN HSIN MING	74
INTRODUCTION	75
TEXT	77
THE HEART SUTRA (PRAJNAPARAMITA HRDAYA)	81

THE HEART SUTRA (PRAJNAPARAMITA HRDAYA) — 81

INTRODUCTION — 82

TEXT — 85

DIAMOND SUTRA (VAJRACCEDIKA SUTRA) — 87

INTRODUCTION — 88

TEXT — 89

THE DHARMA OF MIND TRANSMISSION: HUANG-PO — 99

INTRODUCTION — 100

TEXT: INTRODUCTION — 103

The Preface of P'ei Hsiu — 104

THE CHUNG-LING RECORD — 106

THE WAN-LING RECORD — 123

THE PRECIOUS GARLAND RATNAVALI OF NAGARJUNA — 139

INTRODUCTION — 140

TEXT — 141

SELF-REALISATION OF NOBLE WISDOM (THE LANKAVATARA SUTRA) — 249

INTRODUCTION	**250**
CHAPTER I: DISCRIMINATION	**251**
CHAPTER II: FALSE-IMAGINATIONS AND KNOWLEDGE OF APPEARANCES	**256**
CHAPTER III: RIGHT KNOWLEDGE OR KNOWLEDGE OF RELATIONS	**265**
CHAPTER IV: PERFECT KNOWLEDGE OR KNOWLEDGE OF THE REAL	**270**
CHAPTER V: THE SYSTEM OF THE MIND	**274**
CHAPTER VI: THE TRANSCENDENCE OF INTELLIGENCE	**280**
CHAPTER VII: SELF REALISATION	**286**
CHAPTER VIII: ATTAINING SELF REALISATION	**292**
CHAPTER IX: THE FRUITS OF SELF REALISATION	**297**
CHAPTER X: DISCIPLESHIP - LINEAGE OF THE ARHATS	**302**
CHAPTER XI: THE STAGES OF BODHISATTVAHOOD	**306**
CHAPTER XII: TATHAGATAHOOD AND NOBLE WISDOM	**312**
CHAPTER XIII: NIRVANA	**319**

MASTER XUYUN'S ESSENTIALS OF CH'AN PRACTICE	324
INTRODUCTION	325
THE PREREQUISITES AND UNDERSTANDING NECESSARY TO BEGIN CH'AN PRACTISE	327
LECTURES ON THE METHODS OF PRACTISE IN THE CH'AN HALL	333
THE WRITINGS OF DOGEN ZENJI	347
INTRODUCTION	348
A GENERAL RECOMMENDED WAY OF SITTING MEDITATION	350
BENDOWA	353
GUIDELINES FOR STUDYING THE WAY	365

Forward

Over 2,500 years ago Shakyamuni sat in meditation under the Bodhi Tree at Bodhgaya, and on the morning of the eighth day experienced full enlightenment. This was the true beginning of Buddhism.

Sitting in meditation is known as zazen in the Zen School, with za 坐 meaning "sit" and zen 禅 meaning "meditation." The seated posture is one of stillness and relaxation, and expresses a tranquil mind and a settled body. In the practice of zazen, one maintains the body in a position free of tension and movement, and focuses the mind on a single object of attention. The state is one of union of body and mind deepened through the relaxation and regulation of the breath.

The zen of zazen is the Japanese pronunciation of the character 禅, pronounced chan in Chinese. Chan is an abbreviation of the word channa 禅那, which, in turn, is the Chinese transliteration of the Sanskrit word dhyana. Dhyana is interpreted in various ways, but in Chinese Buddhism it means meditative practice in general. Dhyana brings about a nondualistic state of consciousness through the deep harmonization of body, breath, and mind, a state of unification and profound stillness known as samadhi. Although profoundly still, samadhi is not a state of passivity, unconsciousness, or trance. The stillness of samadhi is vibrant and dynamic, arising from a mind that is completely clear, aware, and open. In this state of awareness the ordinary world is seen in a new light, in which the unexamined "common sense" view of a dualistic world is transcended and the underlying unity of all existence is clearly experienced. This perception of the world through the awakened consciousness gives rise to prajna, "enlightened wisdom." In Zen there is the expression joe enmyo 定慧圓明, meaning that samadhi invariably gives rise to prajna and prajna is always rooted in samadhi, and that the two act in perfect clarity as one integral whole.

The purpose of Zen is to awaken to the bodhisattva within us. This perception, also called kensho 見性, "seeing self-nature," opens the way to a true Zen life lived in unrestricted liberation. To attain such freedom, one must strive in all of one's activities to live in accordance with the Bodhisattva Vows:

Sentient beings are numberless: I vow to liberate them.
Desires are inexhaustible: I vow to end them.
The Dharma gates are infinite: I vow to master them.
The Buddha way is unsurpassable: I vow to attain it.

This does not mean, however, that Zen shuts its door to those whose aspirations are not quite so high. A person can only start from the place where he or she is at that time. Zazen has many benefits for those seeking physical and mental wellbeing, for example. As an ancient saying puts it, "The Great Way has no barrier; there are a thousand different ways [to enter]." Zen is not a system of defined beliefs, but a path to clarity and awareness. As such it has no conflicts with science, and can enrich the inner life of followers of any religious tradition. East, west, north, or south, all are welcome. From wherever one enters, the path to the bodhisattva mind unfolds.

This may make it sound like Zen has no clear goal, but that is not the case. One is free to enter the path to "seeing the bodhisattva within" from whatever gate one wishes, but the ultimate objective is the same: to attain liberation, then to help others according to their needs to attain liberation themselves. This, in Buddhism, is known as bodhicitta, the mind that strives "above, to seek enlightenment, below, to awaken all sentient beings."

It would be easy to spend an entire lifetime studying and contemplating the various source documents of the Zen tradition. The selections herein capture the full flavor and essence of Zen and can easily stand as both the beginning and terminus of one's studies.

The Teachings of Bodhidharma

Introduction

Bodhidharma was a legendary Buddhist monk who lived during the fifth and sixth century C.E. and played a seminal role in the transmission of Zen Buddhism from India to China. He is considered by Zen Buddhists to be the twenty-eighth Patriarch in a lineage that is traced directly back to Gautama Buddha himself.

His teachings point to a direct experience of Buddha-Nature rather than an intellectual understanding of it, and he is best known for his terse style that infuriated some (such as Emperor Wu of Liang), while leading others to enlightenment.

Bodhidharma was not a prolific writer or philosopher like other Buddhist figures, yet the central elements of his teachings can be seen in stories of his life such as his emphasis on zazen, his style of interacting with students (often referred to as "dharma-dueling" and found in many koans), the lack of emphasis on scholarship and intellectual debate, and the importance of personal realization and mind-to-mind transmission from teacher to disciple. These distinctive features that Bodhidharma brought from India to China almost 1,500 years ago still define Zen Buddhism today.

Tradition holds that Bodhidharma's principal text was the Lankavatara Sutra, a development of the Yogacara or "Mind-only" school of Buddhism established by the Gandharan half-brothers Asanga and Vasubandhu. He is described as a "master of the Lankavatara Sutra," and an early history of Zen in China is titled Record of the Masters and Disciples of the Lankavatara Sutra (Chinese, Leng-ch'ieh shih-tzu chi). Some sources go so far as to credit Bodhidharma with being the first to introduce this sutra to China.

He also lectured extensively on the doctrine of emptiness (shunyata), a defining feature of Mahayana thought found in the Prajnaparamita Sutras and the writings of Nagarjuna (c. 150-250) and his school of Madhyamaka. In one example, he states that "the sutras tell us... to see without seeing... to hear without hearing, to know without knowing... Basically, seeing, hearing, and knowing are completely empty" (Red Pine 1987, 27). This passage expresses another distinct feature of Zen: we should act without conceptualization or (as a result) hesitation. All things and all actions are held to be "empty" of any intellectual elaborations, and exist freely and spontaneously as direct expressions of nothing other than themselves. This influence is seen in Zen's insistence on natural and immediate actions and responses, as seen in numerous koans, interactions between teachers and students, and in Zen art. One common example of this is a student shouting in response to a teacher's question as a way of demonstrating their understanding. If the student is able to do so without hesitation and with their whole being, then they are said to have shown their master their 'Zen Mind.'

Another characteristic feature of Bodhidharma's presentation of Buddhism was the emphasis he placed on physical well-being. He taught that keeping our bodies healthy increases our mental energy and prepares us for the rigors that serious meditation practice requires. Bodhidharma's mind-and-body approach to spiritual practice ultimately proved highly attractive to the Samurai class in Japan, who incorporated Zen into their way of life, following their encounter with the martial-arts-oriented Zen Rinzai School introduced to Japan by Eisai in the twelfth century.

During his travels in China, Bodhidharma stopped at the Shaolin temple at Mt. Song but was refused entry. He is said to have subsequently sat in meditation outside the monastery facing its walls (or in a nearby cave in other accounts) for nine years. The Shaolin monks were so impressed with his dedication to his zazen that he was finally granted entry. However, it is reported that after sitting for so many years in meditation, Bodhidharma lost the use of his legs through the process of atrophy. This legend is still alive in Japan, where legless Daruma dolls representing Bodhidharma, and are used to make wishes. Even today, zazen (sitting meditation) is an important part of Zen Buddhist practice. However, the story of Bodhidharma losing the use of his legs contradicts other legends about him founding martial arts to combat physical weakness.

His life and teachings continue to be an inspiration to practitioners of Zen Buddhism today, and he exemplifies hard work, discipline and determination on the path to spiritual realization.

Outline of Practice

There are many roads leading to the Path, but basically there are only two: reason and practice. To enter by reason means to realize the essence through instruction and to believe that all living things share the same true nature, which isn't apparent because it's shrouded by sensation and delusion. Those who turn from delusion back to reality, who meditate on walls,' the absence of self and other, the oneness of mortal and sage, and who remain unmoved even by scriptures are in complete and unspoken agreement with reason. Without moving, without effort, they enter, we say, by reason.

To enter via practice refers to four all-inclusive practices: Suffering injustice, adapting to conditions, seeking nothing, and practicing the Dharma. First, suffering injustice. When those who search for the Path encounter adversity, they should think to themselves, "In ages gone by, I've turned from the essential to the trivial and wandered through all manner of existence, often angry without cause and guilty of numberless transgressions.

Now, though I do no wrong, I'm punished by my past. Neither gods nor men can foresee when an evil deed will bear its fruit. I accept it with an open heart and without complaint of injustice. The sutras say " when you meet with adversity don't be upset because it makes sense." With such understanding you're in harmony with reason. And by suffering injustice you enter the Path. Second, adapting to conditions. As mortals, we're ruled by conditions, not by ourselves. All the suffering and joy we experience depend on conditions. If we should be blessed by some great reward, such as fame or fortune, it's the fruit of a seed planted by us in the past. When conditions change, it ends. Why delight In Its existence? But while success and failure depend on conditions, the mind neither waxes nor wanes. Those who remain unmoved by the wind of joy silently follow the Path.

Third, seeking nothing. People of this world are deluded. They're always longing for something-always, in a word, seeking. But the wise wake up. They choose reason over custom. They fix their minds on the sublime and let their bodies change with the seasons. All phenomena are empty. They contain nothing worth desiring. Calamity forever alternates with Prosperity! To dwell in the three realms is to dwell in a burning house. To have a body is to suffer. Does anyone with a body know peace? Those who understand this detach themselves from all that exists and stop Imagining or seeking anything. The sutras say, "To seek is to suffer.

To seek nothing is bliss." When you seek nothing, you're on the Path. Fourth, practicing the Dharma.' The Dharma is the truth that all natures are pure. By this truth, all appearances are empty. Defilement and attachment, subject and object don't exist. The sutras say, "The Dharma includes no being because it's free from the impurity of being, and the Dharma includes no self because it's free from the impurity of self." Those wise enough to believe and understand these truths are bound to practice according to the Dharma. And since that which is real includes nothing worth begrudging, they give their body, life, and property in charity, without regret, without the vanity of giver, gift, or recipient, and without bias or attachment. And to eliminate impurity they teach others, but without becoming attached to form. Thus, through their own practice they're able to help others and glorify the Way of Enlightenment. And as with charity, they also practice the other virtues. But while practicing the six virtues to eliminate delusion, they practice nothing at all. This is what's meant by practicing the Dharma.

Bloodstream Sermon

Everything that appears in the three realms originates from the mind. Hence Buddhas of the past and future teach mind to mind without bothering about definitions.

Student: But if they don't define it, what do they mean by mind?

Bodhidharma: You ask. That's your mind. I answer. That's my mind. If I had no mind how could I answer? If you had no mind, how could you ask? That which asks is your mind. Through endless kalpas" without beginning, whatever you do, wherever you are, that's your real mind, that's your real buddha. This mind is the buddha" says the same thing. Beyond this mind you'll never find another Buddha. To search for enlightenment or nirvana beyond this mind is impossible. The reality of your own self-nature the absence of cause and effect, is what's meant by mind. Your mind is nirvana. You might think you can find a Buddha or enlightenment somewhere beyond the mind', but such a place doesn't exist.

Trying to find a Buddha or enlightenment is like trying to grab space. Space may have a name but no form. It's not something you can pick up or put down. And you certainly can't grab if. Beyond mind you'll never see a Buddha. The Buddha is a product of the mind. Why look for a Buddha beyond this mind?

Buddhas of the past and future only talk about this mind. The mind is the Buddha, and the Buddha is the mind. Beyond the mind there's no Buddha and beyond the Buddha there's no mind. If you think there is a Buddha beyond the mind', where is he? There's no Buddha beyond the mind, so why envision one? You can't know your real mind as long as you deceive yourself. As long as you're enthralled by a lifeless form, you're not free. If you don't believe me, deceiving yourself won't help. It's not the Buddha's fault. People, though, are deluded. They're unaware that their own mind is the Buddha. Otherwise they wouldn't look for a Buddha outside the mind.

Buddhas don't save Buddhas. If you use your mind to look for a Buddha, you won't see the Buddha. As long as you look for a Buddha somewhere else, you'll never see that your own mind is the Buddha. Don't use a Buddha to worship a Buddha. And don't use the mind to invoke a Buddha." Buddhas don't recite sutras." Buddhas don't keep precepts." And Buddhas don't break precepts. Buddhas don't keep or break anything. Buddhas don't do good or evil.

To find a Buddha, you have to see your nature." Whoever sees his nature is a Buddha. If you don't see your nature, invoking Buddhas, reciting sutras, making offerings, and keeping precepts are all useless. Summoning Buddhas results in good karma, reciting sutras results in a good memory; keeping precepts results in a good rebirth, and making offerings results in future blessings-but no buddha. If you don't understand by yourself, you'll have to find a teacher to get to the bottom of life and death. But unless he sees his nature, such a person isn't a tea6er. Even if he can recite the Twelvefold Canon he can't escape the Wheel of Birth and Death. He suffers in the three realms without hope of release. Long ago, the monk Good Star 21 was able to recite the entire Canon. But he didn't escape the Wheel, because he didn't see his nature. If this was the case with Good Star, then people nowadays who recite a few sutras or shastras and think it's the Dharma are fools. Unless you see your mind, reciting so much prose is useless.

To find a Buddha all you have to do is see your nature. Your nature is the Buddha. And the Buddha is the person who's utterly free: free of plans, free of cares. If you don't see your nature and run around all day looking somewhere else, you'll never find a buddha. The truth is there's nothing to find. But to reach such an understanding you need a teacher and you need to struggle to make yourself understand. Life and death are important. Don't suffer them in vain.

There's no advantage in deceiving yourself. Even if you have mountains of jewels and as many servants as there are grains of sand along the Ganges, you see them when your eyes are open. But what about when your eyes are shut? You should realize then that everything you see is like a dream or illusion.

If you don't find a teacher soon, you'll live this life in vain. It's true, you have the buddha-nature. But the help of a teacher you'll never know it. Only one person in a million becomes enlightened without a teacher's help. If, though, by the conjunction of conditions, someone understands what the Buddha meant, that person doesn't need a teacher. Such a person has a natural awareness superior to anything taught. But unless you're so blessed, study hard, and by means of instruction you'll understand.

People who don't understand and think they can do so without study are no different from those deluded souls who can't tell white from black." Falsely proclaiming the Buddha-Dharma, such persons in fact blaspheme the Buddha and subvert the Dharma. They preach as if they were bringing rain. But theirs is the preaching of devils not of Buddhas. Their teacher is the King of Devils and their disciples are the Devil's minions. Deluded people who follow such instruction unwittingly sink deeper in the Sea of Birth and Death. Unless they see their nature, how can people call themselves Buddhas they're liars who deceive others into entering the realm of devils. Unless they see their nature, their preaching of the Twelvefold Canon is nothing but the preaching of devils. Their allegiance is to Mara, not to the Buddha. Unable to distinguish white from black, how can they escape birth and death?

Whoever sees his nature is a Buddha; whoever doesn't is a mortal. But if you can find your buddha-nature apart from your mortal nature, where is it? Our mortal nature is our Buddha nature. Beyond this nature there's no Buddha. The Buddha is our nature. There's no Buddha besides this nature. And there's no nature besides the Buddha.

Student: But suppose I don't see my nature, cant I still attain enlightenment by invoking Buddhas, reciting sutras, making offerings, observing precepts, Practicing devotions, or doing good works?

Bodhidharma: No, you cannot.

Student: Why not?

Bodhidharma:If you attain anything at all, it's conditional, it's karmic. It results in retribution. It turns the Wheel. And as long as you're subject to birth and death, you'll never attain enlightenment. To attain enlightenment you have to see your nature. Unless you see your nature, all this talk about cause and effect is nonsense. Buddhas don't practice nonsense. A Buddha free of karma free of cause and effect. To say he attains anything at all is to slander a Buddha. What could he possibly attain? Even focusing on a mind, a power, an understanding, or a view is impossible for a Buddha. A Buddha isn't one sided. The nature of his mind is basically empty, neither pure nor impure. He's free of practice and realization. He's free of cause and effect.

A Buddha doesn't observe precepts. A Buddha doesn't do good or evil. A Buddha isn't energetic or lazy. A Buddha is someone who does nothing, someone who can't even focus his mind on a Buddha. A Buddha isn't a Buddha. Don't think about Buddhas. If you dont see what I'm talking about, you'll ever know your own mind. People who don't see their nature and imagine they can practice thoughtlessness all the time are lairs and fools. They fall into endless space. They're like drunks. They can't tell good from evil. If you intend to cultivate such a practice, you have to see your nature before you can put an end to rational thought. To attain enlightenment without seeing your nature is impossible. Still others commit all sorts of evil deeds, claiming karma doesn't exist. They erroneously maintain that since everything is empty committing evil isn't wrong. Such persons fall into a hell of endless darkness with no hope of release. Those who are wise hold no such conception.

Student: But if our every movement or state, whenever it occurs, is the mind, why don't we see this mind when a person's body dies?

The mind is always present. You just don't see it.

Student: But if the mind is present, why don't I see it?

Bodhidharma: Do you ever dream?

Student: Of course.

When you dream, is that you?

Student: Yes, it's me.

And is what you're doing and saying different from you?

Student: No, it isn't.

Bodhidharma: But if it isn't, then this body is your real body. And this real body is your mind. And this mind, through endless kalpas without beginning, has never varied. It has never lived or died, appeared or disappeared, increased or decreased. Its not pure or impure, good or evil, past or future. It's not true or false. It's not mate or female. It doesn't appear as a monk or a layman, an elder or a novice, a sage or a fool, a Buddha or a mortal. It strives 'for no realization and suffers no karma. It has no strength or form. It's like space. You can't possess it and you can't lose it. Its movements can't be blocked by mountains, rivers, or rock walls. Its unstoppable powers penetrate the Mountain of Five Skandhas and cross the River of Samsara." No karma can restrain this real body. But this mind is subtle and hard to see. It's not the same as the sensual mind. Every I one wants to see this mind, and those who move their hands and feet by its light are as many as the grains of sand along the Ganges, but when you ask them, they can't explain it. They're like puppets. It's theirs to use. Why don't they see it?

The Buddha said people are deluded. This Is why when they act they fall into the river of endless rebirth. And when they try to get out they only sink deeper. And all because they don't see their nature. If people weren't deluded why would they ask about something right in front of them? Not one of they understands the movement of his own hands and feet. The Buddha wasn't mistaken. Deluded people don't know who they are. A Buddha and no one else know something so hard to fathom. Only the wise knows mind, this mind call nature, this mind called liberation. Neither life nor death can restrain this mind. Nothing can. It's also called the Unstoppable Tathagata," the Incomprehensible, the Sacred Self, the Immortal, the Great Sage. Its names vary but not its essence. Buddhas vary too, but none leaves his own mind. The mind's capacity is limitless, and its manifestations are inexhaustible. Seeing forms with your eyes, hearing sounds with your ears, smelling odors with your nose, tasting flavors with your tongue, every movement or state is your entire mind. At every moment, where language can't go, that's your mind.

The sutras say, "A Tathagata's forms are endless. And so is his awareness." The endless variety of forms is due to the mind. Its ability to distinguish things, whatever their movement or state, is the mind's awareness. But the mind has no form and its awareness no limit. Hence it's said, "A Tathagata's forms are endless. And so is his awareness." A material body of the four elements" is trouble. A material body is subject to birth and death. But the real body exists without existing, because a Tathagata's real body never changes. The sutras say, "People should realize that the buddha-nature is something they have always had." Kashyapa only realized his own nature.

Our nature is the mind. And the mind is our nature. This nature is the same as the mind of all Buddhas. Buddhas of the past and future only transmit this mind. Beyond this mind there's no Buddha anywhere. But deluded people don't realize that their own mind is the Buddha. They keep searching outside. They never stop invoking Buddhas or worshipping Buddhas and wondering Where is the buddha? Don't indulge in such illusions. Just know your mind. Beyond your mind there's no other Buddha. The sutras say, "Everything that has form is an illusion." They also say, "Wherever you are, there's a Buddha." Your mind is the Buddha. Don't use a Buddha to worship a Buddha.

Even if a Buddha or bodhisattva" should suddenly appear before you, there's no need for reverence. This mind of ours is empty and contains no such form. Those who hold onto appearances are devils. They fall from the Path. Why worship illusions born of the mind? Those who worship don't know, and those who know don't worship. By worshipping you come under the spell of devils. I point this out because 1 afraid you're unaware of it. The basic nature of a Buddha has no such form. Keep this in mind, even if something unusual should appear. Don't embrace it, and don't fear it, and don't doubt that your Mind is basically pure. Where could there be room for any such form? Also, at the appearance of spirits, demons, or divine conceive neither respect nor fear. Your mind is basically empty. All appearances are illusions. Don't hold on to appearances. If you envision a Buddha, a Dharma, or a bodhisattva" and conceive respect for them, you relegate yourself to the realm of mortals. If you seek direct understanding, don't hold on to any appearance whatsoever, and you'll succeed. I have no other advice. The sutras say, "All appearances are illusions." They have no fixed existence, o constant form. They're impermanent. Don't cling to appearances and you'll be of one mind with the Buddha. The sutras say, "'That which is free of all form is the Buddha."

Student: But why shouldn't we worship Buddhas and bodhisattvas?

Bodhidharma: Devils and demons possess the power of manifestation. They can create the appearance of bodhisattvas in all sorts of guises. But they're false. None of them are Buddhas. The Buddha is your own mind. Don't misdirect your worship.

Buddha is Sanskrit for what you call aware, miraculously aware. Responding, arching your brows blinking your eyes, moving your hands and feet, its all your miraculously aware nature. And this nature is the mind. And the mind is the Buddha. And the Buddha is the path. And the path is Zen. But the word Zen is one that remains a puzzle to both mortals and sages. Seeing your nature is Zen. Unless you see your nature, it's not Zen.

Even if you can explain thousands of sutras and shastras, unless you see your own nature yours is the teaching of a mortal, not a Buddha. The true Way is sublime. It can't be expressed in language. Of what use are scriptures? But someone who sees his own nature finds the Way, even if he can't read a word. Someone who sees his nature is a Buddha. And since a Buddha's body is intrinsically pure and unsullied, and everything he says is an expression of his mind, being basically empty, a buddha can't be found in words or anywhere in the Twelvefold Canon.

The Way is inherently perfect. It doesn't require perfecting. The Way has no form or sound. It's subtle and hard to perceive. It's like when you drink water: you know how hot or cold it is, but you can't tell others. Of that which only a

Tathagata knows men and gods remain unaware. The awareness of mortals falls short. As long as ,they're attached to appearances, they're unaware that their minds are empty.

And by mistakenly clinging to the appearance of things they lose the Way. If you know that everything comes from the mind, don't become attached. Once attached, you're unaware. But once you see your own nature, the entire Canon becomes so much prose. Its thousands of sutras and shastras only amount to a clear mind. Understanding comes in midsentence. What good are doctrines? The ultimate Truth is beyond words. Doctrines are words.

They're not the Way. The Way is wordless. Words are illusions. They're no different from things that appear in your dreams at night, be they palaces or carriages, forested parks or lakeside 'lions. Don't conceive any delight for such things. They're all cradles of rebirth. Keep this in mind when you approach death. Don't cling to appearances, and you'll break through all barriers. A moment's hesitation and you'll be under the spell of devils. Your real body is pure and impervious. But because of delusions you're unaware of it. And because of this you suffer karma in vain. Wherever you find delight, you find bondage. But once you awaken to your original body and mind," you're no longer bound by attachments.

Anyone, who gives up the transcendent for the mundane, ill any of its myriad forms, is a mortal. A Buddha is someone who finds freedom in good fortune and bad. Such is his power that karma can't hold him. No matter what kind of karma Buddha transforms it. Heaven and hell are nothing to him. But the awareness of a mortal is dim compared to that of a

Buddha who penetrates everything inside and out. If you're not sure don't act. Once you act, you wander through birth and death and regret having no refuge. Poverty and hardship are created by false thinking. To understand this mind you have to act without acting. Only then will you see things from a Tathagata's perspective.

But when you first embark on the Path, your awareness won't focused. But you shouldn't doubt that all such scenes come from your own mind and nowhere else.

If, as in a dream, you see a light brighter than the sun, your remaining attachments will suddenly come to an end and the nature of reality will be revealed. Such an occurrence serves as the basis for enlightenment. But this is something only you know. You can't explain it to others. Or if, while you're walking, standing, sitting, or lying in a quiet grove, you see a light, regardless of whether it's bright or dim, don't tell others and don't focus on it. It's the light of your own nature.

Or if, while you're walking, standing, sitting, or lying in the stillness and darkness of night, everything appears as though in daylight, don't be startled. It's your own mind about to reveal itself.

Or if, while you're dreaming at night, you see the moon and stars in all their clarity, it means the workings of your mind are about to end. But don't tell others. And if your dreams aren't clear, as if you were walking in the dark, it's because your mind is masked by cares. This too is something of" you know. if you so your nature,, you don't need to read sutras or invoke buddhas. Erudition and Knowledge are not only useless but also cloud your awareness. Doctrines are only for pointing to the mind. Once you see your mind, why pay attention to doctrines?

To go from mortal to Buddha, you have to put an end to karma, nurture your awareness, and accept what life brings. If you're always getting angry, you'll turn your nature against the Way. There's no advantage in deceiving yourself. Buddhas move freely through birth and death, appearing and disappearing at will. They can't be restrained by karma or overcome by devils. Once mortals see their nature, all attachments end. Awareness isn't hidden. But you can only find it right now. It's only now. If you really want to find the Way, don't hold on to anything. Once you put an end to karma and nurture your awareness, any attachments that remain will come to an end. Understanding comes naturally. You don't have to make any effort. But fanatics don't understand what the Buddha meant. And the harder they try, the farther they get from the Sage's meaning. All day long they invoke Buddhas and read sutras. But they remain blind to their own divine nature, and they don't escape the Wheel.

A Buddha is an idle person. He doesn't run around after fortune and fame. What good are such things in the end? People who don't see their nature and think reading sutras, invoking Buddhas', studying long and hard, practicing morning and night, never lying down, or acquiring knowledge is the Dharma, blaspheme the Dharma. Buddhas of the past and future only talk about seeing your nature. All practices are impermanent. Unless they see their nature people who claim to have attained unexcelled, complete enlightenment" are liars. Among Shakyamuni's ten greatest disciples, Ananda was foremost in learning. But he didn't know the Buddha. All he did was study and memorize. Arhats don't know the Buddha. All they know are so many practices for realization, and they become trapped by cause and effect. Such is a mortal's karma: no escape from birth and death. By doing the opposite of what lie intended, Such people blaspheme the Buddha. Killing them would not be wrong. The sutras say, "Since icchantikas are incapable of belief, killing them would be blameless, whereas people who believe reach the state of Buddhahood."

Unless you see your nature, You shouldn't go around criticizing the goodness of others. There's no advantage in deceiving yourself. Good and bad are distinct. Cause and effect are clear. Heaven and hell are right before your eves. But fools don't believe and fall straight into a hell of endless darkness without even knowing it. What keeps them from believing is the heaviness of their karma. They're like blind people who don't believe there's such a thing as light. Even if you explain it to them, they still don t believe, because they're blind. How can they possibly distinguish light?

The same holds true for fools who end up among the lower orders of existence or among the poor and despised. They can't live and they can't die. And despite their sufferings, if you ask them, they say they're as happy as gods. All mortals even those who think themselves wellborn, are likewise unaware. Because of the heaviness of their karma, such fools can't believe and can't get free.

People who see that their mind is the Buddha don't need to shave their head" Laymen are Buddhas too. Unless they see their nature, people who shave their head are simply fanatics.

Student: But since married laymen don't give up sex, bow can they become Buddhas?

Bodhidharma: I only talk about seeing your nature. I don't talk about sex simply because you don't see your nature. Once you see your nature, sex is basically immaterial. It ends along with your delight in it. Even if some habits remain', they can't harm you, because your nature is essentially pure. Despite dwelling in a material body of four elements, your nature is basically pure. It can't be corrupted.

Your real body is basically pure. It can't be corrupted. Your real body has no sensation, no hunger or thirst', no warmth or cold, no sickness, no love or attachment, no pleasure or pain, no good or bad, no shortness or length, no weakness or strength. Actually, there's nothing here. It's only because you cling to this material body that things like hunger and thirst, warmth and cold, sickness appear Once you stop clinging and let things be, you'll- be free, even of birth and death. You'll transform everything. You'll possess Spiritual powers " that cant be obstructed. And you'll be at peace wherever you are. If you doubt this, you'll never see through anything. You're better off doing nothing. Once you act, you can't avoid the cycle of birth and death. But once you see your nature, you're a Buddha even if you work as a butcher.

Student: But butchers create karma by slaughtering animals. How can they be Buddhas?

Bodhidharma: I only talk about seeing your nature. I don't talk about creating karma. Regardless of what we do, our karma has no hold on us. Through endless kalpas without beginning, its only because people don't see their nature that they end up in hell. As long as a person creates karma, he keeps passing through birth and death. But once a person realizes his original nature, he stops creating karma. If he doesn't see his nature, invoking Buddhas won't release him from his karma, regardless of whether or not he's a butcher. But once he sees his nature, all doubts vanish. Even a butcher's karma has no effect on such a person. In India the twenty-seven patriarchs only transmitted the imprint of the mind.

And the only reason I've come to China is to transmit the instantaneous teaching of the Mahayana This mind is the Buddha. I don't talk about precepts, devotions or ascetic practices such immersing yourself in water and fire, treading a wheel of knives, eating one meal a day, or never lying down. These are fanatical, provisional teachings. Once you recognize your moving, miraculously aware nature.

Yours is the mind of all Buddhas. Buddhas of the past and future only talk about transmitting the mind.

They teach nothing else if someone understands this teaching, even if he's illiterate he's a Buddha. If You don't see your own miraculously aware nature, you'll never find a Buddha even if you break your body into atoms.

The Buddha is your real body, your original mind. This mind has no form or characteristics, no cause or effect, no tendons or bones. It's like space. You can't hold it. Its not the mind or materialists or nihilistic ones. Except for a Tathagata, no one else- no mortal, no deluded being-can fathom it.

But this mind isn't somewhere outside the material body of four elements.Without this mind we can't move. The body has no awareness.

Like a plant or stone, the body has no nature. So how does it move? It's the mind that moves. Language and behavior, perception and conception are all functions of the moving mind. All motion is the mind's motion. Motion is its function. Apart from motion there's no mind, and apart from the mind there's no motion. But motion isn't the mind. And the mind isn't motion. Motion is basically mindless. And the mind is basically motionless. But motion doesn't exist without the mind. And the mind doesn't exist without motion. Theres no mind for motion to exist apart from, and no motion for mind to exist apart from. Motion is the mind's function, and its function is its motion. Even so, the mind neither moves nor functions, the essence of its functioning is emptiness and emptiness is essentially motionless. Motion is the same as the mind. And the mind is essentially motionless. Hence the Sutras tell us to move without moving, to travel without traveling, to see without seeing, to laugh without laughing, to hear without hearing, to know without knowing, to be happy, without being happy, to walk without walking, to stand without standing. And the sutras say, "Go beyond language. Go beyond thought." Basically, seeing, hearing, and knowing are completely empty. Your anger, Joy, or pain is like that of puppet. You search but you won't find a thing.

According to the Sutras, evil deeds result in hardships and good deeds result in blessings. Angry people go to hell and happy people go to heaven. But once you know that the nature of anger and joy is empty and you let them go, you free yourself from karma. If you don't see your nature, quoting sutras is no help, I could go on, but this brief sermon will have to do.

Wake-up Sermon

The essence of the Way is detachment. And the goal of those who practice is freedom from appearances. The sutras say, Detachment is enlightenment because it negates appearances. Buddhahood means awareness Mortals whose minds are aware reach the Way of Enlightenment and are therefore called Buddhas. The sutras say, "Those who free themselves from all appearances are called Buddhas." The appearance of appearance as no appearance can't be seen visually but can only be known by means of wisdom. Whoever hears and believes this teaching embarks on the Great Vehicle" and leaves the three realms. The three realms are greed, anger, and delusion. To leave the three realms means to go from greed, anger, and delusion back to morality, meditation, and wisdom. Greed, anger, and delusion have no nature of their own. They depend on mortals. And anyone capable of reflection is bound to see that the nature of greed, anger, and delusion is the buddha-nature. Beyond greed, anger, and delusion there is no other buddha-nature. The sutras say, "Bu as have only become buddhas while living with the three poisons and nourishing themselves on the pure Dharma." The three poisons are greed, anger, and delusion.

The Great Vehicle is the greatest of all vehicles. It's the conveyance of bodhisattvas, who use everything wit out using anything and who travel all day without traveling. Such is the vehicle of Buddhas.

The sutras say, "No vehicle is the vehicle of Buddhas."

Whoever realizes that the six senses aren't real, that the five aggregates are fictions, that no such things can be located anywhere in the body, understands the language of Buddhas. The sutras say, "The cave of five aggregates is the hall of Zen. The opening of the inner eye is the door of the Great Vehicle." What could be clearer?

Not thinking about any particular thing is Zen. Once you know this, walking, standing, sitting, or lying down, everything you do is Zen. To know that the mind is empty is to see the Buddha. The Buddhas of the ten directions" have no mind. To see no mind is to see the Buddha.

To give up yourself without regret is the greatest charity. To transcend motion and stillness is the highest meditation. Mortals keep moving, and Arhats stay still." But the highest meditation surpasses both that of mortals and that of Arhats. People who reach such understanding free themselves from all appearances without effort and cure all illnesses without treatment. Such is the power of great Zen.

Using the mind to look for reality is delusion. Not using the mind to took for reality is awareness. Freeing oneself from words is liberation. Remaining unblemished by the dust of sensation is guarding the Dharma.

Transcending life and death is leaving home."

Not suffering another existence is reaching the Way. Not creating delusions is enlightenment. Not engaging in ignorance is wisdom. No affliction is nirvana. And no appearance of the mind is the other shore.

When you're deluded, this shore exists. When you wake tip, it doesn't exist. Mortals stay on this shore. But those who discover the greatest of all vehicles stay on neither this shore nor the other shore. They're able to leave both shores. Those who see the other shore as different from this shore don't understand Zen.

Delusion means mortality. And awareness means Buddhahood. They're not the same. And they're not different. It's 'List that people distinguish delusion from awareness. When we're deluded there's a world to escape. When we're aware, there's nothing to escape.

In the light of the impartial Dharma, mortals look no different from sages. The sutras say that the impartial Dharma is something that mortals can't penetrate and sages can't practice. The impartial Dharma is only practiced by great bodhisattvas and Buddhas. To look on life as different from death or on motion as different from stillness is to be partial. To be impartial means to look on suffering as no different from nirvana,, because the nature of both is emptiness. By imagining they're putting an end to Suffering and entering nirvana Arhats end up trapped by nirvana. But bodhisattvas know that suffering is essentially empty. And by remaining in emptiness they remain in nirvana. Nirvana means no birth and no death. It's beyond birth and death and beyond nirvana. When the mind stops moving, it enters nirvana. Nirvana is an empty mind. When delusions dont exist, Buddhas reach nirvana. Where afflictions don't exist, bodhisattvas enter the place of enlightenment An uninhabited place is one without greed, anger, or delusion. Greed is the realm of desire, anger the realm of form, and delusion the formless realm. When a thought begins, you enter the three realms. When a thought ends, you leave the three realms. The beginning or end of the three realms, the existence or nonexistence of anything, depends on the mind. This applies to everything, even to such inanimate objects as rocks and sticks.

Whoever knows that the mind is a fiction and devoid of anything real knows that his own mind neither exists nor doesn't exist. Mortals keep creating the mind, claiming it exists. And Arhats keep negating the mind, claiming it doesn't exist. But bodhisattvas and Buddhas neither create nor negate the mind. This is what's meant by the mind that neither exists nor doesn't exist. The mind that neither exists nor doesn't exist is called the Middle Way.

If you use your mind to study reality, you won't understand either your mind or reality. If you study reality without using your mind, you'll understand both. Those who don't understand don't understand understanding. And those who understand, understand not understanding. People capable of true vision know that the mind is empty. They transcend both understanding and not understanding. The absence of both understanding and not understanding is true understanding Seen with true vision, form isn't simply form, because form depends on mind. And mind isn't simply mind, because mind depends on form. Mind and form create and negate each other. That which exists exists in relation to that which doesn't exist. And that which doesn't exist doesn't exist in relation to that which exists. This is true vision. By means of such vision nothing is seen and nothing is not seen. Such vision reaches throughout the ten directions without seeing: because nothing is seen; because not seeing is seen; because seeing isn't seeing. What mortals see are delusions. True vision is detached from seeing. The mind and the world are opposites, and vision arises where they meet. When your mind doesn't stir inside, the world doesn't arise outside. When the world and the mind are both transparent, this is true vision. And such understanding is true understanding.

To see nothing is to perceive the Way, and to understand nothing is to know the Dharma, because seeing is neither seeing nor not seeing and because understanding is neither understanding nor not understanding. Seeing without seeing is true vision. Understanding without understanding is true understanding.

True vision isn't just seeing seeing. It's also seeing not seeing. And true understanding isn't just understanding understanding. It's also understanding not understanding. If you understand anything, you don't understand. Only when you understand nothing is it true understanding. Understanding is neither understanding nor not understanding.

The sutras say, "Not to let go of wisdom is stupidity." When the mind doesn't exist, understanding and not understanding are both true. When the mind exists, understanding and not understanding are both false. When you understand, reality depends on you. When you don't understand, you depend on reality. When reality depends on you, that which isn't real becomes real. When you depend on reality, that which is real becomes false. When you depend on reality, everything is false. When reality depends on you, everything is true. Thus, the sage doesn't use his mind to look for reality, or reality to look for his mind, or his mind to look for his mind, or reality to look for reality. His mind doesn't give rise to reality. And reality doesn't give rise to his mind. And because both his mind and reality are still, he's always in samadhi.

When the mortal mind appears, buddhahood disappears. When the mortal mind disappears, buddhahood appears. When the mind appears, reality disappears. When the mind disappears, reality appears. Whoever knows that nothing depends on anything has found the Way. And whoever knows that the mind depends on nothing is always at the place of enlightenment.

When you don't understand, your wrong. When you understand, you re not wrong. This is because the nature of wrong is empty. When you don't understand right seems wrong. When you understand, wrong isn't wrong, because wrong doesn't exist. The sutras say, "Nothing has a nature of its own." Act. Don't question. When you question, you're wrong. Wrong is the result of questioning. When you reach such an understanding, the wrong deeds of your past lives are wiped away. When you're deluded, the six senses and five shades are constructs of suffering and mortality When you wake up, the six senses and five shades are constructs of nirvana and immortality.

Someone who seeks the Way doesn't look beyond himself. He knows that the mind is the Way. But when he finds the mind, he finds nothing. And when he finds the Way, he finds nothing. If you think you can use the mind to find the Way, you're deluded. When you, re deluded, buddhahood exists. When you're aware, it doesn't exist. This is because awareness is buddhahood.

If you're looking for the Way, the Way won't appear until your body' disappears. It's like stripping bark from a tree. This karmic body undergoes constant change. It has no fixed reality. Practice according to your thoughts. Don't hate life and death or love life and death. Keep your every thought free of delusion, and in life you'll witness the beg- inning of nirvana and in death you'll experience the assurance of no rebirth.

To see form but not be corrupted by form or to hear sound but not to be corrupted by sound is liberation. Eyes that aren't attached to form are the gates of Zen. In short, those who perceive the existence and nature of phenomena and remain unattached are liberated. Those who perceive the external appearance of phenomena are at their mercy. Not to be subject to afflictions is what's meant by liberation. There's no other liberation. When you know how to look at form, form doesn't give rise to mind and mind doesn't give rise to form. Form and mind are both pure.

When delusions have absented themselves, the mind is the land of Buddhas. When delusions are present, the mind is hell. Mortals create delusions. And by using the mind to give birth to mind they always find themselves in hell. Bodhisattvas see through delusions. And by not using the mind to give birth to mind they always find themselves in the land of Buddhas. If you don't use your mind to create mind, every state of mind is empty and every thought is still. You go from one buddhaland to another. If you use your mind to create mind, every state of mind is disturbed and every thought is in motion. You go from one hell to the next. When a thought arises, there's good karma and bad karma, heaven and hell. When no thought arises, there's no good karma or bad karma, no heaven or hell.

The body neither exists nor doesn't exist. Hence existence as a mortal and nonexistence as a sage are conceptions with which a sage has nothing to do. His heart is empty and spacious as the sky. That which follows is witnessed on the Way. It's beyond the ken of Arhats and mortals.

When the mind reaches nirvana, you don't see nirvana, because the mind is nirvana. If you see nirvana somewhere outside the mind, you're deluding yourself.

Every suffering is a buddha-seed, because suffering impels mortals to seek wisdom. But you can only say that suffering gives rise to Buddhahood. You can't say that suffering is Buddhahood. Your body and mind are the field. Suffering is the seed, wisdom the sprout, and Buddhahood the grain. The Buddha in the mind is like a fragrance in a tree. The Buddha comes from a mind free of suffering, just as a fragrance comes from a tree free of decay. There's no fragrance without the tree and no Buddha without the mind. If there's a fragrance without a tree, it's a different fragrance. If there's a Buddha without your mind, it's a different Buddha.

When the three poisons are present in your mind, you live in a land of filth.

When the three poisons are absent from your mind, you live in a land of purity.

The sutras say, "if you fill a land with impurity and filth, no Buddha will ever appear." Impurity and filth refer to on and the other poisons. A Buddha refers to a pure and awakened mind. There's no language that, isn't the Dharma. To talk all day without saying anything is the Way. To be silent all day and still say something isn't the Way. Hence neither does a Tathagata speech depend on silence, nor does his silence depend on speech, nor does his speech exist apart from his silence. Those who understand both speech and silence are in samadhi. If you speak when you know, Your speech is free. If you're silent when you don't know, your silence is tied. If speech isn't attached to appearances its free. If silence is attached to appearances, it's tied. Language is essentially free. It has nothing to do with attachment. And attachment has nothing to do with language. Reality has no high or low. If you see high or low, It isn't real. A raft isn't real. But a passenger raft is. A person who rides such a raft can cross that which isn't real. That's why it's real.

According to the world there's male and female, rich and poor. According to the Way there's no male or female, no rich or poor. When the goddess realized the Way, she didn't change her sex. When the stable boy" awakened to the Truth, he didn't change his status. Free of sex and status, they shared the same basic appearance. The goddess searched twelve years for her womanhood without success. To search twelve years for ones manhood would likewise be fruitless. The twelve years refer to the twelve entrances. Without the mind there s no Buddha. Without the Buddha there is no mind.

Likewise, without water there's no ice, and without ice there is no water. Whoever talks about leaving the mind doesn't get very far. Don't become attached to appearances of the mind. The sutras say, "When you see no appearance, you see the Buddha." This is what's meant by being free from appearances of the mind. Without the mind there's no Buddha means that the-buddha comes from the mind. The mind gives birth to the Buddha. But although the Buddha comes from the mind, the mind doesn't come from the Buddha, just as fish come from water, but water doesn't come from fish. Whoever wants to see a fish sees the water before lie sees the fish. And whoever wants to see a Buddha sees the mind before he sees the Buddha. Once you've seen the fish, You forget about the water. And once you've seen the Buddha, you forget about the mind. If you don't forget about the mind, the mind will confuse you, just as the water will confuse you if you don't forget about it.

Mortality and Buddhahood are like water and ice. To be afflicted by the three poisons is mortality. To be purified by the three releases" is Buddhahood. That which freezes into ice in the winter melts into water in summer. Eliminate ice and there's no more water. Get rid of mortality and there's no more Buddhahood. Clearly, the nature of ice is the nature of water. And the nature of water is the nature of ice. And the nature of mortality is the nature of Buddhahood. Mortality and Buddhahood share the same nature, just as Wutou and Futzu share the same root but not the same season. It's only because of the delusion of differences that we have the words mortality and buddhahood. When a snake becomes a dragon, it doesn't change its scales. And when a mortal becomes a sage, he doesn't change his face. He knows his mind through internal wisdom and takes care of his body through external discipline.

Mortals liberate Buddhas and Buddhas liberate mortals. This is what's meant by impartiality. Mortals liberate Buddhas because affliction creates awareness. And Buddhas liberate mortals because awareness negates affliction. There can't help but be affliction. And there can't help but be awareness. If it weren't for affliction, there would be nothing to create awareness. And if it weren't for awareness, there would be nothing to negate affliction. When you're deluded, Buddhas liberate mortals. When you're aware, mortals liberate Buddhas. Buddhas don't become Buddhas on their own. They're liberated by mortals. Buddhas regard delusion as their father and greed as their mother. Delusion and greed are different names for mortality. Delusion and mortality are like the left hand and the right hand. There's no other difference.

When you're deluded, you're on this shore. When you're aware, you're on the other shore. But once you know your mind is empty and you see no appearances, you're beyond delusion and awareness. And once you're beyond delusion and awareness, the other shore doesn't exist. The tathagata isn't on this shore or the other shore. And he isn't in midstream. Arhats are in midstream and mortals are on this shore. On the other shore is Buddhahood. Buddhas have three bodies: a transformation body a reward body, and a real body. The transformation body is also called the incarnation body. The transformation body appears when mortals do good deeds, the reward body when they cultivate wisdom, and the real body when they become aware of the sublime. The transformation body is the one you see flying in all directions rescuing others wherever it can. The reward body puts an end to doubts. The Great Enlightenment occurred in the Himalayas suddenly becomes true. The real body doesn't do or say anything. It remains perfectly still. But actually, there's not even one buddha-body, much less three. This talk of three bodies is simply based on human understanding, which can be shallow, moderate, or deep. People of shallow understanding imagine they're piling up blessings and mistake the transformation body for the Buddha. People of moderate understanding imagine they're putting an end to Suffering and mistake the reward body for the Buddha.

And people of deep understanding imagine they're experiencing Buddhahood and mistake the real body for the Buddha. But people of the deepest understanding took within, distracted by nothing. Since a clear mind is the Buddha they attain the understanding of a Buddha without using the mind. The three bodies, like all other things, are unattainable and indescribable. The unimpeded mind reaches the Way. The sutras say, " Buddhas don't preach the Dharma. They don't liberate mortals. And they don't experience Buddhahood." This is what I mean. Individuals create karma; karma doesn't create individuals. They create karma in this life and receive their reward in the next. They never escape. Only someone who's perfect creates no karma in this life and receives no reward. The sutras say, "Who creates no karma obtains the Dharma." This isn't an empty saying. You can create karma but you can't create a person. When you create karma, you're reborn along with your karma. When you don't create karma, you vanish along with your karma. Hence, wit karma dependent on the individual and the individual dependent on karma, if an individual doesn't create karma, karma has no hold on him. In the same manner, "A person can enlarge the Way. The Way can't enlarge a person."

Mortals keep creating karma and mistakenly insist that there's no retribution. But can they deny suffering? Can they deny that what the present state of mind sows the next state of mind reaps? How can they escape? But if the present state of mind sows nothing, the next state of mind reaps nothing. Don't misconceive karma.

The sutras say, "Despite believing in Buddhas, people who imagine that Buddhas practice austerities aren't Buddhists. The same holds for those who imagine that Buddhas are subject to rewards of wealth or poverty. They're icchantikas. They're incapable of belief." Someone who understands the teaching of sages is a sage. Someone who understands the teaching of mortals is a mortal. A mortal who can give up the teaching of mortals and follow the teaching of sages becomes a sage. But the fools of this world prefer to look for sage a away. They don't believe that the wisdom of their own mind is the sage. The sutras say, "Among men of no understanding, don't preach this sutra. And the sutras say, "Mind is the teaching." But people of no understanding don't believe their own mind or that by understanding this teaching they can become a sage. They prefer to look for distant knowledge and long for things in space, buddha-images, light, incense, and colors. They fall prey to falsehood and lose their minds to Insanity.

The sutras say, "When you see that all appearances are not appearances, you see the tathagata." The myriad doors to the truth all come from the mind. When appearances of the mind are as transparent as space, they're gone. Our endless sufferings are the roots of illness. When mortals are alive, they worry about death. When they're full, they worry about hunger. Theirs is the Great Uncertainty. But sages don't consider the past. And they don't worry about the future. Nor do they cling to the present. And from moment to moment they follow the Way. If you haven't awakened to this great truth, you'd better look for a teacher on earth or in the heavens. Don't compound your own deficiency.

Breakthrough Sermon

Student: If someone is determined to reach enlightenment, what is the most effective method he can practice?

Bodhidharma: The most essential method, which includes all other methods, is beholding the mind.

Student: But how can one method include all others?

Bodhidharma: The mind is the root from which all things grow if you can understand the mind, everything else is included. It's like the root of a tree. All a tree's fruit and flowers, branches and leaves depend on its root. If you nourish its root, a tree multiplies. If you cut its root, it dies. Those who understand the mind reach enlightenment with minimal effort. Those who don't understand the mind practice in vain. Everything good and bad comes from your own mind. To find something beyond the mind is impossible.

Student: But bow can beholding the mind be called understanding?

Bodhidharma: When a great bodhisattva delves deeply into perfect wisdom, he realizes that the four elements and five shades are devoid of a personal self. And he realizes that the activity of his mind has two aspects: pure and impure. By their very nature, these two mental states are always present. They alternate as cause or effect depending on conditions, the pure mind delighting in good deeds, the impure mind thinking of evil. Those who aren't affected by impurity are sages. They transcend suffering and experience the bliss of nirvana. All others, trapped by the impure mind and entangled by their own karma, are mortals. They drift through the three realms and suffer countless afflictions and all because their impure mind obscures their real self.

The Sutra of Ten Stages says, "in the body of mortals is the indestructible buddha-nature. Like the sun, its light fills endless space, But once veiled by the dark clouds of the five shades, it's like a light 'inside a 'at, hidden from view." And the Nirvana Sutra says, "All mortals have the buddha-nature. But it's covered by darkness from which they can't escape. Our buddha-nature is awareness: to be aware and to make others aware. To realize awareness is liberation," Everything good has awareness for its root. And from this root of awareness grow the tree of all virtues and the fruit of nirvana. Beholding the mind like this is understanding.

Student: You say that our true Buddha-nature and all virtues have awareness for their root. But what is the root of ignorance?

Bodhidharma: The ignorant mind, with its infinite afflictions, passions, and evils, is rooted in the three poisons. Greed, anger, and delusion. These three poisoned states of mind themselves include countless evils, like trees that have a single trunk but countless branches and leaves.

Yet each poison produces so many more millions of evils that the example of a tree is hardly a fitting comparison. The three poisons are present in our six sense organs' as six kinds of consciousness' or thieves. They're called thieves because they pass in and out of the gates of the senses, covet limitless possessions, and mask their true identity. And because mortals are misled in body and mind by these poisons or thieves, they become lost in life and death, wander through the six states of existence, and suffer countless afflictions. These afflictions are like rivers that surge for a thousand miles because of the constant flow of small springs.

But if someone cuts off their source, rivers dry up. And if someone who seeks liberation can turn the three poisons into the three sets of precepts and the six thieves into the six paramitas, he rids himself of affliction once and for all.

Student: But the three realms and six states -of existence are infinitely vast. How can we escape their endless afflictions if all we do is behold the mind?

Bodhidharma: The karma of the three realms comes from the mind alone. If your mind isn't within the three realms, it's beyond them. The three realms correspond to the three poisons- greed corresponds to the realm of desire, anger to the realm of form, and delusion to the formless realm. And because karma created by the poisons can be gentle or heavy, these three realms are further divided into six places known as the six states of existence.

Student: And how does the karma of these six differ?

Bodhidharma: Mortals who don't understand true practice and blindly perform good deeds are born into the three higher states of existence within the three realms. And what are these three higher states? Those who blindly perform the ten good deeds and foolishly seek happiness are born as gods in the realm of desire. Those who blindly observe the five precepts and foolishly indulge in love and hate are born as men in the realm of anger, And those who blindly cling to the phenomenal world, believe in false doctrines, and pray for blessings are born as demons in the realm of delusion. These are the three higher states of existence.

And what are the three lower states? They're where those who persist in poisoned thoughts and evil deeds are born. Those whose karma from greed is greatest become hungry ghosts. Those whose karma from anger is greatest become sufferers in hell. And those whose karma from delusion is greatest become beasts. These three lower states together with the previous three higher states form the six states of existence. From this you should realize that all karma, painful or otherwise, comes from your own mind. If you can just concentrate your mind and transcend its falsehood and evil, the suffering of the three realms and six states of existence will automatically disappear. And once free from suffering, you're truly free.

Student: But the Buddha said, "Only after undergoing innumerable hardships for three asankhya kalpas did I achieve enlightenment," Why do you now say that simply beholding the mind and over-coming the three poisons is liberation?

Bodhidharma: The words of the Buddha are true. But the three-asankhya kalpas refer to the three poisoned states of mind. What we call asankhya in Sanskrit you call countless. Within these three poisoned states of mind are countless evil thoughts, And every thought lasts a kalpa. Such an infinity is what the Buddha meant by the three asankhya kalpas, Once the three poisons obscure your real self, how can you be called liberated until you overcome their countless evil thoughts? People who can transform the three poisons of greed, anger, and delusion into the three releases are said to pass through the three-sankhya kalpas. But people of this final age are the densest of fools. They don't understand what the Tathagata really meant by the three-asankhya kalpas. They say enlightenment is only achieved after endless kalpas and thereby mislead disciples to retreat on the path to Buddhahood.

Student: But the great bodbisattvas have achieved enlightenment only by observing the three sets of precepts"' and practicing the six Paramitas, Now you tell disciples merely to behold the mind. How can anyone reach enlightenment without cultivating the rules of discipline?

Bodhidharma: The three sets of precepts are for overcoming the three poisoned states of mind, When you overcome these poisons, you create three sets of limitless virtue, A set gathers things together-in this case, countless good thoughts throughout your mind. And the six paramitas are for purifying the six senses. What we call paramitas you call means to the other shore. By purifying your six senses of the dust of sensation, the paramitas ferry you across the River of Affliction to the Shore of Enlightenment.

Student: According to the sutras, the three sets of precepts are, "I vow, to put an end to all evils. I vow to cultivate all virtues. And I vow to liberate all beings." But now you say they're only for controlling the three poisoned states of mind. Isn't this contrary to the meaning of the scriptures?

Bodhidharma: The sutras of the Buddha are true. But long ago, when that great bodhisattva was cultivating the seed of enlightenment, it was to counter the three poisons that he made his three vows. Practicing moral prohibitions to counter the poison of greed, he vowed to put an end to all evils. Practicing meditation to counter the poison of anger, he vowed to cultivate all virtues. And practicing wisdom to counter the poison of delusion, he vowed to liberate all beings. Because he persevered in these three pure practices of morality, meditation, and wisdom, he was able to overcome the three poisons and reach enlightenment. By overcoming the three poisons he wiped out everything sinful and thus put an end to evil. By observing the three sets of precepts he did nothing but good and thus cultivated virtue. And by putting an end to evil and cultivating virtue lie consummate all practices, benefited himself as well as others, and rescued mortals everywhere. Thus he liberated beings.

You should realize that the practice you cultivate doesn't exist apart from your mind. If your mind is pure, all buddha-lands are pure. The sutras say, "if their minds are impure, beings are impure. If their minds are pure, beings are pure," And "To reach a buddha-land, purify your mind. As your mind becomes pure, buddha-lands become pure." Thus by overcoming the three poisoned states of mind the three sets of precepts are automatically fulfilled.

Student: But the sutras say the six Paramitas are charity, morality, patience, devotion, meditation, and wisdom. Now you say the paramitas refer to the purification of the senses. What do you mean by this? And why are they called ferries?

Bodhidharma: Cultivating the paramitas means purifying the six senses by overcoming the six thieves. Casting out the thief of the eye by abandoning the visual world is charity. Keeping out the thief of the ear by not listening to sound is morality. Humbling the thief of the nose by equating smells as neutral is patience. Controlling the thief of the mouth by conquering desires to taste, praise, and explain is devotion. Quelling the thief of the body by remaining unmoved by sensations of touch is meditation. And taming the thief of the mind by not yielding to delusions but practicing wakefulness is wisdom, These six paramitas are transports. Like boats or rafts, they transport beings to the other shore. Hence they're called ferries.

Student: But when Sbakyamuni was a bodhisattva, he consumed three bowls of milk and six ladles of gruel prior to attaining enlightenment. If he bad to drink milk before be could taste the fruit of buddhahood, how can merely beholding the mind result in liberation?

Bodhidharma: What you say is true. That is how he attained enlightenment. He had to drink milk before he could become a Buddha. But there are two kinds of milk. That which Shakyamuni drank wasn't ordinary impure milk but Pure Dharma-talk. The three bowls were the three sets of precepts. And the six ladies were the six paramitas. When Shakyamuni attained enlightenment, it was because he drank this pure dharma-rnilk that he tasted the fruit of Buddhahood. To say that the Tathagata drank the worldly concoction of impure, rank-smelling cow's milk is the height of slander. That which is truly so, the indestructible, passionless Dharma-self, remains forever free of the world's afflictions. Why would it need impure milk to satisfy its hunger or thirst?

The sutras say, "This ox doesn't live in the highlands or the lowlands. It doesn't eat grain or chaff. And it doesn't graze with cows. The body of this ox is the color of burnished gold." The ox refers to Vairocana. Owing to his great compassion for all beings, he produces from within his pure Dharma-body the sublime Dharma-milk of the three sets of precepts and six paramitas to nourish all those who seek liberation. The pure milk of such a truly pure ox not only enabled the 'tathagata to achieve buddhahood but also enables any being who drinks it to attain unexcelled, complete enlightenment.

Student: Throughout the sutras the Buddha tells mortals they can achieve enlightenment by performing such meritorious works as building monasteries, casting statues, burning incense, scattering flowers, lighting eternal lamps, practicing all six periods" of the day and night, walking around stupas, observing fasts, and worshipping. But if beholding the mind includes all other practices, then such works as these would appear redundant.

Bodhidharma: The sutras of the Buddha contain countless metaphors. Because mortals have shallow minds and don't understand anything deep, the Buddha used the tangible to represent the sublime. People who seek blessings by concentrating on external works instead of internal cultivation are attempting the impossible, What you call a monastery we call a sangbarama, a place of purity. But whoever denies entry to the three poisons and keeps the gates of his senses pure, his body and mind still, inside and outside clean, builds a monastery.

Casting statues refers to all practices cultivated by those who seek enlightenment. The Tathagata's sublime form can't be represented by metal. Those who seek enlightenment regard their bodies as the furnace, the Dharma as the fire, wisdom as the craftsmanship, and the three sets of precepts and six paramitas as the mold. They smelt and refine the true buddha-nature within themselves and pour it into the mold formed by the rules of discipline. Acting in perfect accordance with the -Buddha's teaching, they naturally create a perfect likeness. 'Me eternal, sublime body isn't subject to conditions or decay. If you seek the Truth but dont learn how to make a true likeness, what will you use in its place?

And burning incense doesn't mean ordinary material incense but the incense of the intangible Dharma, which drives away filth, ignorance, and evil deeds with its perfume. There are five kinds of such Dharma-incense. First is the incense of morality, which means renouncing evil and cultivating virtue. Second is the incense of meditation, which means deeply believing in the Mahayana with unwavering resolve. Third is the incense of wisdom, which means contemplating the body and mind, inside and out. Fourth is the incense of liberation, which means severing the bonds of ignorance. And fifth is the incense of perfect knowledge, which means being always aware and nowhere obstructed. These five are the most precious kinds of incense and far superior to anything the world has to offer.

When the Buddha was in the world, he told his disciples to light such precious incense with the fire of awareness as an offering to the Buddhas of the ten directions. But people today don't understand the Tathagata's real meaning. They use an ordinary flame to light material incense of sandalwood or frankincense and pray for some future blessing that never comes.

For scattering flowers the same holds true. This refers to speaking the Dharma, scattering flowers of virtue, in order to benefit others and glorify the real sell. These flowers of virtue are those praised by the Buddha. They last forever and never fade. And whoever scatters such flowers reaps infinite blessings. If you think the Tathagata meant for people to harm plants by cutting off their flowers, you're wrong. Those who observe the precepts don't injure any of the myriad life forms of heaven and earth. If you hurt something by mistake, you suffer for it. But those who intentionally break the precepts by injuring the living for the sake of future blessings suffer even more, How could they let would-be blessings turn into sorrows?

The eternal lamp represents perfect awareness. Likening the illumination of awareness to that of a lamp, those who seek liberation see their body as the lamp, their mind as its wick, the addition of discipline as its oil, and the power of wisdom as its flame. By lighting this lamp of perfect awareness they dispel all darkness and delusion. And by passing this Dharma on to others they're able to use one lamp to light thousands of lamps. And because these lamps likewise light countless other lamps, their light lasts forever.

A long time ago, there was a Buddha named Dipamkara, or lamplighter. This was the meaning of his name. But fools don't understand the metaphors of the Tathagata. Persisting in delusions and clinging to the tangible, they light lamps of everyday vegetable oil and think that by illuminating the interiors of buildings they're following the Buddha's teaching. How foolish! The light released by a Buddha from one curl between his brows can illuminate countless worlds. An oil lamp is no help. Or do you think otherwise?

Practicing all six periods of the day and night means constantly cultivating enlightenment among the six senses and persevering in every form of awareness. Never relaxing control over the six senses is what's meant by all six periods. As for walking around stupas, the stupa is your body and mind. When your awareness circles your body and mind without stopping, this is called walking around a stupa. The sages of long ago followed this path to nirvana. But people today don't understand what this means. Instead of looking inside they insist on looking outside. They use their material bodies to walk around material stupas. And they keep at it day and night, wearing themselves out in vain and coming no closer to their real self.

The same holds true for observing a fast. It's useless unless you understand what this really means. To fast means to regulate, to regulate your body and mind so that they're not distracted or disturbed. And to observe means to uphold, to uphold the rules of discipline according to the Dharma. Fasting means guarding against the six attractions on the outside and the three poisons on the inside and striving through contemplation to purify your body and mind.

Fasting also includes five kinds of food. First there's delight in the Dharma. This is the delight that comes from acting in accordance with the Dharma. Second is harmony in meditation. This is the harmony of body and mind that comes from seeing through subject and object. Third is invocation, the invocation of Buddhas with both your month and your mind. Fourth is resolution, the resolution to pursue virtue whether walking, standing, sitting, or lying down. And fifth is liberation, the liberation of your mind from worldly contamination. These five are the foods of fasting. Unless a person eats these five pure foods, he's wrong to think he's fasting.

Also, once you stop eating the food of delusion, if you touch it again you break your fast. And once you break it, you reap no blessing from it. The world is full of deluded people who don't see this. They indulge their body and mind in all manner of evil. They give free rein to their passions and have no shame. And when they stop eating ordinary food, they call it fasting. How absurd!

It's the same with worshipping. You have to understand the meaning and adapt to conditions. Meaning includes action and nonaction. Whoever understands this follows the Dharma.

Worship means reverence and humility it means revering your real self and humbling delusions. If you can wipe out evil desires and harbor good thoughts, even if nothing shows its worship. Such form is its real form. The Lord wanted worldly people to think of worship as expressing humility and subduing the mind. So he told them to prostrate their bodies to show their reverence, to let the external express the internal, to harmonize essence and form. Those who fail to cultivate the inner meaning and concentrate instead on the outward expression never stop indulging in ignorance, hatred, and evil while exhausting themselves to no avail. They can deceive others with postures, remain shameless before sages and vain before mortals, but they'll never escape the Wheel, much less achieve any merit.

Student: But the Bathhouse Sutra says, "By contributing to the bathing of monks, people receive limitless blessings." This would appear to be an instance of external practice achieving merit. How does this relate to beholding the mind?

Bodhidharma: Here, the bathing of monks doesn't refer to the washing of anything tangible. When the Lord preached the Bathhouse Sutra, he wanted his disciples to remember the Dharma of washing. So he used an everyday concern to convey his real meaning, which he couched in his explanation of merit from seven offerings. Of these seven, the first is clear water, the second fire, the third soap, the fourth willow catkins, the fifth pure ashes, the sixth ointment, and the seventh the inner garment He used these seven to represent seven other things that cleanse and enhance a person by eliminating the delusion and filth of a poisoned mind. The first of these seven is morality, which washes away excess just as water washes away dirt. Second is wisdom, which penetrates subject and object, just as fire warms water. Third is discrimination, which gets rid of evil practices, just as soap gets rid of grime. Fourth is honesty, which purges delusions, just as chewing willow catkins purifies the breath. Fifth is true faith, which resolves all doubts, just as rubbing pure ashes on the body prevents illnesses. Sixth is patience, which overcomes resistance and disgrace, just as ointment softens the skin. And seventh is shame, which redresses evil deeds, just as the inner garment covers up an ugly body. These seven represent the real meaning of the sutra. When he spoke this sutra, the Tathagata was talking to farsighted followers of the Mahayana, not to narrow-minded people of dim vision. It's not surprising that people nowadays don't understand.

The bathhouse is the body. When you light the fire of wisdom, you warm the pure water of the precepts and bathe the true Buddha nature within you. By upholding these seven practices you add to your virtue. The monks of that age were perceptive. They understood the Buddha's meaning. They followed his reaching, perfected their virtue, and tasted the fruit of Buddhahood. But people nowadays can't fathom these things. They use ordinary water to wash a physical body and think they're following the sutra. But they're mistaken. Our true buddha-nature has no shape. And the dust of affliction has no form. How can people use ordinary water to wash an intangible body? It won't work. When will they wake up? To clean such a body you have to behold it. Once impurities and filth arise from desire, they multiply until they cover you inside and out. But if you try to wash this body of yours, you have to scrub until it's nearly gone before it's clean. From this you should realize that washing something external isn't What the Buddha meant.

Student: The sutras say that someone who wholeheartedly invokes the Buddha is sure to be reborn in the Western Paradise. Since is door leads to Buddhahood, why seek liberation in beholding the mind?

Bodhidharma: If you're going to invoke the Buddha, you have to do it right. Unless you understand what invoking means, you'll do it wrong. And if you do it wrong, you'll never go anywhere.

Buddha means awareness, the awareness of body and mind that prevents evil from arising in either. And to invoke means to call to mind, to call constantly to mind the rules of discipline and to follow them with all your might. This is what's meant by invoking. Invoking has to do with thought and not with language. If you use a trap to catch fish, once you succeed you can forget the trap. And if you use language to find meaning, once you find it you can forget language. To invoke the Buddha's name you have to understand the Dharma of invoking. If it's not present in your mind, your mouth chants an empty name. As long as you're troubled by the three poisons or by thoughts of yourself, your deluded mind will keep you from seeing the Buddha and you'll only waste your effort. Chanting and invoking are worlds apart, Chanting is done with the mouth. Invoking is done with the mind. And because invoking comes from the mind, it's called the door to awareness. Chanting is centered in the mouth and appears as sound. If you cling to appearances while searching for meaning, you won't find a thing. Thus, sages of the past cultivated introspection and not speech. This mind is the source of all virtues. And this mind is the chief of all powers, The eternal bliss of nirvana comes from the mind at rest. Rebirth in the three realms also comes from the mind. The mind is the door to every world and the mind is the ford to the other shore. Those who know where the door is don't worry about reaching it. Those who know where the ford is don't worry about crossing it.

The people I meet nowadays are superficial. They think of merit as something that has form. They squander their wealth and butcher creatures of land and sea. They foolishly concern themselves with erecting statues and stupas, telling people to pile up lumber and bricks, to paint this blue and that green. They strain body and mind, injure themselves and mislead others. And they don't know enough to be ashamed. How will they ever become enlightened?

They see something tangible and instantly become attached. If you talk to them about formlessness, they sit there dumb and confused. Greedy for the small mercies of this world, they remain blind to the great suffering to come. Such disciples wear themselves out in vain. Turning from the true to the false, they talk about nothing but future blessings.

If you can simply concentrate your mind's Inner Light and behold its outer illumination, you'll dispel the three poisons and drive away the six thieves once and for all. And without effort gain possession of an infinite number of virtues, perfections, and doors to the truth, Seeing through the mundane and witnessing the sublime is less than an eye-blink away, Realization is now. Why worry about gray hair? But the true door is hidden and can't be revealed. I have only touched upon beholding the mind.

The Zen Teaching of Instantaneous Awakening by Baizhang Huahai

Introduction

Baizhang Huaihai (720–814) was a Chinese Zen master during the Tang Dynasty. He was a dharma heir of Mazu Daoyi and his students included Huangbo and Linji.

Traditional Chan/Zen mythology holds Baizhang established an early set of rules for Chan monastic discipline, the Pure Rules of Baizhang famous for the saying One day not work, one day not eat. As the Zen monks farmed, it helped them to survive the Great Anti-Buddhist Persecution more than other sects which rely more on donations. The rules are used today in many Zen monasteries, but some believe these rules developed much later in Chan history, and are agreed by the monks Taixu and Hsu Yun.

A Treatise on Entering the Tao of Sudden Enlightenment

I, disciple Hui-Hai, humbly bow before all Bodhisattvas in each of the ten directions. Even though I have written this thesis, I fear that it does not correspond to holy thought. If this is so, I hope that all Buddhas and Bodhisattvas in the ten directions will give me a chance to repent. However, if the treatise tallies with the holy doctrines, then I desire that all merit acquired therefrom be returned and contributed to all sentient beings; and I wish all of them to become Buddhas in the future.

Q: What method must be practiced to attain liberation?

A: Only by practicing the Dharma of Sudden Enlightenment can we attain liberation.

Q: What is Sudden Enlightenment?

A: "Sudden" means instantly stopping false thought. "Enlightenment" means [awareness] that one attains nothing.

Q: What method is used to begin this practice?

A: Just practice using the fundamental teaching.

Q: What is it and how does one practice using the fundamental teaching?

A: Mind is the fundamental source.

Q: How do you know that mind is the fundamental source?

A: The Lankavatara Sutra says: "When the mind comes into being, then various conceptions (dharmas) come to be; and when the mind ceases to be, then these various conceptions cease to be." The Vimalakirti Nirdesa Sutra says: "If you wish to attain the Pure Land, you should purify your own mind, because if your mind is pure, all Buddha-Lands are also pure." The Sutra of Transforming Teaching says: "Just concentrate the mind on one point and all things are achieved." Another sutra says: "The holy person seeks Mind and does not seek Budha. The foolish man seeks Buddha and does not seek Mind. The wise man regulates the mind and does not regulate the body, while the foolish man regulates the body but does not regulate the mind." The Sutra of the Buddha's Names says: "The evil arising from the mind can be extinguished only by the mind." Thus, we see that all good and evil arise from one's own mind and that the mind itself is the fundamental source. Therefore, if one wishes to seek liberation, he should recognize this fundamental source. On the other hand, if one does not understand this truth, he will seek liberation outside himself, always laboring in vain. The Dhyanaparamita Sutra says: "As long as you seek it from external forms, you cannot come to complete Enlightenment even after many kalpas. However, through perceptive insight Bodhi is suddenly attained."

Q: How is the fundamental Dharma to be practiced?

A: Only through meditation and insightful contemplation in samadhi. The Dhyanaparamita Sutra says: "To seek the wisdom of Buddha, you need both dhyana and contemplation. Without dhyana and contemplation together, thought will be disordered and break the root of goodness."

Q: What is dhyana and what is contemplation?

A: The non-arising of a single thought is dhyana. The original nature is your increate Mind. Contemplation in samadhi happens when opposites and external objects do not cause a single thought to arise. In contemplation (samadhi), the mind cannot be moved by the so-called eight winds: benefit and loss; fame and ignominy; praise and ridicule; suffering and happiness. If only one can abide in this kind of contemplation, then, even though he is a worldly person, he, nevertheless, can enter Buddhahood. The Sutra of Bodhisattva Discipline says: "All sentient beings who receive the discipline of the Buddha thus assume the position of all Buddhas." Achieving this state is called "liberation". It is also described as arriving on the other shore by leaping over the three realms of samsara ... Such a one is a great, powerful Bodhisattva with immeasurable sway and influence as well as a conqueror of all obstacles.

Q: Where does the mind dwell in its real abode?

A: Dwelling nowhere is its real abode.

Q: What is dwelling nowhere?

A: It is the mind not dwelling anywhere or on anything.

Q: What does "not dwelling anywhere or on anything" mean?

A: Not to dwell anywhere or on anything means not to dwell on good or evil, existence or non-existence, within or without or on the middle, nor on concentration nor dispersion, and neither to dwell on the void nor on the non-void. This is the meaning of "not dwelling anywhere or on anything". Just this alone is real abiding. This stage of achievement is also the non-abiding Mind, and the non-abiding Mind is the Buddha Mind.

Q: What is the non-abiding Mind like?

A: The non-abiding Mind is not green, yellow, red or white. It is not long or short, nor does it come or go. It is not pure or impure, nor does it have birth or death. It is only deep and permanent stillness. This is the non-abiding Mind, which is also called the Original Body. The Original Body is the Buddha's Body, which is also called the Dharmakaya.

Q: In perception through body and mind, are there several forms, such as eye perception, ear perception, nose perception, body perception, mind perception, etc.?

A: No, there are not several forms like these.

Q: If there are not several ways of perceiving, what, then, is perception?

A: This so-called "perception" is one's own Nature. One's own Nature, originally pure and clean, deep and still, is, in fact, in its voidness, perception.

Q: Since this pure, clean "substance" cannot be located, where does perception come from?

A: It is like a great, bright mirror that, even though it has no images inside it, can perceive and reflect all kinds of shadows. It is just utterly void no-mind. If the mind of the practicer does not grasp anything, then false thought will not arise; and the ego and its objects will vanish. Then the mind would naturally be pure and clean because it would be one with the pure and clean perception of void Original Nature. The Dharmapada Sutra says: "Perception manifesting itself in the Absolute Void -- this is the learned master."

Q: What is the meaning of the sentence in "The Diamond-Body Chapter" of The Mahaparinirvana Sutra, which goes as follows: "To perceive nothing -- neither not knowing nor without not knowing -- this only is clear perception"?

A: To perceive nothing describes the Self-Nature, which is without shape and so cannot be grasped; therefore, it is described as perceiving nothing. Also, because it is deep and still, it cannot be grasped. It neither comes nor goes; it is not separate from worldly concerns, but neither do worldly concerns disturb it. "Clear perception" means being fully at ease. "Not-knowing" means the Self-Nature has no shape and is non-discriminating. "Without not-knowing" means that the "substance" of non-discrimination has as many functions as the numberless sandgrains in the Ganges River and can discriminate all things clearly. The Prajna Gatha says: "Unknowing, Prajna knows all; unseeing, Prajna sees all."

Q: One sutra says: "To perceive neither existence nor non-existence is real liberation." What does this mean?

A: Attaining pure Mind is known as perceiving existence, while no thought of pure Mind arising at that time is known as not perceiving existence. Furthermore, when the stage of no continuation is attained, no thought of no birth and no continuation should arise. This is known as not seeing anything as existent or as non-existent. The Surangama Sutra says: "Intellect acts as the knower, and this is the root of your ignorance; but if it is free from perception, it will be Nirvana, which is also known as Liberation."

Q: What does "There is no object to perceive" mean?

A: To see men and women and all objects and not let a single thought of love or hate relative to any of them arise -- as if they were not beheld at all -- is the meaning of "There is no object to perceive".

Q: Regarding all objects is called perception, so can not perceiving any object whatsoever still be called perception?

A: Yes, it is still called perception.

Q: When regarding objects, we perceive them as existing; so how can there be any perception at all if there are no existent objects to be perceived?

A: Perception does not depend on the existence or non-existence of objects. The nature of perception is permanent. For example, to behold an object is seeing, but even without an object, seeing remains. Thus, you should understand that even though things come and go, the nature of seeing neither comes nor goes. The same is true with all your other sense organs as well.

Q: If I see an object, does something really exist within that focus of perception?

A: No, nothing really exists within that focus of perception.

Q: When there is sound, there is hearing. When there is no sound, is there still hearing?

A: Yes, There is still hearing.

Q: When there is sound, we say we hear, so how can there, logically, still be hearing without sound?

A: In hearing, it does not matter whether there is sound or no sound. Since the nature of hearing is permanent, when there is sound there is hearing; and when there is no sound there is still hearing.

Q: Who is the knower of hearing?

A: It is one's own nature that is generally referred to as the knower of hearing.

Q: What is wrong thinking, and what is right thinking?

A: Thoughts of existence and non-existence are wrong thinking, while no thoughts of existence and non-existence are right thinking. Thoughts of good and evil are wrong thinking, while no thoughts of good and evil are right thinking. Also, thoughts of suffering and happiness, birth and death, acceptance and rejection, like and dislike, love and hate, etc., are all wrong thinking, while no thoughts of suffering and happiness, etc., are right thinking.

Q: So what, in a nutshell, is right thought?

A: In a nutshell, right thought means thinking only of Bodhi.

Q: Can Bodhi be acquired?

A: No! You cannot acquire Bodhi.

Q: Since it cannot be acquired, how can one, reasonably. think only of Bodhi?

A: To name Bodhi is false, because it cannot be described or possessed. It is neither in front nor in back of one who tries to acquire it, because it cannot be acquired or thought about. Only not thinking about it is true and right thought. Bodhi, then, is not a thought-object and, thus, there is no mind whatsoever anywhere. However, all the various kinds of non-thinking which have been touched upon accord with the needs of particular circumstances, being merely expedient terms; and even though different names are used expediently, there is no difference whatsoever in the substance. There is only no mind whatsoever dwelling nowhere at all. When this stage is reached, one is, quite naturally, liberated.

Q: How can one perform the actions of the Buddha?

A: Not to engage in or perform any action whatsoever is the Buddha's action. It is also called right action or holy action, which is, as I have said before, not acting with concepts of existence and non-existence, love and hate, etc. The chapter on the discipline of the Bodhisattva in the fifth volume of The Great Vinaya says: "The Holy Ones do not act like other sentient beings, nor do ordinary sentient beings act like the Holy Ones."

Q: What is the right view?

A: To perceive without perceiving any object whatsoever is the right view.

Q: What does "to perceive without perceiving any object whatsoever" mean?

A: Perceiving all sorts of things without grasping -- that is, not being clouded by the arising of any thought of love or hate, etc. -- is perceiving without any objects. If one can see without seeing any object whatsoever, that is using the Buddha-Eye, which is like no other eye. On the other hand, if one sees all sorts of things that cause thoughts of love and hate, etc., to arise, that is known as "perceiving objects" with ordinary eyes, and sentient beings have no other kind of eyes. This is true, likewise, with all of the other sense organs.

Q: You said earlier that wisdom is the function of the Way of Sudden Enlightenment, but what is wisdom?

A: If you understand that the nature of non-duality is voidness, then you are liberated. However, if you understand that the nature of duality is not void, then you are not liberated. Thus, wisdom is understanding what is right and what is wrong. It is also recognizing universal substance and its functions. The understanding of the voidness of duality is the substance of wisdom, while liberation, which is never allowing any thought whatsoever of existence or non-existence, good of evil, love or hate, etc., to arise, is known as understanding the function of the voidness of duality.

Q: Where can one enter the doorway to this understanding?

A: Through the perfection of charity (dana-paramita).

Q: Buddha has said that the six paramitas are the action of the Bodhisattva path, so how can we enter the doorway to this understanding by practicing, as you have said, only the dana-paramita?

A: People who are confused or deluded do not understand that the other five paramitas all evolve from the dana-paramita. Therefore, in practicing the dana-paramita, one also fulfills the practice of the other five paramitas.

Q: For what reason is it called the dana-paramita?

A: "Dana" means the perfection of charity.

Q: What things can be given up in the name of charity?

A: Clinging to thoughts of duality can be given up.

Q: Just what does this mean?

A: It means to give up clinging, in the name of charity, to thoughts of good and evil, existence and non-existence, love and hate, emptiness and fullness, concentration and non-concentration, pure and impure, etc. In the name of charity, give up all of them. Then, and only then, can you attain the stage of the voidness of duality, while, at the same time, letting neither a thought about the voidness of opposites nor about charity arise. This is the genuine practice of the dana-paramita, which is also known as absolute detachment from all phenomena. This is only the voidness of all dharma-nature, which means that always and everywhere is just no-mind. If one can attain the stage of no-mind everywhere, no form will be perceived, because our self-nature is void, containing no form. This, then, is true Reality, which is also called the wonderful form or body of the Tathagata. The Diamond Sutra says: "Those who have abandoned all forms are called Buddhas."

Q: But the Buddha spoke about six paramitas, so how can you reasonably say that one paramita (the dana-paramita) can include the other five?

A: The Sutra of the Benefits of Thinking says: "The Jalavidyadeva spoke to Brahmadeva as follows: 'Bodhisattvas who abandon all defilements are said to have completed the dana-paramita. This is the perfection of charity. If there is the non-arising of a single thought, they are said to have completed the sila-paramita. This the perfection of discipline. If there is no injury to or harm by any dharma, they are said to have completed the ksanti-paramita. This is the perfection of patience. If there is non-attachment to all dharmas, they are said to have completed the virya-paramita. This is the perfection of zeal. If there is non-dwelling on any dharma whatsoever, they are said to have completed the dhyana-paramita. This is the perfection of serenity. If there is no use of sophistry in speaking of any dharma, they are said to have completed the prajna-paramita. This is the perfection of wisdom. These are also known as the six Dharmas without any difference. The first one involves giving; the second one, non-arising of sensation; the third one, the non-arising of thought; the fourth one, being detached from form; the fifth one, non-dwelling in any dharma; and the sixth one, speaking without sophistry. These six paramitas are given different names expediently to meet different needs, but the wonderful principle underlying them all is not different. Thus, if one thing is abandoned, then everything is abandoned; and if one thing does not arise, then nothing whatsoever arises. Deluded people cannot understand this, and even insist that these six paramitas, or methods, are different. Thus, these foolish people, clinging to the variety of methods, revolve endlessly on the Wheel-of-Life-and-Death. Therefore, I urge all you students just to practice the one method of the dana-paramita, which, since it includes completely all dharmas, must, logically, include the other five paramitas.'"

Q: What are the three methods of study, and how can they be used equally?

A: The three methods of study are discipline, meditation and wisdom.

Q: Can you describe these methods of study: discipline, meditation and wisdom?

A: Discipline is centered upon purity and non-defilement. Meditation is centered upon stilling the mind so that it is moved by no object whatsoever. Wisdom is reached when the knowing mind is agitated by no object, but yet does not hold any thought of being unagitated. Wisdom is reached only when the knowing mind is clear and pure but has no thought of being clear and pure. Wisdom is reached when you can discriminate between good and evil, as well as other dualities, but, grasping none if them, remain free. Finally, if you realize that the "substances" of discipline, of meditation and of wisdom, none of which can be possessed, are indistinguishable -- i.e., are of only one substance -- this, in itself, is equal to the three studies undertaken and completed separately.

Q: If the mind dwells in purity, does it not, then, grasp the pure?

A: When the mind dwells in purity, not allowing a thought of purity to arise, it is not grasping the pure.

Q: If the mind abides in voidness, is it not, then, grasping the void?

A: If you have a thought of voidness, that is grasping the void.

Q: If the mind dwells in non-dwelling, is it not, then, grasping non-dwelling?

A: If your mind is void of thinking, then there is no grasping. If you wish to recognize clearly the non-dwelling mind, then during your meditation just be aware that your mind does not think about any object or hold on to any dualities, such as good and evil, etc. Since past things are already past, you should not think about them anymore; and, thus, any thought about the past vanishes. This is known as being without the past. Furthermore, since future things have not yet arrived, you should neither seek nor wish for them; and, thus, any thought of the future vanishes. This is known as being without the future. Finally, since present things are already present, you should not grasp them nor allow a thought of love or hate to arise; and, thus, any thought about the present vanishes. This is known as being without the present. In summary, if no thought about these three time periods arises, then the three time periods do not exist. If a thought of moving arises, do not follow it; and the thought of moving will vanish. If a thought of dwelling arises, do not follow it; and the thought of dwelling will vanish. However, grasping at the thought of non-dwelling is abiding in non-dwelling. On the other hand, if you understand clearly that your mind does not abide anywhere whatsoever that is abiding, then you are neither abiding nor not abiding anywhere. If you understand clearly that your mind does not abide anywhere at all, then you are clearly seeing your Original Mind, which is also referred to as "clearly seeing the nature of seeing." Just this Mind, that abides nowhere at all, is the Mind of Buddha and the Mind of liberation, the Mind of Bodhi and the Mind of the Uncreate. It is also referred to as realizing that the nature of form is void. Finally, it is what the sutra calls "Attaining the patient endurance of the Uncreate." If you have not yet arrived at this stage, then you should dedicate yourself to the task, make a great effort and practice diligently. When you have succeeded completely, you will then know that you have come to the understanding of truth from your own self. You will then understand from a non-abiding mind -- that is to say, a mind dwelling neither upon the real nor the unreal. What is the unreal? Any thought of love or hate. What is real? Any thought without love or hate. Only a mind without thoughts of love or hate is void of duality. And it follows that when the mind is void of duality, liberation naturally ensues.

Q: Does he who practices stilling the mind do it only while sitting in meditation?

A: The practice of stilling the mind means not only doing it while sitting, but also while walking, standing or lying down and, uninterruptedly, during all other actions at all times. This is referred to as truly abiding in permanence.

Q: The Vaipulya Sutra lists five kinds of Dharmakaya: (1) The Absolute Reality-Dharmakaya; (2) The Merit Dharmakaya; (3) The Dharma-Nature Dharmakaya; (4) The Infinite-Transformation Dharmakaya; and (5) The Voidness Dharmakaya. Which of these refers to one's own body?

A: The awareness that mind cannot be destroyed is the Absolute-Reality Dharmakaya. The awareness that mind includes all things is the Merit Dharmakaya. The awareness that mind is no-mind is the Dharma-Nature Dharmakaya. The potentiality to spread the Dharma is the Infinite-Transformation Dharmakaya. The awareness that the mind is without shape or form and cannot be grasped is the Voidness Dharmakaya. If you understand this doctrine, you should also understand that there is nothing whatsoever to be attained. Knowing that there is nothing to be gained or attained is the realization of the Dharmakaya of Buddhadharma. If one harbors any thought whatsoever of gaining or attaining, he holds the wrong view and, being a person of overweening pride, is labeled heterodox. The Vimalakirti Nirdesa Sutra says: "Then Sariputra asked of the devakanya, 'What have you gained or attained that has given you supernatural powers?' The devakanya answered, 'Just because I have really neither gained nor attained anything whatsoever, I can be as I am.'" So if one thinks he has gained or attained something, he is, in Buddhadharma, known as a man of overweening pride.

Q: The sutra speaks about both Universal Enlightenment and Wonderful Enlightenment. What is Universal Enlightenment and what is Wonderful Enlightenment?

A: To realize that form is void is known as Universal Enlightenment. To realize the voidness of dualities is known as Wonderful Enlightenment. Also, to realize there is really neither enlightenment nor non-enlightenment is known as Wonderful Enlightenment.

Q: Are Universal Enlightenment and Wonderful Enlightenment different or not?

A: Actually, the two names are used only as an expedient, but, since their substance is the same, there is really no difference between them. Likewise, this mutual substantiality is true of all phenomena.

Q: What does it mean when The Diamond Sutra says: "There is really no Dharma to expound, and this is really expounding the Dharma?"

A: Since the substance of Prajna is absolutely pure and bright, not even a single thing can be attained. This is the meaning of "There is really no Dharma to expound". Also, the substance of Prajna is stillness, but it, nevertheless, includes functions as numerous as sandgrains in the Ganges; thus, it is aware of everything. This is known as "really expounding the Dharma". Therefore, it is said that having no Dharma whatever to expound is really expounding the Dharma.

Q: What does it mean in The Diamond Sutra when it says, "If a virtuous man or woman receives, reads, holds in mind and recites this Sutra and is despised by other people, then this person, who was bound to suffer an evil destiny in retribution for his past sins, will now have his bad karma eradicated by the others' contempt"? Will he then attain Anuttara-samyak-sambodhi?

A: He is just like a person who has not yet met a great and learned master. Even though his original mind is pure and bright, it is covered by evil karma, ignorance and the three poisons; and so it cannot manifest itself. Thus, he is held in contempt by others. Because he is shown contempt by others, he makes up his mind to seek the Tao of Buddha. Then the three poisons cannot arise, his ignorance is also destroyed and all evil karma vanishes. He recovers his original, bright, pure mind and never becomes confused again. So we can then say that he has found liberation and attained Anuttara-samyak-sambodhi.

Q: What are the five eyes of the Tathagata, and what are their functions?

A: The Tathagata's fleshly eye sees form as pure. The Tathagata's deva eye sees substance as pure. The Tathagata's wisdom eye sees all sorts of forms and can discriminate among them regarding their qualities of good or evil but, by not grasping, remains free. The Tathagata's Dharma eye sees formlessness. The Tathagata's Buddha eye neither sees nor does not see either form or formlessness.

Q: What is the difference between the Mahayana and the Supreme Vehicle?

A: The Mahayana is the Bodhisattva's vehicle, and the Supreme Yana is the Buddha's vehicle.

Q: How can one practice to attain these vehicles?

A: To practice the Bodhisattva's vehicle is simply Mahayana practice. After attaining the Bodhisattva stage, where there is no longer any need to practice, one arrives at the stage of no-practice, which is permanently still and deep and where there is neither increase nor decrease. This is called the Supreme Vehicle or the Buddha's Vehicle.

Q: What is the meaning of the passage in The Mahaparinirvana Sutra which states, "More meditative contemplation than wisdom cannot separate one from ignorance, while more wisdom than meditative contemplation merely multiplies wrong views; thus, only with an equal balance of meditative contemplation and wisdom can there be liberation"?

A: To discriminate among the various kinds of good and evil is wisdom, while, during such discrimination, never allowing thoughts of love and hate to arise -- and if they do, not being defiled by them -- is meditative contemplation. This is the functioning of meditative contemplation and wisdom in equal balance.

Q Having neither words nor speech is referred to as concentration of mind, but can this concentration still take place even while one is speaking?

A: When I spoke of concentration, I was referring to that deep and constant concentration, which is held both during speaking and non-speaking. Since the function of concentration is constant, it continues even while we discriminate among things and are speaking. If one uses the mind of voidness to see forms, then forms are void. Oppositely, if one uses the mind of voidness not to see forms and not to discriminate, the result is also void. This is true, likewise, of our senses -- seeing, hearing, feeling and cognition. Because our Self-Nature is void, it continues to be void everywhere and under all circumstances. Thus, because voidness is non-attachment, this non-attachment is identical with the sense functions. Bodhisattvas use this Dharma of Voidness to attain the stage of the Absolute. It is, therefore, identical with concentration and wisdom and is also known as liberation. But allow me to give you a vivid example to end your doubt once and for all. When a bright mirror illuminates things, does its brightness fluctuate? No! When the mirror does not illuminate things, does its brightness fluctuate? Again, no! And why not? Just because the brightness of the mirror possesses no feeling or sensation of illumination. Therefore, during illumination, the brightness does not fluctuate. Again, why not? Since the mirror has no feeling or sensation, there is neither movement nor non-movement of its brightness. We can use the sun as another example. The light of the sun illuminates the world. Does its light fluctuate when it is shining? No! Does its light fluctuate when it is not shining? Again, no! And why not? Since the light has no feeling or sensation when it illuminates, it, therefore, shines or does not shine, all the while never fluctuating. Wisdom is illumination, while concentration of mind is no fluctuation whatsoever. All Bodhisattvas depend upon an equal balance of concentration and wisdom to attain perfect Enlightenment. Thus, it can be said that a perfect balance of wisdom and concentration is liberation. Finally, let me emphasize, in using these examples, that although to have no feeling in the meditative concentration of mind means to be without worldly feeling, I do not imply that it means to be without holy feeling.

Q: What, then, is worldly feeling, and what is holy feeling?

A: If you give rise to a thought of duality, that is worldly feeling. On the other hand, if you do not give rise to a thought of duality, that is holy feeling.

Q: What does it mean when the sutra says: "The sound of discussion has ceased, and the role of thought is done"?

A: Words are used to manifest the doctrine. After understanding the doctrine, then, words are useless. The doctrine is void, voidness is the Tao, and the Tao is without words. This is the meaning of "The sound of discussion has ceased". Since the real meaning of the doctrine does not give rise to a single thought or perception and because no thought or perception arises, it is unborn. Furthermore, because it is unborn, then the fundamental nature of all forms is void, Next, since the fundamental nature of all forms is void, then everything in the world is non-existent. Finally, since all things are fundamentally non-existent, "the role of thought is done".

Q: What is the meaning of "The immutability of the Absolute is maintained in every state"?

A: "The immutability of the Absolute is maintained in every state" means, simply, that it is both never moved and forever unmoving. This is the mind of Bhutatathata, which is also referred to as Suchness. In reality, all Buddhas in the past attained Enlightenment by means of the principle of immutability. Also, all Buddhas in the present have attained Enlightenment in this way. Finally, all Buddhas in the future who practice in this way will attain Enlightenment. The Vimalakirti Nirdesa Sutra says: "It has ever been like this with all Buddhas; and it will ever be like this with Maitreya as well as with all sentient beings, because none of them can ever be dissociated from their Buddha-Nature."

Q: Is the awareness that form is void and that the worldly is holy the same as Sudden Enlightenment?

A: Yes!

Q: Just what is the meaning of "form is void and the worldly is holy"?

A: The mind defiled is the same as form, but the mind undefiled is void. Similarly, the mind defiled is worldly, but the mind undefiled is holy. To say it in another way, the Absolute Void mysteriously exists as form, but because its "form" cannot be grasped, it is void. Here, when we refer to "void", we are speaking of the voidness of Self-Nature. We are not referring, in this instance, to the voidness which occurs after the destruction of form. Similarly, when we refer to "form", in this context, we mean the form of the void-nature of the Absolute Void; but we are not speaking, in the usual sense, of form that creates other forms.

Q: What does it mean when the sutra speaks of "the Dharma of the exhaustible and the inexhaustible"?

A: The nature of both the exhaustible and the inexhaustible is void. Thus, when there is no further creation of forms by the senses -- such as seeing and hearing -- then that is the end, or exhaustion, of all things in the world. In contrast, the untreated substance, with functions as numerous as the sandgrains in the Ganges River and which manifests all kinds of activities in response to circumstances, is inexhaustible and includes all dharmas. Also, in the original substance there is no decrease in spite of its infinite manifestations. This, then, is the meaning of "the Dharma of the exhaustible and the inexhaustible".

Q: Are the exhaustible and the inexhaustible the same or different?

A: Their substance is identical; but when spoken of, they seem to be different.

Q: Since their substance is identical, how can they appear to be different when spoken of?

A: Their "sameness" is the substance of speech, and speech is the function of their substance, which is used appropriately to respond to all kinds of circumstances. Therefore, we say that their substance is identical; but when spoken of, they appear to be different. To illustrate this let's use a vivid example. Although there is only one sun in the sky, when it is reflected in many containers of water below, there appears to be one sun in each container. Each reflected sun is perfect and complete like the real sun in the sky; and since there is no difference among them, it can be said that they are of one substance. However, when each sun is spoken of relative to its own container, it appears to be different from all the others. Therefore, we can say that even though their substance is identical in reality, they, nevertheless, appear to be different when pointed out and spoken about separately. Finally, all the reflected suns are perfect, and there has been no decrease of the original sun in the sky. Therefore, original substance is spoken of as being inexhaustible.

Q: One sutra says that nothing is born and nothing dies. Which dharmas are not born and which dharmas do not die?

A: Evil dharmas are not born, and good dharmas do not die.

Q: What dharmas are good and what dharmas are evil?

A: Evil dharmas are produced by the flowing or agitated mind. Non-defilement and stillness do not increase evil dharmas. When one arrives at the stage of non-defilement and non-flowing stillness, then the mind is perfectly pure and bright, deep, still and permanent, neither creating nor destroying. This is truly the condition of no birth and no death.

Q: What does it mean in The Sutra of Bodhisattva Discipline when it says: "When sentient beings practice the Buddha's Discipline, they assume the position of all Buddhas, which is the same as Great Enlightenment, thus becoming authentic sons of all Buddhas"?

A: The Buddha's Discipline in the Buddhadharma is the practice of pure mind. If one can make up his mind to practice the conduct of purity of mind without attachment, he can be said to have received the Buddha's Discipline. All Buddhas in the past engaged in pure-mind practice and consequently attained the Tao of Enlightenment. If one can engage in the practice of pure mind without attachment, then his merit is equal to and no different from the merit of the Buddhas; and he can be said to have gained the position of all Buddhas. If one attains enlightenment like this, it is the same as the enlightenment of a Buddha; and, therefore, it can be said that his state is completely identical with the Great Enlightenment. He, then, becomes the authentic son of all Buddhas. Finally, if one engages in pure-mind practice, then the mind is pure and everything else is pure. Such a one is then called the son of all Buddhas as well as the authentic son of all Buddhas.

Q: Concerning the Buddha and the Dharma, which preceded the other? Did the Buddha come first or did the Dharma come first? If the Buddha came first, upon what Dharma did the Buddha depend to attain enlightenment?

A: In one way of speaking, the Buddha precedes the Dharma, but succeeds it in another.

Q: How can this reasonably be so?

A: If you are speaking about the Dharma of stillness and voidness, then the Dharma precedes the Buddha. However, if you are speaking about the Dharma of words, then the Buddha precedes the Dharma. Furthermore, we can observe that because all Buddhas depend on the Dharma of stillness and voidness to attain Perfect Enlightenment, the Dharma must, logically, precede the Buddha. However, the opposite of this is, also, logical and reasonable, when the sutra says: "The Dharma is the teacher of all

Buddhas." After attaining Perfect Enlightenment, they begin to expound on the twelve divisions of the Sutras in order to convert all sentient beings. In turn, all sentient beings depend upon the teaching of the Dharma to practice and to attain Enlightenment, which is an example of the Buddha preceding the Dharma.

Q: What is the meaning of transmitting Dharma through words but not through Tsung (Ch'an)?

A: When words are different from action, then what is transmitted though words is not conveyed through action.

Q: How can Dharma be transmitted through both Tsung and words?

A: When words and action are not different, then Dharma can be transmitted through both Tsung and words.

Q: What is meant when the sutra says: "To arrive is not to arrive, while not to arrive is to arrive"?

A: Just to speak of arriving (at intuitive understanding) but not yet having arrived in action is known as "arriving that has not yet arrived". Having arrived in action but not speaking about arriving is known as "not arriving that has arrived". However, arriving in both speech and action is known as Complete Arrival.

Q: The Buddhadharma neither rejects the existent (activity) nor clings to the transcendental (non-activity). What does this mean?

A: From the beginning of his practice to generate his Bodhi-Mind until he attained Perfect Enlightenment under the Bodhi tree and, finally, even to the moment he entered the forest and sat under the twin Sala trees to enter Parinirvana, the Buddha never abandoned a single dharma or a single sentient being. This is the meaning of not rejecting the existent. On the other hand, even though he engaged in the practice of no-mind, he did not have even a single thought about the attainment of no-mind. Also, even though he concentrated on voidness, he did not have even a single thought about the attainment of voidness. Finally, even though he contemplated the nirvana of Bodhi, which is without form and without activity, yet he did not have even a single thought about the attainment of no-form and no-activity. This is the meaning of not clinging to the transcendental.

Q: Does hell exist or not?

A: One can say that there really is a hell, and one can also say that there really is no hell.

Q: What reason is there to say that hell both exists and does not exist?

A: All evil karma is created by the mind, and, thus, hell may be held to exist. However, if the mind is without defilement and void of self-nature, then hell may be held not to exist.

Q: Do suffering sentient beings have the Buddha-Nature?

A: Yes! All of them have the same Buddha-Nature.

Q: This being the case, do they have their Buddha-Nature when they enter hell? That is, does their Buddha-Nature enter hell along with them?

A: No, it does not enter hell along with them.

Q: So, just at that very moment when they enter hell, where is their Buddha-Nature?

A: It also enters hell along with them.

Q: Since it enters hell along with them and since those sentient beings encounter suffering, does their Buddha-Nature also encounter suffering?

A: Even though their Buddha-Nature enters hell with sentient beings, only those sentient beings themselves bear the suffering. Their Buddha-Nature never encounters any suffering.

Q: Since it enters hell along with sentient beings, why doesn't their Buddha-Nature encounter any suffering?

A: All sentient beings grasp at thought and form; and since they have form, they are, therefore, subject to creation and destruction. The Buddha-Nature does not possess form, and, having no form is, thus, in its nature, void. Because its nature is perfectly void, it, therefore, is subject neither to creation nor destruction. Let me use a vivid example to illustrate this. A person who tries to store up firewood in the sky is really trying to do the impossible, so this delusory firewood is inevitably destroyed by itself. However, the sky itself, which is permanent, can never be destroyed. The sky is void like the Buddha-Nature, while the firewood is subject to creation and destruction like sentient beings. Therefore, we can say that even though they enter hell together, only sentient beings encounter suffering, while the Buddha-Nature does not.

Q: The eight consciousnesses are turned into the Four Wisdoms, and the Four Wisdoms are bound together to become the Three Bodies. Which Wisdoms are the transformation of multiple consciousnesses? Which Wisdoms are the transformation of only one consciousness?

A: Eyes, ears, nose, tongue and body -- these five consciousnesses together become Perfecting Wisdom. The sixth consciousness alone becomes Wonderful-Observing Wisdom. The seventh consciousness alone becomes Equality-Nature Wisdom. The eighth consciousness alone becomes Great-Perfect-Mirror Wisdom.

Q: Are these four kinds of wisdom the same or different?

A: Their substance is the same, but their names are different.

Q: Since their substance is the same, why are there different names for it? Also, if it is true that these differentiating names are used only as expedients, then what is it that -- even though it is, in reality, just one substance -- is, nevertheless, named Great-Perfect-Mirror Wisdom?

A: Deep and still void that is bright and completely motionless -- this describes Great-Perfect-Mirror Wisdom. When no object causes a single thought of love or hate to arise, then duality is void. This voidness of duality is Equality-Nature Wisdom. When all the sense organs and all objects can discriminate and be discriminated, but no confused thought arises to limit freedom -- this is Wonderful-Observing Wisdom. When all the sense organs experience in a correct way with no discrimination of form -- this is Perfecting Wisdom.

Q: In relationship to the binding together of the Four Wisdoms to become the Three Bodies, which Wisdom alone becomes one Body, and which Wisdoms come together to form one Body?

A: Only Great-Perfecting-Mirror Wisdom becomes the Dharmakaya. Only Equality-Nature Wisdom becomes the Sambhogakaya. However, Wonderful-Observing Wisdom and Perfecting Wisdom combine to become the Nirmanakaya. These Three Bodies are set up as names and differentiated as concepts only as an expedient to assist those who do not yet understand. If one readily understands this doctrine, the expedient concept of "Three Bodies" is not necessary, for he clearly comprehends that their nature and substance are formless and that they are rooted neither in impermanence nor in non-impermanence.

Q: How can one see the True Body of Buddha?

A: Neither to see anything as existent nor as non-existent is to see the True Body of Buddha.

Q: What does it mean when you state that neither to see anything as existent nor as non-existent is to see the True Body of Buddha?

A: Since the idea of existence depends upon the idea of non-existence to be conceived of and since the idea of non-existence depends upon the idea of existence for its manifestation, then if, originally, the idea of existence is not conceived of, the idea of non-existence cannot be sustained. If it were separated from non-existence, where would existence come from? Existence and non-existence are interdependent; and since both of them cause each other, both of them relate to the endless round of birth and death. If one can detach himself from this duality of existence versus non-existence, then he perceives the True Body of Buddha.

Q: If even the concepts of existence and non-existence have no validity, then how or where can the concept of the True Body of Buddha have validity?

A: It can be conceptualized just because one asks about it. If no one asked about it, the concept of the True Body of Buddha would never arise again. It is just like a bright mirror that reflects objects that face it but reflects nothing if nothing is there before it.

Q: What is the meaning of "never ever departing from the Buddha"?

A: The mind that is free from the concepts of birth and death and that is still and silent in the face of things, so that it is forever motionless and void, is eternally with the Buddha.

Q: What is the meaning of the Dharma of the Supramundane?

A: It is solely mundane.

Q: I asked about the supramundane. So why do you reply that it is mundane?

A: Because the idea of the existent is set up by that of the non-existent, and the notion of the non-existent is made manifest by that of the existent. However, if originally the existent is not postulated, then the non-existent has nowhere from which to arise. Truthfully, the Real Supramundane is neither existent nor non-existent. This is the Dharma of True Activity. The Diamond Sutra says: "If one grasps the concept of Dharma, that is attachment to the false notion of an ego and a personality. In contrast, if one grasps at the concept of non-Dharma, that also is attachment to the false notion of an ego and a personality. Therefore, one should not hold either the notion of Dharma or of non-Dharma." This is really holding the True Dharma. If one can understand this doctrine and the Dharma of non-duality, then he is truly liberated.

Q: What is meaning of "the Middle Way"?

A: It designates the extremes.

Q: I asked about the Middle Way, so why do you reply that it designates the extremes?

A: The concept of the extremes is derived from that of the middle, and the concept of the middle is derived from that of the extremes. However, if originally there is no extreme, where would the middle come from? Thus, we talk about the Middle Way because we conceive of extremes; therefore, we know that the concepts of the Middle Way and the extremes are derived from each other and that both are impermanent. This is also true of form, feeling, conception, impulse and consciousness.

Q: What are the five aggregates (skandhas)?

A: When non-form grasps form and then follows form, this leads one to be born. This is the aggregate of form. Thereafter, the eight winds are embraced, which cause the accumulation of wrong thoughts and views, which are followed for pleasure and which lead one to be born. This is the aggregate of feeling. Then, using the confused mind to follow false thought, one allows conceptions to arise that lead one to be born. This is the aggregate of conception. Consequently, collecting and pursuing actions, one allows impulses to arise that lead one to be born. This is the aggregate of impulse. Finally, in uniform, pure substance a false thought arises that discriminates and grasps at false consciousness that leads one to be born. This is the aggregate of consciousness. The first aggregate relates to the body and objects, while the second, third, fourth and fifth aggregates relate to the mind.

Q: What is meant when the sutra talks about "the twenty-five elements of existence"?

A: This relates to the body undergoing future incarnations -- i.e., rebirths in the six conditions. All sentient beings have confused their minds in their present lifetimes, creating all sorts of karma; and later they must follow that karma to their rebirth, which is known as reincarnation. However, if one exists in the world with great ambition to practice the Absolute Liberation and to attain the Patient Endurance of the Uncreate, he will transcend the three realms forever, never again going through reincarnation. Rather, he will then attain only the Dharmakaya, which is nothing other than the Body of Buddha.

Q: What are the different names of the twenty-five elements of existence?

A: Their substance is one, but, depending on their functions, the twenty-five elements of existence are given different names, which are the ten virtues, the ten vices and the five aggregates.

Q: What are the ten virtues and the ten vices?

A: The ten vices are as follows: killing, stealing, carnality, lying, slander, coarse language, affected speech, cupidity, anger and perverse views. The ten virtues are quite simply defined as not engaging in the ten vices.

Q: I am still not clear about the idea of "no thought", which you referred to earlier. Can you please explain it further?

A: No thought means no mind grasping anything whatsoever. It is being without any view whatever, not even the thought of seeking something or not seeking anything. Having no thought means that in the face of any object or form, not even a single thought arises. This being-without-thought is called Real Mind. However, if one grasps the thought that this being-without-thought is the Real Mind, then it is not right thought but merely the wrong view. The sutra says: "Abandoning the six thoughts is True Thought." Again, the sutra says: "Virtuous ones abide in the Dharma of No Thought and obtain the golden color and the thirty-two characteristics of Buddha, which emit great, radiant light that illuminates the whole universe." If the merits thus gained are inconceivable and indescribable even by the Buddhas, then how much less can be known about them by the followers of other Vehicles! When the stage of no thought is arrived at, the six sense organs no longer grasp anything; and then the perception of all Buddhas is realized quite naturally. When this state is realized, it is called the Storehouse of the Buddhas and the Dharma, which includes all Buddhas and all Dharmas, because it is without mind. This same sutra says: "All Buddhas have become enlightened through this sutra."

Q Since it is without mind, how is it possible to conceive of and realize Buddha-Perception?

A: It is possible just because it is conceived of and realized without mind. A sutra says: "On original non-abiding all dharmas are based." The same sutra states further: "Take the example of a bright mirror. Even though there is no reflection in the mirror, yet it can manifest all forms." And just how is this possible? Just because the mirror's brightness is void, it can, therefore, manifest all forms. Similarly, if one can maintain no-mind, then false thoughts do not arise anymore, and the sense of an ego and a personality comes to an end. Only Absolute Purity remains, which makes one capable of boundless wisdom and Sudden Enlightenment. Sudden Enlightenment means liberation during this lifetime. Just as a lion-cub, from the moment it is born, is a real lion, likewise anyone who practices the Sudden-Enlightenment method has, from the moment he begins his practice, already entered the Buddha-Stage. Just as the bamboo-shoots growing in springtime are not different from the parent bamboo-shoots, because they are also empty inside, likewise anyone who practices the Sudden-Enlightenment method to rid himself suddenly of false thought abandons, like the Buddhas, the sense of an ego and a personality forever. Being absolutely deep, still and void, he is, then, without an iota of difference, equal to the Buddhas. Thus, in this sense it can be said that the worldly is holy. If one practices the Sudden-Enlightenment method, he can transcend the three realms during this lifetime. The sutra also states: "Do not annihilate the world; rather, transcend the world. Do not abandon defilements; rather, enter Nirvana." If one does not practice the Sudden-Enlightenment method, he is just like a wild fox that, though following and pretending to be a lion, can never become a lion even after hundreds of thousands and endless kalpas of trying.

Q: Is the nature of Absolute Reality truly void or not? If it is not really void, that suggests form; however, if it is truly void, that suggests annihilation. So upon which Dharma should sentient beings depend in their practice to attain Liberation?

A: The nature of Absolute Reality is neither void nor not void. Since the "wonderful substance" of Absolute Reality is without shape or form and cannot be perceived, it is void. On the other hand, since in the "substance" of Absolute Reality functions are included. as numerous as the sandgrains of the Ganges, that respond to everything, it is also not void. A sutra says: "If one can understand this point, one can understand a thousand others. However, if one is confused about this point, then ten thousand delusions envelop him. In no-mind practice, all problems vanish." This is the wonderful way of Enlightenment. The sutra also says: "All kinds of views result from one Dharma." Why and how can all kinds of views result from one Dharma? All merit depends upon practice. If one cannot subdue his own mind and depends only upon words to attain Enlightenment, he will never achieve anything. He is just deceiving himself, and will fail on both counts. Everyone should be extremely careful, neither grasping anything nor letting the mind dwell anywhere. If one is able to practice like this, then he can enter Nirvana and attain the Patient Endurance of the Uncreate. It is also known as attaining the Dharma Door of Non-Duality, the absence of debate and the samadhi of single, perfect Wisdom, because it is absolutely pure. Being without ego and personality, knowing neither love nor hate, and having no need of the concept of self versus objects, the practicer realizes the voidness of all duality. This is the stage of absolute eloquence with no disputation whatsoever.

This doctrine should not be transmitted to those who do not believe but should only be entrusted to those who share the same view and practice. You should see that someone having some potential is also totally sincere, possesses deep faith and will not backslide before expounding to him this doctrine directing him to Enlightenment. I have not written this thesis for fame or personal benefit, but only for those whose past conditions make it possible for them to receive it wholeheartedly. Thus, I follow all the Buddhas of the past who expounded a thousand different sutras and ten thousand different sastras appropriate for all kinds of sentient beings with all the different sorts of mental confusion. To follow this doctrine of Absolute Liberation, just do not form mental concepts about anything, allow the mind to dwell nowhere, always keep it still and void, and maintain it in a state of absolute purity; then Liberation will follow quite naturally.

Furthermore you should not seek false fame, because the ordinary mind, like an overactive monkey, is unstill and constantly grasping so that words and acts are forever in conflict with each other. Seeking false fame, we deceive only ourselves and surely will fall into evil ways. Thus, to repeat, you should not seek false fame and happiness in this lifetime that could cause suffering forever. Every person should be very careful.

Sentient beings must seek to save themselves and not wait for the Buddha to do it. If the Buddha could liberate sentient beings, then, since there have been Buddhas as numerous as all the dust motes that have ever existed, surely all of them would have been delivered by now. So why do we still loaf about in these realms of birth and death, unable to become Buddhas? Everyone should understand that sentient beings must save themselves. The Buddha will not do it. Make an effort! Practice yourself! Do not depend upon the power of other Buddhas. Therefore, the sutra says appropriately: "To seek and find the Dharma, do not depend upon the Buddha."

Q: In the future, there will be many followers who hold mixed views. How can we live together with them?

A: You can be on friendly terms with them, but do not follow them in their pursuits. That is why one sutra says: "It follows worldly affairs, but its nature is permanent." Students of the Way should not brag that only they themselves possess the causes and conditions for Liberation and Enlightenment. Do not disrespect those who do not study the Dharma, and never boast about your own merit. Do not downgrade others' goodness and capabilities, and never expose the faults of others. Rather, examine yourself! If you do this, you will meet with no obstacles anywhere; and happiness will, quite naturally, ensue. Let me epitomize all this in a gatha:

> Patience is the foremost way,
>
> But first let go of ego and personality.
>
> Just do not form concepts about anything --
>
> This is the true Body of Buddha.

The Diamond Sutra says: "If a Bodhisattva knows the non-ego Dharma completely, the Tathagata declares him to be a true Bodhisattva." The sutra also declares: "If you neither take nor reject anything, you are freed from the Wheel-of-Birth-and-Death forever. To practice non-dwelling everywhere is to be a real son of the Buddhas." The Mahaparinirvana Sutra says: "When the Tathagata attained Nirvana, he freed himself from the Wheel-of-Birth-and-Death forever." Let me epitomize all this in some additional gathas:

> I am wonderfully fine in my mind
>
> And feel not defiled when abused.

In "no words" there's no right or wrong;

Samsara, Nirvana -- the same.

Recognizing my own sect,

I ignore petty weeds and grass.

Every false thought discriminates,

But the worldly do not understand.

Hopefully all people in the future

Will rid their minds of weeds and grass.

I am wonderfully free in my mind;

With "no words" there's nothing there.

Knowing liberation and freedom,

I wander easily everywhere.

With "no words" and still all day long,

I focus on the Doctrine each moment.

To see the Tao naturally

Ends the birth-and-death cycle.

All my circumstances are wonderful:

Old clothes, simple food are enough;

Knowing fame and wealth are both false,

I do not cheat in the world.

Meeting people, I do not speak,

So they all say I am foolish.

Manifestly dull in appearance,

I am crystal-bright in my mind,

Holding Rahula's recondite practice,

That the worldly can't understand.

Q: The Vimalakirti Nirdesa Sutra says: "If you wish rebirth in the Pure Land, you should first purify your mind." What does "purify the mind" mean?

A: The mind is purified when it is absolutely pure.

Q: But what does "the purified mind is absolutely pure" mean?

A: When it is neither pure nor impure, but beyond both, it is absolutely pure.

Q: But what does "neither pure nor impure" mean?

A: Mind that dwells nowhere is pure; but when the pure mind is attained, there should be no thought of being pure, for that would no longer be pure. Also, conversely, when the impure is encountered, there should be no thought of being impure; and then there remains only the pure.

Q: What is the meaning of "attainment" (of the goal) for a practicer of the Way?

A: Only Absolute Attainment is attainment.

Q: But what is "Absolute Attainment"?

A: Neither attaining something nor not attaining something is Absolute Attainment.

Q: What is the meaning of "neither having non-attainment nor not having non-attainment"?

A: Neither grasping at form and sound outside nor allowing a false thought to arise inside is known as attainment. However, when there is attainment, there should be no thought of attainment; and this is known as having non-attainment. Furthermore, when non-attainment is realized, there should be no thought of non-attainment; and this is known as not having non-attainment.

Q: What does "a liberated mind" mean?

A: A mind that does not grasp concepts of a liberated mind or a non-liberated mind is truly liberated. The Diamond Sutra says: "If even the Dharma must be cast aside, then how much more so the non-Dharma." Dharma, in this context, means existence, and non-Dharma means nonexistence. Thus, grasping neither the Dharma nor the non-Dharma is real, total liberation.

Q: What does "attainment of the Tao" mean?

A: Absolute Attainment is attainment of the Tao.

Q: But what does "Absolute Attainment" mean?

A: As I said before, neither attaining anything nor not attaining anything is Absolute Attainment.

Q: What does "Absolute Voidness" mean?

A: Having no concept of voidness or voidlessness is Absolute Voidness.

Q: What does "concentration on Reality" mean?

A: Having no attachment to concentration or non-concentration is Reality Concentration. The Diamond Sutra says: "There is no fixed Dharma called Supreme Enlightenment, and there is no fixed Dharma the Tathagata can expound." Another sutra also means this when it says: "In your practice of meditating on and perceiving the void, do not think you have attained the void." When engaged in the practice of concentrating your mind, do not ever think you have attained the highest realization; for even if one attains Pure Mind, there should never be any thought whatsoever of having attained it. When the goal of mind-concentration is realized, there is only purity and non-dwelling mind everywhere. If anyone has a thought of attaining something, that is a false thought; he is then bound by grasping thought, which cannot possibly be called Liberation. One who truly realizes this stage understands clearly in himself that he cannot grasp this attainment nor even hold a thought of having attained something. This is true self-mastery and Real Liberation. Finally, if one allows the thought of vigorous perseverance toward attainment to arise, that is false, not real, vigorous perseverance. However, if one does not allow a false thought to arise regarding vigorous perseverance, then that is real, boundless perseverance.

Q: What does "the Middle Way" mean?

A: The way that has neither a middle nor the two extremes is the true Middle Way.

Q: But why do the two extremes exist?

A: The two extremes exist because we have thoughts of this and that.

Q: Just what do "thisness" thought and "thatness" thought really mean?

A: If one is bound by sounds and forms, he is controlled by "thatness" thought; conversely, if one allows a false thought to arise inwardly, he is controlled by "thisness" thought. However, if one does not grasp outside forms, he is no longer controlled by "thatness" thought; and if he does not allow a false thought to arise inwardly, he is no longer controlled by "thisness" thought. This is known as abandoning the two extremes. If the mind does not contain the two extremes, then where can the middle be? When this awareness is attained, it is know as the Middle Way, the Way of Tathagata, the Way of Bodhi, and the Way of Liberation. The sutra says: "The void has neither a middle nor extremes, and it is the same with the Body of the Buddha." The voidness of all forms means that mind dwells on nothing whatsoever; and dwelling upon nothing anywhere implies the void nature of all forms. As such, the meaning of these two extremes is the same. This is known as the Dharma of the voidness of form as well as the voidness of non-form. If you do not accept the non-dwelling of mind anywhere, then, in your practice, you cannot realize Bodhi, Liberation, Nirvana, stillness, extinction, concentration in dhyana or the six paramitas. On the other hand, if you do accept the non-dwelling of mind anywhere, then, in your practice, you will realize Bodhi, Liberation, Nirvana, stillness, extinction, concentration in dhyana and the six paramitas -- all of which means seeing your Original Nature. Apropos of this, The Diamond Sutra says: "I have not gained even the least Dharma from Supreme Enlightenment; therefore, it is known as Supreme Enlightenment."

Q: If one performs all sorts of good deeds and is completely successful in his practice, can it be reasonably predicted that he will realize his Original Nature?

A: No, that cannot be predicted.

Q: If one does not practice any Dharma at all, can it be reasonably predicted that he will realize his Original Nature?

A: No, that, also, cannot be predicted.

Q: If this is true, is there any kind of Dharma whatsoever that can be used to bring about such a prediction?

A: When you practice non-dwelling on the existence of good deeds or the non-existence of good deeds, then the prediction will be fulfilled. The Vimalakirti Nirdesa Sutra says: "The form and the nature of all deeds are impermanent." Also, The Mahaparinirvana Sutra says: "The Buddha declared to Mahakashyapa, "All phenomena are impermanent and are void of self." You need only have no-mind about anything -- neither in the realm of phenomena nor in the realm of non-phenomena -- and just this, in itself, is the fulfillment of the very prediction you asked about. Having no-mind anywhere whatsoever means being free of love and hate. Being free of love and hate means that when you see good things, you do not allow a thought of love to arise, which is known as the "no-love" mind. Conversely, when you see evil things, you do not allow a thought of hate to arise, which is known as the "no-hate" mind. A mind that is void of love and hate is also known as a non-defiled mind, wherein the voidness of all forms is realized. This is also known as the termination of all conditions, and the termination of all conditions means attaining Liberation naturally and spontaneously.

Think deeply about all this. If there is anything that you do not understand, you should ask questions about it immediately. Don't waste time! If you all depend upon this teaching, that I have delivered, in your practice and still do not attain salvation, may I fall into the deepest hell! If I have misled or fooled you in any way, may I be seized and devoured by a tiger or a wolf! However, if you do not have faith in this teaching and diligently practice accordingly, I really don't know what may happen to you! Just remember this: once you have lost your human body, you might not acquire another one for ten thousand kalpas. Therefore, you should understand how to use your present opportunity and make a determined effort to attain Liberation.

Hsin Hsin Ming

Introduction

Although the third patriarch Seng-ts'an has historically been accepted as the author of the Hsin-hsin Ming, contemporary scholarship doubts whether he was in fact the author. There is no record that Hui-k'o or Seng-ts'an ever wrote anything. The expressions and idioms used in the work have caused certain scholars to place the date of its composition in a later year.

Niu-t'ou Fa-jung[1] (594-657), a disciple of Tao-hsin, composed a poem called Mind Inscription[2] (Hsin Ming) and the similarity between the Hsin-hsin Ming and the Hsin Ming has caused scholars to speculate that Hsin-hsin Ming was actually written after the time of the sixth patriarch Hui-neng[3] (638-713), as an improved, condensed version of the Mind Inscription.

According to Japanese scholars Nishitani Keiji and Yanagida Seizan, the Hsin-hsin Ming was composed in the eighth century, two centuries after Seng-ts'an (see Nishitani Keiji and Yanagida Seizan, eds., Zenke Goroku[4] vol.2; Tōkyō: Chikuma Shobō, 1974, pp. 105-112). Yanagida Seizan also suspects that the Hsin-hsin Ming is the work of the fourth patriarch Tao-hsin (580-651). Chinese scholar Yin-shun shares this opinion in his Chung-kuo Ch'an-tsung Shih[5], pp. 52-60.

Some scholars also believe that the author of the Hsin-hsin Ming was not Seng-ts'an but the fourth Ch'an patriarch Tao-hsin. As observed in most religious and spiritual traditions, putting down to writing what one's master recited was a common practice. It is therefore also possible, as some scholars suspect, that Seng-ts'an only recited the poem, and it was later written by one of his disciples. The title of the Hsin-hsin Ming may be explained in the following way:

信

Hsin means "belief" or "faith." This is not the faith in the ordinary sense, it is a belief that comes from firsthand experience, a faith which arise out of supreme knowledge and wisdom of enlightenment. This "believing" is an affirmation that all existence or reality is essentially the Buddha mind, which is our true nature. Hsin is the conviction that at the bottom of all phenomena lies the One Mind, the Buddha mind, which is one with our real nature, the Buddha-nature.

心

Hsin literally means "heart." It means mind, not the deluded mind of the ignorant but the Buddha-mind. Hsin is the mind that merge with the all-encompassing One Mind.

銘

Ming literally means "inscription." It means written expression or record. Ming also means warnings or admonitions.

Hsin-hsin Ming is one of the earliest and most influential Zen writings. It is usually referred to as the first Zen poem. It consists of 146 unrhymed four-character[1] verses[2] (lines), total 584 characters[3]. The Hsin-hsin Ming was composed in shih[4] form. Shih was the principal poetic form in use in the early period, it is first used in the Book of Odes (Shih-ching, Shikyō). Like the early shih, the Hsin-hsin Ming consists of lines that are 4-characters in length, but contrary to most shih, no end rhyme is employed in the poem.

As a characteristic of shih, one line usually constitutes a single syntactical unit. Since one character represents one syllable, and since classical Chinese is basically monosyllabic, this means that there are usually four words to a line. Lines tend to be end-stopped, with few run-on lines, so that the efffect is of a series of brief and compact utterances.

This concise form of four characters a line is shorter than the general run of Chinese verse, which usually has five or seven characters per line. Economy, even starkness of expression is a characteristic of the Hsin-hsin Ming. It is more of a verse than poetry and its brevity is one of the peculiar characteristics of this famous work. Its contents is closer to the Buddhist sûtras than poems. In fact, the Hsin-hsin Ming can be regarded as a sûtra. Many verses are like a short Zen saying and therefore can be taken as if they are a single-sentence Zen maxim. The original text was not divided in stanzas. Some translators divided the poem in different ways, with or without adding numbers to them.

The Hsin-hsin Ming has an important place In Ch'an Buddhist tradition. The poem has been very influential in Zen circles and many important commentaries were written on it. The opening stanza, "The best way is not difficult. It only excludes picking and choosing," is quoted by many Zen masters as well as in the classical Zen works such as the Blue Cliff Records and it reveals the essence of Zen philosophy.

Text

The Way of the Supreme is not difficult,

If only people will give up preferences.

Don't like, don't dislike.

Be illuminated.

Make the slightest distinction
And heaven and earth are set apart.
If you wish to see the truth,
Don't think for or against.
Likes and dislikes
Are diseases of the mind.
Without understanding the deep meaning
You cannot still your thoughts.
It is clear like space,
Nothing missing, nothing extra.
If you want something
You cannot see things as they are.
Outside, don't get tangled in things.
Inside, don't get lost in emptiness.
Be still and become One
And all opposites will disappear.
If you stop moving to become still,
This stillness always moves.
If you hold on to opposites,
How can you know Oneness?
If you don't understand Oneness,
This and that cannot function.
Denied, the world asserts itself.
Pursued, emptiness is lost.
The more you think and talk,
The more you lose the Way.
Cut off all thinking
And pass freely anywhere.
Return to the root and understand.
Chase appearances and lose the source.
One moment of enlightenment
Illuminates the emptiness before you.

Emptiness changing into things
Is only our deluded view.
Do not seek the truth.
Only set aside your opinions.
Do not live in the world of opposites.
Be careful! Never go that way.
If you make right and wrong,
Your mind is lost in confusion.
Two comes from One,
But do not cling even to this One.
When your mind is undisturbed
The ten thousand things are faultless.
No fault, no ten thousand things,
No disturbance, no mind.
No world, no one to see it.
No one to see it, no world.
This becomes this because of that.
That becomes that because of this.
If you wish to understand both,
See them as originally one emptiness.
In emptiness the two are the same,
And each holds the ten thousand things.
If you no longer see them as different,
How can you prefer one to another?
The Way is calm and wide,
Not easy, not difficult.
But small minds get lost.
Hurrying, they fall behind.
Clinging, they go too far,
Sure to take a wrong turn,
Just let it be! In the end,
Nothing goes, nothing stays.
Follow nature and become one with the Way,
Free and easy and undisturbed.
Tied by your thoughts, you lose the truth,
Become heavy, dull, and unwell.
Not well, the mind is troubled.
Then why hold or reject anything?
If you want to get the One Vehicle
Do not despise the world of the senses.
When you do not despise the six senses,
That is already enlightenment.

The wise do not act.
The ignorant bind themselves.
In true Dharma there is no this or that,
So why blindly chase your desires?
Using mind to stir up the mind
Is the original mistake.
Peaceful and troubled are only thinking.
Enlightenment has no likes or dislikes.
All opposites arise
From faulty views.
Illusions, flowers in the air –
Why try to grasp them?
Win, lose, right, wrong –
Put it all down!
If the eye never sleeps,
Dreams disappear by themselves.
If the mind makes no distinctions,
The ten thousand things are one essence.
Understand this dark essence
And be free from entanglements.
See the ten thousand things as equal
And you return to your original nature
Enlightened beings everywhere
All enter this source.
This source is beyond time and space.
One moment is ten thousand years.
Even if you cannot see it,
The whole universe is before your eyes.
Infinitely small is infinitely large:
No boundaries, no differences.
Infinitely large is infinitely small:
Measurements do not matter here.
What is is the same as what is not.
What is not is the same as what is.
Where it is not like this,
Don't bother staying.
One is all,
One in All,

All in One—

If only this is realized,

No more worry about your not being perfect!

Where Mind and each believing mind are not divided,

And undivided are each believing mind and Mind,

This is where words fail;

For it is neither of the past, present, and future.

The Heart Sutra (Prajnaparamita Hrdaya)

Introduction

The Heart Sutra, possibly the best known text of Mahayana Buddhism, is said to be the pure distillation of wisdom (prajna). The Heart Sutra is also among the shortest of sutras. An English translation can easily be printed on one side of a piece of paper.

The teachings of the Heart Sutra are deep and subtle, and I do not pretend to completely understand them myself. This article is a mere introduction to the sutra for the completely baffled.

The Heart Sutra is part of the much larger Prajnaparamita (perfection of wisdom) Sutra, which is a collection of about 40 sutras composed between 100 BCE and 500 CE. The precise origin of the Heart Sutra is unknown. According to the translator Red Pine, the earliest record of the sutra is a Chinese translation from Sanskrit by the monk Chih-ch'ien made between 200 and 250 CE.

In the 8th century another translation emerged that added an introduction and conclusion. This longer version was adopted by Tibetan Buddhism. In Zen and other Mahayana schools that originated in China, the shorter version is more common.

As with most Buddhist scriptures, simply "believing in" what the Heart Sutra says is not its point. It is important also to appreciate that the sutra cannot be grasped by intellect alone. Although analysis is helpful, people also keep the words in their hearts so that understanding unfolds through practice.

In this sutra, Avalokiteshvara Bodhisattva is speaking to Shariputra, who was an important disciple of the historical Buddha. The early lines of the sutra discuss the five skandhas -- form, sensation, conception, discrimination, and consciousness. The bodhisattva has seen that the skandhas are empty, and thus has been freed from suffering. The bodhisattva speaks:

> Shariputra, form is no other than emptiness; emptiness no other than form. Form is exactly emptiness; emptiness exactly form. Sensation, conception, discrimination, and consciousness are also like this.

Emptiness (in Sanskrit, shunyata) is a foundational doctrine of Mahayana Buddhism. It is also possibly the most misunderstood doctrine in all of Buddhism. Too often, people assume it means that nothing exists. But this is not the case.

His Holiness the 14th Dalai Lama said, "The existence of things and events is not in dispute; it is the manner in which they exist that must be clarified." Put another way, things and events have no intrinsic existence and no individual identity except in our thoughts.

The Dalai Lama also teaches that "existence can only be understood in terms of dependent origination." Dependent origination is a teaching that no being or thing exists independently of other beings or things.

In the Four Noble Truths, the Buddha taught that our distresses ultimately spring from thinking ourselves to be independently existing beings with an intrinsic "self." Thoroughly perceiving that this intrinsic self is a delusion liberates us from suffering.

The Heart Sutra continues, with Avalokiteshvara explaining that all phenomena are expressions of emptiness, or empty of inherent characteristics. Because phenomena are empty of inherent characteristics, they are neither born nor destroyed; neither pure nor defiled; neither coming nor going.

Avalokiteshvara then begins a recitation of negations -- "no eye, ear, nose, tongue, body, mind; no color, sound, smell, taste, touch, thing," etc. These are the six sense organs and their corresponding objects from the doctrine of the skandhas.

What is the bodhisattva saying here? Red Pine writes that because all phenomena exist interdependently with other phenomena, all distinctions we make are arbitrary.

"There is no point at which the eyes begin or end, either in time or in space or conceptually. The eye bone is connected to the face bone, and the face bone is connected to the head bone, and the head bone is connected to the neck bone, and so it goes down to the toe bone, the floor bone, the earth bone, the worm bone, the dreaming butterfly bone. Thus, what we call our eyes are so many bubbles in a sea of foam."

Another doctrine associated with the Heart Sutra is that of the Two Truths. Existence can be understood as both ultimate and conventional (or, absolute and relative). Conventional truth is how we usually see the world, a place full of diverse and distinctive things and beings. The ultimate truth is that there are no distinctive things or beings.

The important point to remember with the two truths is that they are two truths, not one truth and one lie. Thus, there are eyes. Thus, there are no eyes. People sometimes fall into the habit of thinking that the conventional truth is "false," but that's not correct.

Avalokiteshvara goes on to say there is no path, no wisdom, and no attainment. Because no individual being comes into existence, neither does a being cease to exist.

Because there is no cessation, there is no impermanence, and because there is no impermanence, there is no suffering. Because there is no suffering, there is no path to liberation from suffering, no wisdom, and no attainment of wisdom. Thoroughly perceiving this is "supreme perfect enlightenment," the bodhisattva tells us.

Text

When the Bodhisattva Avalokiteshvara

was coursing in the deep Prajnaparamita,

he perceived that all five skandhas are empty,

thereby transcending all sufferings.

Sariputra, form is not other than emptiness

and emptiness not other than form.

Form is precisely emptiness and emptiness precisely form.

So also are sensation, perception, volition, and consciousness.

Sariputra, this voidness of all dharmas

is not born, not destroyed,

not impure, not pure, does not increase or decrease.

In voidness there is no form,

and no sensation, perception, volition or consciousness;

no eye, ear, nose, tongue, body, mind;

no sight, sound, smell, taste, touch, thought;

there is no realm of the eye

all the way up to no realm of mental cognition.

There is no ignorance and there is no ending of ignorance

through to no aging and death and no ending of aging and death.

There is no suffering, no cause of suffering,

no cessation of suffering, and no path.

There is no wisdom or any attainment.

With nothing to attain, Bodhisattvas relying on Prajnaparamita

have no obstructions in their minds.

Having no obstructions, there is no fear

and departing far from confusion and imaginings,

they reach Ultimate Nirvana.

All past, present and future Buddhas,

relying on Prajnaparamita, attain Anuttara-Samyak-Sambodhi.

Therefore, know that Prajnaparamita

is the great mantra of power,

the great mantra of wisdom, the supreme mantra,

the unequalled mantra,

which is able to remove all sufferings.

It is real and not false.

Therefore recite the mantra of Prajnaparamita:

Gate, Gate, Paragate, Parasamgate, Bodhi Svaha.

Diamond Sutra (Vajraccedika Sutra)

Introduction

No other text is as important to Buddhists, especially Zen Buddhists, and this translation includes commentary from major Chinese and Japanese historical sources.

Zen Buddhism is often said to be a practice of "mind-to-mind transmission" without reliance on texts —in fact, some great teachers forbid their students to read or write. But Buddhism has also inspired some of the greatest philosophical writings of any religion, and two such works lie at the center of Zen: The Heart Sutra, which monks recite all over the world, and The Diamond Sutra, said to contain answers to all questions of delusion and dualism. This is the Buddhist teaching on the "perfection of wisdom" and cuts through all obstacles on the path of practice.

The Diamond Sutra may look like a book, but it's really the body of the Buddha. It's also your body, my body, all possible bodies. But it's a body with nothing inside and nothing outside. It doesn't exist in space or time. Nor is it a construct of the mind. It's no mind.

And yet because it's no mind, it has room for compassion. This book is the offering of no mind, born of compassion for all suffering beings. Of all the sutras that teach this teaching, this is the diamond."

Text

1. Thus have I heard.

At one time the Lord Buddha stayed at Anathapindaka's Garden in the grove of jeta in the kingdom of Sravasti; he was together with 1,250 great Bhikshus. When the meal time came the World-honoured One put on his cloak and, holding his bowl, entered the great city of Sravasti, where he begged for food. Having finished his begging from door to door, he came back to his own place, and took his meal. When this was done, he put away his cloak and bowl, washed his feet, spread his feet, and sat down.

2. Then the Venerable Subhuti, who was among the assembly, rose from his seat, bared his right shoulder, set his right knee on the ground, and, respectfully folding his hands, addressed the Lord Buddha thus:

"It is wonderful, World-honoured One, that the Tathagata thinks so much of all the Bodhisattvas, and so instructs them so well. World-honoured One, in case good men and good women ever raise the desire for the Supreme Enlightenment, how would they abide in it? How would they keep their thoughts under control?"

The Lord Buddha declared: "Well said, indeed, O Subhuti! As you say, the Tathagata thinks very much of all the Bodhisattvas, and so instructs them well. But now listen attentively and I will tell you. In case good men and good women raise the desire for the Supreme Enlightenment, they should thus abide in it, they should thus keep their thoughts under control."

"So be it, World-honoured One, I wish to listen to you."

3. The Lord Buddha declared to Subhuti:

"All the Bodhisattva-Mahasattvas should thus keep their thoughts under control. All kinds of beings such as the egg-born, the womb-born, the moisture born, the miraculously-born, those with form, those without form, those with consciousness, those without consciousness, those with no-consciousness and those without no-consciousness - they are all led by me to enter Nirvana that leaves nothing behind and to attain final emancipation. Though thus beings immeasurable, innumerable, and unlimited are emancipated, there are in reality no beings that are ever emancipated. Why, Subhuti? If a Bodhisattva retains the thought of an ego, a person, a being, or a soul, he is no more a Bodhisattva.

4. "Again, Subhuti, when a Bodhisattva practices charity he should not be cherishing any idea, that is to say, he is not to cherish the idea of a form when practising charity, nor is he to cherish the idea of a sound, an odour, a touch, or a quality. Subhuti, a Bodhisattva should thus practice charity without cherishing any idea of form, his merit will be beyond conception. Subhuti, what do you think? Can you have the conception of space extending eastward?"

"No, World-honoured One, I cannot."

Subhuti, can you have the conception of space extending towards the south, or west, or north, or above, or below?"

"No, World-honoured One, I cannot."

"Subhuti, so it is with the merit of a Bodhisattva who practices charity without cherishing any idea of form; it is beyond conception. Subhuti, a Bodhisattva should cherish only that which is taught to him.

5. "Subhuti, what do you think? Is the Tathagata to be recognised after a body-form?"

"No, World-honoured One, he is not to be recognised after a body-form. Why? According to the Tathagata, a body-form is not a body-form."

The Lord Buddha declared to Subhuti, "All that has a form is an illusive existence. When it is perceived that all form is no-form, the Tathagata is recognised."

6. Subhuti said to the Lord Buddha: "World-honoured One, if beings hear such words and statements, would they have a true faith in them?"

The Lord Buddha declared to Subhuti: "Do not talk that way. In the last five hundred years after the passing of the Tathagata, there may be beings who, having practised rules of morality and, being thus possessed of merit, happen to hear of these statements and rouse a true faith in them. Such beings, you must know, are those who have planted their root of merit not only under one, two, three, four, or five Lord Buddhas, but already under thousands of myriads of asamkhyeyas of Lord Buddhas have they planted their root of merit of all kinds. Those who hearing these statements rouse even one thought of pure faith, Subhuti, are all known to the Tathagata, and recognised by him as having acquired such an immeasurable amount of merit. Why? Because all these beings are free from the idea of an ego, a person, a being, or a soul; they are free from the idea of a dharma as well as from that of a no-dharma. Why? Because if they cherish in their minds the idea of a form, they are attached to an ego, a person, a being, or a soul. If they cherish the idea of a dharma, they are attached to an ego, a person, a being, or a soul. Why? If they cherish the idea of a no-dharma, they are attached to an ego, a person, a being, or a soul. Therefore, do not cherish the idea of a dharma, nor that of a no-dharma. For this reason, the Tathagata always preaches thus: `O you Bhikshus, know that my teaching is to be likened unto a raft. Even a dharma is cast aside, much more a no-dharma.'

7. "Subhuti, what do you think? Has the Tathagata attained the supreme enlightenment? Has he something about which he would preach?"

Subhuti said:

"World-honoured One, as I understand the teaching of the Lord Buddha, there is no fixed doctrine about which the Tathagata would preach. Why? Because the doctrine he preaches is not to be adhered to, nor is it to be preached about; it is neither a dharma nor a no-dharma. How is it so? Because all wise men belong to the category known as non-doing (asamskara), and yet they are distinct from one another.

8. "Subhuti, what do you think? If a man should fill the three thousand chilocosms with the seven precious treasures and give them all away for charity, would not the merit he thus obtains be great?"

Subhuti said:

"Very great, indeed, World-honoured One."

"Why? Because their merit is characterised with the quality of not being a merit. Therefore, the Tathagata speaks of the merit as being great. If again there is a man who, holding even the four lines in this sutra, preaches about it to others, his merit will be superior to the one just mentioned. Because, Subhuti, all the Lord Buddhas and their supreme enlightenment issue from this sutra. Subhuti, what is known as the teaching of the Lord Buddha is not the teaching of the Lord Buddha.

9. "Subhuti, what do you think? Does a Srotapanna think in this wise: `I have obtained the fruit of Srotappatti'?"

Subhuti said:

"No, Universally-Honored One, he does not. Why? Because while Srotapanna means `entering the stream' there is no entering here. He is called a Srotapanna who does not enter (a world of) form, sound, odour, taste, touch, and quality.

"Subhuti, what do you think? Does a Sakridagamin think in this wise, `I have obtained the fruit of a Sakridagamin'?"

Subhuti said:

"No, Universally-Honored One, he does not. Why? Because while Sakridagamin means 'going-and-coming for once', there is really no going-and-coming here, and he is then called a Sakridagamin."

"Subhuti, what do you think? Does an Anagamin think in this wise: `I have obtained the fruit of an Anagamin'?"

Subhuti said:

"No, Universally-Honored One, he does not. Why? Because while Anagamin means `not-coming' there is really no not-coming and therefore he is called an Anagamin."

"Subhuti, what do you think? Does an Arhat think in this wise: 'I have obtained Arhatship'?"

Subhuti said:

"No, Universally-Honored One, he does not. Why? Because there is no dharma to be called Arhat. If, Universally-Honored One, an Arhat thinks in this wise: `I have obtained Arhatship,' this means that he is attached to an ego, a person, a being, or a soul. Although the Lord Buddha says that I am the foremost of those who have attained Arana-samadhi, that I am the foremost of those Arhats who are liberated from evil desires, Universally-Honored One, I cherish no such thought that I have attained Arhatship. Universally-Honored One, (if I did,) you would not tell me: `O Subhuti, you are one who enjoys the life of non-resistance.' Just because Subhuti is not at all attached to this life, he is said to be the one who enjoys the life of non-resistance."

10. The Lord Buddha declared to Subhuti:

"What do you think? When the Tathagata was anciently with Dipankara Lord Buddha did he have an attainment in the dharma?"

"No, Universally-Honored One, he did not. The Tathagata while with Dipankara Lord Buddha had no attainment whatever in the dharma."

"Subhuti, what do you think? Does a Bodhisattva set any Lord Buddha land in array?"

"No, Universally-Honored One, he does not."

"Why? Because to set a Lord Buddha land in array is not to set it in array, and therefore it is known as setting it in array. Therefore, Subhuti, all the Bodhisattva-Mahasattvas should thus rouse a pure thought. They should not cherish any thought dwelling on form; they should not cherish any thought dwelling on sound, odour, taste, touch, and quality; they should cherish thoughts dwelling on nothing whatever. Subhuti, it is like unto a human body equal in size to Mount Sumeru; what do you think? Is not this body large?"

Subhuti said:

"Very large indeed, Universally-Honored One. Why? Because the Lord Buddha teaches that that which is no-body is known as a large body."

11. "Subhuti, regarding the sands of the Ganga, suppose there as many Ganga rivers as those sands, what do you think? Are not the sands of all those Ganga rivers many?"

Subhuti said:

"Very many, indeed, Universally-Honored One."

Lord Buddha declared to Subhuti:

"If a good man or a good woman holding even four lines from this sutra preach it to others, this merit is much larger than the preceding one.

12. "Again, Subhuti, wherever this sutra or even four lines of it are preached, this place will be respected by all beings including Devas, Asuras, etc., as if it were the Lord Buddha's own shrine or chaitya; how much more a person who can hold and recite this sutra! Subhuti, you should know that such a person achieves the highest, foremost, and most wonderful deed. Wherever this sutra is kept, the place is to be regarded as if the Lord Buddha or a venerable disciple of his were present."

13. At that time, Subhuti said to the Lord Buddha:

"Universally-Honored One, what will this sutra be called? How should we hold it?"

The Lord Buddha declared to Subhuti:

"This sutra will be called the Vajra-prajna-paramita, and by this title you will hold it. The reason is, Subhuti, that, according to the teaching of the Lord Buddha, Prajnaparamita is not Prajnaparamita and therefore it is called Prajnaparamita. Subhuti, what do you think? Is there anything about which the Tathagata preaches?"

Subhuti said to the Lord Buddha:

"Universally-Honored One, there is nothing about which the Tathagata preaches."

"Subhuti, what do you think? Is the Tathagata to be recognised by the thirty-two marks (of a great man)?"

"No, Universally-Honored One, he is not."

"The Tathagata is not to be recognised by the thirty-two marks because what are said to be the thirty-two marks are told by the Tathagata to be no-marks and therefore to be the thirty-two marks. Subhuti, if there be a good man or a good woman who gives away his or her lives as many as the sands of the Ganga, his or her merit thus gained does not exceed that of one who, holding even one gatha of four lines from this sutra, preaches them for others."

14. At that time Subhuti, listening to this sutra, had a deep understanding of its significance, and, filled with tears of gratitude, said this to the Lord Buddha:

"Wonderful, indeed, Universally-Honored One, that the Lord Buddha teaches us this sutra full of deep sense. Such a sutra has never been heard by me even with an eye of wisdom acquired in my past lives. Universally-Honored One, if there be a man who listening to this sutra acquires a true believing heart he will then have a true idea of things. This one is to be known as having achieved a most wonderful virtue. Universally-Honored One, what is known as a true idea is no-idea, and for this reason it is called a true idea.

"Universally-Honored One, it is not difficult for me to believe, to understand, and to hold this sutra to which I have now listened; but in the ages to come, in the next five hundred years, if there are beings who listening to this sutra are able to believe, to understand, and to hold it, they will indeed be most wonderful beings. Why? Because they will have no idea of an ego, of a person, of a being, or of a soul. For what reason? The idea of an ego is no-idea (of ego), the idea of a person, a being, or a soul is no-idea (of a person, a being, or a soul). For what reason? They are Lord Buddhas who are free from all kinds of ideas."

The Lord Buddha declared to Subhuti,

"It is just as you say. If there be a man who, listening to this sutra, is neither frightened nor alarmed nor disturbed, you should know him as a wonderful person. Why? Subhuti, it is taught by the Tathagata that the first Paramita is no-first-Paramita and therefore it is called the first Paramita. Subhuti, the Paramita of humility is no-Paramita of humility and therefore it is called the Paramita of humility . Why? Subhuti, anciently, when my body was cut to pieces by the King of Kalinga, I had neither the idea of an ego, nor the idea of a person, nor the idea of a being, nor the idea of a soul. Why? When at that time my body was dismembered, limb after limb, joint after joint, if I had the idea of an ego, or of a person, or of a being, or of a soul, the feeling of anger and ill-will would have been awakened in me. Subhuti, I remember in my past hundred births, I was a rishi called Kshanti, and during those times I had neither the idea of an ego, nor that of a person, nor that of a being, nor that of a soul.

"Therefore, Subhuti, you should, detaching yourself from all ideas, rouse the desire for the supreme enlightenment. You should cherish thoughts without dwelling on form, you should cherish thoughts without dwelling on sound, odour, taste, touch, or quality. Whatever thoughts you may have, they are not to dwell on anything. If a thought dwells on anything, this is said to be no-dwelling. Therefore, the Lord Buddha teaches that a Bodhisattva is not to practice charity by dwelling on form. Subhuti, the reason he practices charity is to benefit all beings.

"The Tathagata teaches that all ideas are no-ideas, and again that all beings are no-beings. Subhuti, the Tathagata is the one who speaks what is true, the one who speaks what is real, the one whose words are as they are, the one who does not speak falsehood, the one who does not speak equivocally.

"Subhuti, in the Dharma attained by the Tathagata there is neither truth nor falsehood. Subhuti, if a Bodhisattva should practice charity, cherishing a thought which dwells on the Dharma, he is like unto a person who enters the darkness, he sees nothing. If he should practice charity without cherishing a thought that dwells on the Dharma, he is like unto a person with eyes, he sees all kinds of forms illumined by the sunlight.

"Subhuti, if there are good men and good women in the time to come who hold and recite this sutra, they will be seen and recognised by the Tathagata with his Lord Buddha-knowledge, and they will all mature immeasurable and innumerable merit.

15. "Subhuti, if there is a good man or a good woman who would in the first part of the day sacrifice as many bodies of his or hers as the sands of the Ganga, and again in the middle part of the day sacrifice as many bodies of his or hers as the sands of the Ganga, and again in the latter part of the day sacrifice as many bodies of his or hers as the sands of the Ganga, and keep up these sacrifices through hundred-thousands of myriads of kotis of kalpas; and if there were another who listened to this sutra would accept it with a believing heart, the merit the latter would acquire would far exceed that of the former. How much more the merit of one who would copy, hold, learn, and recite and expound it for others!

"Subhuti, to sum up, there is in this sutra a mass of merit, immeasurable, innumerable, and incomprehensible. The Tathagata has preached this for those who were awakened in the Mahayana (great vehicle), he has preached it for those who were awakened in the Sreshthayana (highest vehicle). If there were beings who would hold and learn and expound it for others, they would all be known to the Tathagata and recognised by him, and acquire merit which is unmeasured, immeasurable, innumerable, and incomprehensible. Such beings are known to be carrying the supreme enlightenment attained by the Tathagata. Why? Subhuti, those who desire inferior doctrines are attached to the idea of an ego, a person, a being, and a soul. They are unable to hear, hold, learn, recite, and for others expound this sutra. Subhuti, wherever this sutra is preserved, there all beings, including Devas and Asuras, will come and worship it. This place will have to be known as a chaitya, the object of worship and obeisance, where the devotees gather around, scatter flowers, and burn incense.

16. "Again, Subhuti, there are some good men and good women who will be despised for their holding and reciting this sutra. This is due to their previous evil karma for the reason of which they were to fall into the evil paths of existence; but because of their being despised in the present life, whatever evil karma they produced in their previous lives will be

thereby destroyed, and they will be able to obtain the supreme enlightenment.

"Subhuti, as I remember, in my past lives innumerable asamkhyeya kalpas ago I was with Dipankara Lord Buddha, and at that time I saw Lord Buddhas as many as eighty-four hundred-thousands of myriads of nayutas and made offerings to them and respectfully served them all, and not one of them was passed by me.

If again in the last (five hundred) years, there have been people who hold and recite and learn this sutra, the merit they thus attain (would be beyond calculation), for when this is compared with the merit I have attained by serving all the Lord Buddhas, the latter will not exceed one hundredth part of the former, no, not one hundred thousand ten millionth part. No, it is indeed beyond calculation, beyond analogy.

"Subhuti, if there have been good men and good women in the last five hundred years who hold, recite, and learn this sutra, the merit they attain thereby I cannot begin to enumerate in detail. If I did, those who listen to it would lose their minds, cherish grave doubts, and not believe at all how beyond comprehension is the significance of this sutra and also how also beyond comprehension the rewards are."

18. The Lord Buddha declared to Subhuti:

"Of all beings in those innumerable lands, the Tathagata knows well all their mental traits. Why? Because the Tathagata teaches that all those mental traits are no-traits and therefore they are known to be mental traits. Subhuti, thoughts of the past are beyond grasp, thoughts of the present are beyond grasp, and thoughts of the future are beyond grasp."

23. "Again, Subhuti, this Dharma is even and has neither elevation nor depression; and it is called supreme enlightenment. Because a man practices everything that is good, without cherishing the thought of an ego, a person, a being, and a soul, he attains the supreme enlightenment. Subhuti, what is called good is no-good, and therefore it is known as good."

26. "Subhuti what do you think? Can a man see the Tathagata by the thirty-two marks (of a great man)?"

Subhuti said:

"So it is, so it is. The Tathagata is seen by his thirty-two marks."

The Lord Buddha declared to Subhuti:

"If the Tathagata is to be seen by his thirty-two marks, can the Cakravartin be a Tathagata?"

Subhuti said to the Lord Buddha:

"Universally-Honored One, as I understand the teaching of the Lord Buddha, the Tathagata is not to be seen by the thirty-two marks."

Then the Universally-Honored One uttered this gatha:

"If any one by form sees me,

By voice seeks me,

This one walks the false path,

And cannot see the Tathagata."

29. "Subhuti, if a man should declare that the Tathagata is the one who comes, or goes, or sits, or lies, he does not understand the meaning of my teachings. Why? The Tathagata does not come from anywhere, and does not depart to anywhere; therefore he is called the Tathagata.

32. "How does a man expound it for others? When one is not attached to form, it is of Suchness remaining unmoved. Why?

"All composite things (samskrita)

Are like a dream, a phantasm, a bubble, and a shadow,

Are like a dew-drop and a flash of lightening;

They are thus to be regarded."

The Dharma of Mind Transmission: Huang-po

Introduction

Huángbò Xīyùn (Huang-po Hsi-yün) was an influential Chinese master of Zen Buddhism. He was born in Fujian, China in the Tang Dynasty. Huángbò was a disciple of Baizhang Huaihai (720-840) and the teacher of Linji Yixuan (died 866).

Although Huángbò often railed against traditional Buddhist textual practices, pointing to the necessity of direct experience over sutra study, his record shows that he was familiar with a wide selection of Buddhist doctrines and texts, including the Diamond Sutra, the Vimalakīrti Sutra and the Lotus Sutra. Huángbò's disdain for written texts is exemplified by the story of Pei Xiangguo presenting Huángbò with a text he had written on his understanding of Chan. Huángbò placed the text down without looking at and after a long pause asked, "Do you understand?" Pei replied, "I don't understand." Huángbò said, "If it can be understood in this manner, then it isn't the true teaching. If it can be seen in paper and ink, then it's not the essence of our order." Huángbò was also noted for the manner of his teaching, incorporating the hitting and shouting pioneered by Mazu. There are a number of instances in the record of Huángbò slapping students. The Blue Cliff Record tells the story of the future emperor of China, hiding in the Chan community as a novice monk, receiving slaps from Huángbò for questioning why Huángbò was bowing to an image of the Buddha. The most famous instance was when Linji was directed by the head monk, Muzhou Daoming, to question Huángbò on the meaning of Buddhism after he (Linji) had been practicing in Huángbò's monastery for three years without an interview. Three times Linji went to Huángbò and three times the only answer he got was a slap.

Huángbò's teaching centered on the concept of "mind" (Chinese: hsin), a central issue for Buddhism in China for the previous two centuries or more. He taught that mind cannot be sought by the mind and one of his most important sayings was "mind is the Buddha". He said: "All the Buddhas and all sentient beings are nothing but the One Mind, beside which nothing exists. ...The One Mind alone is the Buddha, and there is no distinction between the Buddha and sentient beings..."He also said: "...to awaken suddenly to the fact that your own Mind is the Buddha, that there is nothing to be attained or a single action to be performed---this is the Supreme Way."

If, as Huángbò taught, all is Buddha-mind, then all actions would reflect the Buddha, be actions of a Buddha. Huángbò's teaching on this reflected the Indian concept of the tathāgatagarbha, the idea that within all beings is the nature of the Buddha. Therefore, Huángbò taught that seeking the Buddha was futile as the Buddha resided within: "If you know positively that all sentient beings already one with Bodhi [enlightenment, Supreme Wisdom], you will cease thinking of Bodhi as something to be attained". Huángbò was adamant that any form of "seeking" was not only useless, but obstructed clarity: "…sentient beings are attached to forms and so seek externally for Buddhahood. By their very seeking they lose it." Furthermore, he claimed that "'Studying the Way' is just a figure of speech….In fact, the Way is not something which can be studied. …You must not allow this name [the Way] to lead you into forming a mental concept of a road." "…any search is doomed to failure"

What Huángbò knew was that students of Chan often became attached to "seeking" enlightenment and he constantly warned against this (and all attachment) as an obstruction to enlightenment: "If you students of the Way wish to become Buddhas, you need study no doctrines whatever, but learn only how to avoid seeking for and attaching yourselves to anything."

He also firmly rejected all dualism, especially between the "ordinary" and "enlightened" states: "If you would only rid yourselves of the concepts of ordinary and Enlightened, you would find that there is no other Buddha than the Buddha in your own Mind. …The arising and the elimination of illusion are both illusory. Illusion is not something rooted in Reality; it exists because of your dualistic thinking. If you will only cease to indulge in opposed concepts such as 'ordinary' and 'Enlightened', illusion will cease of itself."

While Huángbò was an uncompromising and somewhat fearsome Chan teacher, he understood the nature of fear in students when they heard the doctrine of emptiness and the Void: "Those who hasten towards it [the Void] dare not enter, fearing to hurtle down through the void with nothing to cling to or to stay their fall. So they look to the brink and retreat." He taught that 'no activity' was the gateway of his Dharma but that "all who reach this gate fear to enter." To overcome this fear, one "must enter it with the suddenness of a knife-thrust".Huang Po: Ch'an Buddhist, Chinese master of Zen Buddhism, born circa 750-800.

His teachings are primarily attributed to two texts, Essential of Mind Transmission and Record of Wan-Ling); he was adamant about direct experience over sutra study.

Huángbò's disdain for written texts is exemplified by the story of Pei Xiangguo presenting Huángbò with a text he had written on his understanding of Chan. Huángbò placed the text down without looking at and after a long pause asked,

"Do you understand?" Pei replied, "I don't understand." Huángbò said, "If it can be understood in this manner, then it isn't the true teaching. If it can be seen in paper and ink, then it's not the essence of our order."

Big on hitting and shouting, Huangbo taught that the mind cannot by the mind, with mind being consciousness: "All the Buddhas and all sentient beings are nothing but the One Mind, beside which nothing exists. …The One Mind alone is the Buddha, and there is no distinction between the Buddha and sentient beings…"

Thus, Huang Po insisted that all seeking was futile: "…sentient beings are attached to forms and so seek externally for Buddhahood. By their very seeking they lose it." There is no way to Buddhahood, he would argue, and, as such, can not be studied: "You must not allow this name (he was referring to The Way) to lead you into forming a mental concept of a road"

Seeking enlightenment is a roadblock to it's realization, he would argue. What was necessary was to avoid attachment of any kind and any form of seeking.

"If you would only rid yourselves of the concepts of ordinary and Enlightened, you would find that there is no other Buddha than the Buddha in your own Mind. …The arising and the elimination of illusion are both illusory. Illusion is not something rooted in Reality; it exists because of your dualistic thinking. If you will only cease to indulge in opposed concepts such as 'ordinary' and 'Enlightened', illusion will cease of itself."

As to the Gateless gate, he had these words of Wisdom: No activity is the gateway but " all who reach this gate fear to enter." One must, then, ""enter it with the suddenness of a knife-thrust".

Text: Introduction

The Mind is neither large nor small; it is located neither within nor without. It should not be thought about by the mind nor be discussed by the mouth. Ordinarily, it is said that we use the Mind to transmit the Mind, or that we use the Mind to seal the Mind. Actually, however, in transmitting the Mind, there is really no Mind to receive or obtain; and in sealing the Mind, there is really no Mind to seal. If this is the case, then does the Mind exist or does it not exist? Actually, it cannot be said with certainty that the Mind either exists or does not exist, for it is Absolute Reality. This is expressed in the Ch'an Sect by the maxim: "If you open your mouth, you are wrong. If you give rise to a single thought, you are in error." So, if you can quiet your thinking totally, all that remains is voidness and stillness.

The Mind is Buddha; Buddha is the Mind. All sentient beings and all Buddhas have the same Mind, which is without boundaries and void, without name and form and is immeasurable.

What is your Original Face and what is Hua-Tou? Your Original Face is without discrimination. Hua-Tou is the Reality before the arising of a single thought. When this Mind is enlightened, it is the Buddha; but when it is confused, it remains only the mind of sentient beings.

The Ch'an Master Huang-po Tuan-Chi was a major Dharma descendent of the Sixth Patriarch and was the Dharma-son of the Ch'an Master Pai-Chang. He was enlightened by the Supreme Vehicle to realize the Truth. Transmission of Mind is this alone nothing else!

The Dharma of Mind Transmission, the teaching of Ch'an Master Huang-po Tuan-Chi, is a cover-title that includes both The Chung-Ling Record and The Wan-Ling Record. These Records are sermons and dialogues of the Master that were collected and recorded by his eminent follower P'ei Hsiu. Both a government official and great scholar, P'ei Hsiu set down what he could recollect of the Master's teaching in 857 C.E., during the T'ang Dynasty, eight years after the Master's death (ca. 850 C.E.), fifteen years after his first period of instruction by the Master at a temple near Chung Ling (842 C.E.), and nine years after his second period of instruction at a temple near Wan Ling (848 C.E.). The Records were presumably edited and published somewhat later in the T'ang Dynasty by an unknown person, and they contain a "Preface" by the recorder, P'ei Hsiu.

The Preface of P'ei Hsiu

The great Ch'an Master, whose Dharma-name was Hsi Yun, resided below Vulture Peak on Huang-po Mountain, which is in Kao-An County in Hung-Chou. He was a major disciple of Ts'ao-Ch'i, the Sixth Patriarch, and the Dharma-son of Pai-Chang. He admired the Supreme Mahayana Vehicle and sealed it without words, teaching the transmission of Pure Mind only and no other Dharma whatsoever. He held that both Pure Mind and substance are void and that the interrelationships of phenomena are motionless. Thus, everything is, in reality, void and still like the radiant light of the great sun in the sky, shining brightly and purely throughout the world. If one has attained this understanding, he holds no concept of duality such as new versus old or shallow versus deep in his Pure Mind. If one has attained this understanding, he does not attempt to explain its meaning, nor does he hold biased views, one way or another, regarding particular sects. The Master just pointed out that " It is!" alone is the correct understanding. So, even allowing a single thought to arise is wrong. He made clear that the profound meaning beyond words is the Tao, which is subtle and the action of which is solitary and uniform.

Thus, many disciples came to him from the four directions, most of them becoming enlightened merely upon first seeing the Master; and usually a company of more than one thousand disciples accompanied him at any one time.

In the second year of Hui-Ch'ang (842 C.E.), I stayed in Chung-Ling, inviting the Master to come to the city from the mountain. While residing together at Lung-Hsing Temple, I asked the Master, every day, to transmit the Dharma to me. Also, later, in the second year of Ta-Chung (848 C.E.), I stayed in Wan-Ling, again inviting the Master to the city. At that time, while residing together at K'ai Yuan Temple, I received Dharma from the Master every day. A few years later, I made a record of the Dharma that the Master had transmitted to me, but I could recall only a small portion of it. Nevertheless, I regard what is set down here to be the genuine Pure Mind-Seal Dharma. Initially I had some reservations about making this Doctrine public, but, afterwards, fearing that this wonderful and profound Teaching might not be available to or known by future truth-seekers, I decided to publish it.

With this in Pure Mind, I have sent the manuscript to the Master's disciple, Tai-Chou Fa-Chien, asking him to return to Kuang-T'ang Temple, on the ancient mountain, and discuss my record with certain elder monks and other Sangha members to determine how much it agrees with or how much it differs from what they themselves had heard and learned from the Master. T'ang Dynasty

The Chung-Ling Record

All Buddhas and all sentient beings are no different from the One Pure Mind. In this One Pure Mind there is neither arising nor ceasing, no name or form, no long or short, no large or small, and neither existence nor non-existence. It transcends all limitations of name, word and relativity, and it is as boundless as the great void. Giving rise to thought is erroneous, and any speculation about it with our ordinary faculties is inapplicable, irrelevant and inaccurate. Only Pure Mind is Buddha, and Buddhas and sentient beings are not different. All sentient beings grasp form and search outside themselves. Using Buddha to seek Buddha, they thus use Pure Mind to seek Pure Mind. Practicing in this manner even until the end of the kalpa, they cannot attain the fruit. However, when thinking and discrimination suddenly halt, the Buddhas appear.

The Pure Mind is Buddha, and the Buddha is no different from sentient beings. The Pure Mind of sentient beings does not decrease; the Buddha's Pure Mind does not increase. Moreover, the six paramitas and all sila, as countless as the grains of sand of the Ganges, belong to one's own Pure Mind. Thus there is no need to search outside oneself to create them. When causes and conditions unite, they will appear; as causes and conditions separate, they disappear. So if one does not have the understanding that on'es very own Pure Mind itself is Buddha, he will then grasp the form of the practice merely and create even more delusion. This approach is exactly the opposite of the Buddha's practice path. Just this Pure Mind alone is Buddha! Nothing else is!

The Pure Mind is transparent, having no shape or form. Giving rise to thought and discrimination is grasping and runs counter to the natural Dharma. Since time without beginning, there never has been a grasping Buddha. The practice of the six paramitas and various other disciplines is known as the gradual method of becoming a Buddha. This gradual method, however, is a secondary idea, and it does not represent the complete path to Perfect Awakening. If one does not understand that one's Pure Mind is Buddha, no Dharma can ever be attained.

The Buddhas and sentient beings possess the same fundamental Pure Mind, neither mixing nor separating the quality of true voidness. When the sun shines over the four directions, the world becomes light, but true voidness is never light. When the sun sets, the world becomes dark, but voidness is never dark. The regions of dark and light destroy each other, but the nature of voidness is clear and undisturbed. The True Pure Mind of both Buddhas and sentient beings enjoys this same nature.

If one thinks that the Buddha is clean, bright and liberated and that sentient beings are dirty, dark and entangled in samsara, and, further, if one also uses this view to practice, then even though one perseveres through kalpas as numerous as the sand grains of the Ganges, one will not arrive at Bodhi. What exists for both Buddhas and for sentient beings, however, is the unconditioned Pure Mind (Asamskrta citta) with nothing to attain. Many Ch'an students, not understanding the nature of this Pure Mind, use the Pure Mind to create Pure Mind, thus grasping form and searching outside themselves. However, this is only to follow the path of evil and really is not the practice path to Bodhi.

Making offerings to one "without Pure Mind" surpasses in merit offerings made to countless others. Why is this? Because without Pure Mind we have unconditioned Buddha, who has neither movement nor obstruction. This alone is true emptiness, neither active nor passive, without form or place, without gain or loss.

Manjusri Bodhisattva symbolizes great substance (principle) and Samantabhadra Bodhisattva symbolizes the great function (action). Substance means emptiness, being without obstacles; functions means no form, being inexhaustible. Avalokitesvara Bodhisattva symbolizes great compassion (mahakaruna), and Mahasthama Bodhisattva symbolizes great wisdom (mahaprajna). Vimalakirti means "pure name". Purity is nature and name is form. Name and form are not different, and, therefore, Vimalakirti is called "pure name". These great Bodhisattvas symbolize those wholesome qualities or perfections that all of us intrinsically possess. There is no Pure Mind to search for outside ourselves. Understanding "thus it is", people awaken immediately. Many contemporary Dharma students do not investigate their own Pure Minds, but instead search outside and grasp the region of form. Fearing failure, they cannot enter the region of dhyana and, therefore, experience powerlessness and frustration and return to seeking intellectual understanding and knowledge. Hence, many students strive for doctrinal or intellectual understanding, but very few attain to the state of True Awakening. They just proceed, in their error, in the direction the very opposite to Bodhi.

One should be like the great earth. All Buddhas, Bodhisattvas, devas and human beings tread upon the earth, but the earth does not rejoice because of this. When the sheep, oxen, ants, etc., tread upon it, the earth does not become angry. Adorned with jewelry or rare fragrances, the earth does not give rise to greed. Bearing excrement and foul smells, the earth does not exhibit hatred or disgust. The unconditioned Pure Mind is without Pure Mind, beyond form. All sentient beings and Buddhas are not different; the Perfectly Awakened Pure Mind is thus. If Dharma students are unable to let go of conditioned Pure Mind suddenly, and instead practice in other ways, many kalpas may pass but they still will not have reached Bodhi. Because they are tied down by their thinking of the merits of the Three Vehicles, they do not attain genuine liberation.

Some students attain the state of liberated Pure Mind quickly, others slowly. After listening to a Dharma talk, some reach "no Pure Mind" directly. In contrast, some must first pass gradually through the ten grades of Bodhisattva faith, the Dasabhumi of Bodhisattva development, and the ten stages before attaining the Perfectly Awakened Pure Mind. Whether one takes a long or a short time, however, once attained, "no Pure Mind" can never be lost. With nothing further to cultivate and nothing more to attain, one realizes that this "no Pure Mind" is true, not false, Pure Mind. Whether reaching this stage quickly or after passing through the various stages of Bodhisattva development gradually, the attainment of "no Pure Mind" cannot be characterized in terms of shallow or deep. Those students who cannot win this state of understanding and liberation go on to create the wholesome and unwholesome mental states by grasping form, thus creating further suffering in samsara.

In short, nothing is better than the sudden recognition of the Original Dharma. This Dharma is Pure Mind, and outside of Pure Mind there is no Dharma. This Pure Mind is Dharma, and outside of this Dharma there is no Pure Mind. Self Pure Mind is "no Pure Mind" and no "no Pure Mind". Awaken the Pure Mind to "no Pure Mind" and win silent and sudden understanding. Just this!!

A Ch'an master said: "Break off the way of speech and destroy the place of thinking!" This Pure Mind itself is the ultimately pure Source of Buddha; and all Buddhas, Bodhisattvas and sentient beings possess this same Pure Mind. However, some people, because of delusion and discrimination, create much karma fruit. Original Buddha contains nothing. Awaken suddenly, profoundly and completely to the emptiness, peace, brilliance, wonder and bliss of this Original Buddha!!

The attainment of one who has practiced the myriad Dharma doors throughout three kalpas, having passed through the many Bodhisattva stages, and the attainment of one who has suddenly awakened to the One Pure Mind are equal. Both of them have just attained their own Original Buddha. The former type of disciple, the gradual attainer, upon arriving at his Original Buddha, looks back on his three kalpas of past practice as if he were looking at himself acting totally without principle in a dream.

Therefore, the Tathagata said: "There was really no Dharma by means of which the Tathagata attained Supreme Awakening. If there had been, Dipamkara Buddha would not have predicted my future attainment of Buddhahood." In addition the Tathagata said: "This Dharma is universal and impartial; therefore, it is called Supreme Awakening."

This ultimate pure source of Pure Mind encompasses all Buddhas, sentient beings and the world of mountains, rivers, forms and formlessness. Throughout the ten directions, all and everything reflects the equality of pure Pure Mind, which is always universally penetrating and illuminating. However, those with merely worldly understanding cannot recognize this truth and so identify seeing, hearing, touching and thinking as the Pure Mind. Covered by seeing, hearing, touching and thinking, one cannot see the brightness of Original Pure Mind. If suddenly one is without Pure Mind, Original Pure Mind will appear like the great sun in the sky, illuminating everywhere without obstruction.

Most Dharma students only know seeing, hearing, touching and thinking as movement and function and are, therefore, unable to recognize Original Pure Mind at the moment of seeing, hearing, touching and thinking. However, Original Pure Mind does not belong to seeing, hearing, touching and thinking but also is not distinct or separate from these activities. The view that one is seeing, hearing, touching and thinking does not arise; and yet one is not separate from these activities. This movement does not dim the Pure Mind, for it is neither itself a thing nor something apart from things. Neither staying nor grasping, capable of freely moving in any direction whatsoever, everywhere, this Pure Mind becomes the Bodhimandala.

When people hear that all Buddhas transmit the Pure Mind Dharma, they fantasize that there is a special Dharma they might attain. They then try to use the Pure Mind to find Dharma, not realizing that this very Pure Mind is the Dharma and that the Dharma is this very Pure Mind. Using the Pure Mind to search out Pure Mind, one can pass through thousands and thousands of kalpas of cultivation and still not acquire it. However, if a person can be suddenly without Pure Mind, then he and Original Dharma are one. A prodigal son forgot that a pearl was hidden in the cuff of his own clothes and searched outside, here and there, running everywhere in bewilderment and wonder. Then a wise friend pointed out the pearl to him, so thus he found it where it had always been.

Most Dharma students are confused about Original Pure Mind, not knowing that Original Dharma is non-existing, neither dependent nor staying. Neither active nor passive and without stirring thought, they can suddenly attain the stage of Perfect Awakening and see that they have reached the condition of Original Pure Mind that alone is Buddha. Looking back on their prior cultivation throughout many kalpas, they see it now only as labor expended in vain. Thus the prodigal son found his original pearl, and he realized then that the time and energy spent looking for it, heretofore, outside himself were all completely unnecessary. Therefore, Sakyamuni Buddha stated: " There was really no Dharma by means of which the Tathagata attained Supreme Awakening." Because most people find this Dharma profound and difficult to believe, one is forced to make use of analogies to express the Supreme Reality.

Dharma students should harbor no doubts concerning the body, and they should realize that, comprised, as it is, of four elements, there is within it no self or master to be found. The skandhas are Pure Mind, but no self or master can be found there either. The six sense-organs, six sense-objects and six sense-consciousnesses form the eighteen sense-realms, which are, likewise, void. Birth, death and all things everywhere are empty. Only Original Pure Mind is vast and clear. If one maintains the four elements of this body and allays the ulcer of hunger in a manner free from grasping, one nourishes oneself with wisdom food. On the other hand, if one pursues taste, having no regard for rules of moderation, and uses discrimination to seek things to please the palate and sate his desire-nature, one is gorging on consciousness food.

The disciple depends on the sound of the Dharma Teaching to attain the state of Perfect Awakening, but he still does not know the reality of unconditioned Pure Mind. This is because he erroneously gives rise to thoughts concerning the Teaching, sounds, yogic power, auspicious signs, speaking and activity. If such a person were to hear about Bodhi or Nirvana and then set about to practice in order to achieve Liberation even for the duration of three great Asankhyeya kalpas his practice would never, indeed, attain the Supreme Buddha Fruit. This cultivation belongs to the Sravaka stage and is called Sravaka Buddha. Suddenly awakening to one's own Pure Mind, one finds real Buddha. Nothing to practice, nothing to attain this alone is the Supreme Tao, the genuine Dharma. Without seeking the Pure Mind, there is no birth; without grasping the Pure Mind, there is no death. That which is neither birth nor death is Buddha. The 84,000 Dharmas are useful for curing the ills of sentient beings, but they are merely expedients used to teach and convert and receive all sentient beings. However, only Original Emptiness, without defilement, is Bodhi.

If Dharma students wish to know the key to successful cultivation, they should know that it is the Pure Mind that dwells on nothing. Emptiness is the Buddha's Dharmakaya, just as the Dharmakaya is emptiness. People's usual understanding is that the Dharmakaya pervades emptiness, and that it is contained in emptiness. However, this is erroneous, for we should understand that the Dharmakaya is emptiness and that emptiness is the Dharmakaya.

If one thinks that emptiness is an entity and that this emptiness is separate from the Dharmakaya or that there is a Dharmakaya outside of emptiness, one is holding a wrong view. In the complete absence of views about emptiness, the true Dharmakaya appears. Emptiness and Dharmakaya are not different. Sentient beings and Buddhas are not different. Birth and death and Nirvana are not different. Klesa and Bodhi are not different. That alone which is beyond all form is Buddha.

Worldly people grasp worldliness; Dharma students grasp Pure Mind. If they let go of both worldliness and Pure Mind, they can encounter real Dharma. Dwelling without worldliness is easy; dwelling without Pure Mind is difficult. People fear dwelling without Pure Mind and fear failure in their attempts to do so because they think that they would have nothing to hold onto. However, Original Emptiness is not emptiness but genuine Dharmadhatu.

Since time without beginning, the nature of Awakened Pure Mind and Emptiness has consisted of the same, absolute non-duality of no birth or death, no existence or non-existence, no purity or impurity, no movement or stillness, no young or old, no inside or outside, no shape and form, no sound and color. Neither striving nor searching, one should not use intellect to understand nor words to express Awakened Pure Mind. One should not think that it is a place or things, name or form. One should not think that it is a place or things, name or form. Only then is it realized that all Buddhas, Bodhisattvas and sentient beings possess the same natural state of great Nirvana.

True Nature is Pure Mind; the Pure Mind is Buddha; the Buddha is Dharma. One should not use the Pure Mind to seek Pure Mind, the Buddha to seek Buddha, nor the Dharma to seek Dharma. Therefore, Dharma students should suddenly realize no-Pure Mind and suddenly attain stillness and silence. Stirring thoughts is wrong, but using the Pure Mind to transmit Pure Mind is right. Be careful not to search outside yourself. If you consider the Pure Mind to be outside yourself, it is the same as mistaking a thief for your own son.

Because of our craving, aversion and delusion, we must utilize sila, samadhi and prajna to purify our Pure Minds of grasping and delusion. If there originally is no defilement, then what is Bodhi? Relative to this, a Ch'an Master said: "All Dharma taught by Lord Buddha is taught solely to wipe out all Pure Mind, Without any Pure Mind at all, what use is Dharma?" So, there is nothing at all to hold onto at the original and ultimate source of pure Buddha. Even if emptiness were to be adorned with countless jewels and other treasures, these things could not remain. Similarly, even if the Buddha Nature is adorned with immeasurable wisdom and virtue, that adornment has no place to stay. Most people are deluded about their own nature and thus cannot or will not awaken to their own Pure Minds.

In short, all things are dependent on the Pure Mind. When causes and conditions meet, things appear. When causes and conditions separate, they disappear. Dharma students should not sully their pure nature by giving rise to thoughts. The mirror of sila and prajna is bright and tranquil and allows one to reflect on seeing, hearing, touching and thinking. This view of the Pure Mind's sphere is only an expedient used to teach those of average or inferior capabilities and is not a vision of Supreme Bodhi. One who aspires to Supreme Bodhi should not hold such a view. The existent and non-existent are both within the grasping Pure Mind's sphere. Without existence and non-existence, there is no-Pure Mind and everything is Dharma.

A Ch'an Master has said: "From the time of his arrival in China, Patriarch Bodhidharma taught only the view of unconditioned Pure Mind and spread only the view of unconditioned Dharma." Using Dharma to transmit Dharma, there is no other Dharma. Using Buddha to transmit Buddha, there is no other Buddha. This Dharma is "without-words" Dharma; this Buddha is "without-words" Buddha. Hence, they are the ultimate source of Pure Pure Mind. This is the true Ch'an teaching. All others are false!

Prajna is Original Pure Mind without form. Worldly people do not have a natural inclination towards the Tao, but prefer instead to indulge in the six emotions that arise due to the six conditions of sentient existence -- i.e., the emotional effects, like desire or aversion, that arise when sense-objects contact the internal sense-bases or, afterwards, in recollection of this contact. Dharma students who allow a thought of birth and death to arise fall into the realm of Mara. If one allows a thought to arise while seeing, one falls into heresy. When one desires to exterminate birth and death, one falls into the Sravaka realm. One who sees neither birth nor death and is aware only of cessation falls into the Pratyekabuddha realm. However, one might ask: Originally the dharmas know no arising, so how can they be subject to cessation? The answer one might receive is : With this non-dualistic outlook -- that is, having neither desire nor aversion everything is Pure Mind. This alone is the Buddha of Supreme Awakening!

Worldly people allow thoughts to arise concerning the Pure Mind's sphere and thus harbor like and dislike. If one does not want this entanglement, one must forget the Pure Mind. Without Pure Mind, the sphere is empty. If one does not want "without Pure Mind", but only wants to end entanglement in the various realms of the Pure Mind, then one is simply creating more disturbance. Therefore, one must realize that all phenomena are dependent on Pure Mind and that Pure Mind itself is unattainable, if one is to attain the Buddha of Supreme Awakening.

Prajna students, even if you seek the one Dharma and give no thought to the Three Vehicles, this one Dharma is also unobtainable, If someone says he can obtain it, he is indeed an arrogant person and indeed is one with those who left the Lotus Assembly, refusing to listen to the Lotus Teaching Thus the Tathagata said: "There was really no Dharma by means of which the Tathagata attained Supreme Awakening." However, there is the unspoken, silent understanding. There is just this!

Those who are near death just then realize that the five skandhas are empty, the real Pure Mind is without form, and that the four elements are devoid of self. Neither coming nor going, the Buddhas nature does not depart. If one suddenly understands the unconditioned Pure Mind and realizes that the Pure Mind-sphere is non-differentiated, he is not restricted by the three periods. This is the true Arya, who is free of defiling tendencies. Encountering pleasing sense objects and even being greeted by all Buddhas, he does not pursue them. Terrible or loathsome sense objects cause no fear to such a one. Dwelling without Pure Mind, like the Dharmadhatu, the Pure Mind is free of all delusions.

A Ch'an Master said: "The expedient teachings of Sravaka, Bodhisattva, Dasabhumi and Samyak Sambodhi all belong to the path of gradual awakening." What is perfect Nirvana? Perfect Nirvana is the sudden understanding that one's own nature is original Buddha and True Pure Mind. It is the sudden realization that there is neither Buddha nor sentient beings, neither subject nor object. If this present place is illusion city, where then is perfect Nirvana? Perfect Nirvana cannot be pointed out because we are only able to point out a place. Whatever is thought of as a place cannot be the condition of true, perfect Nirvana. One can give indications as to which direction it lies in, but one cannot give a definite location. However, one may come to a correct and silent understanding of it.

An Icchantika is a person abandoned as unteachable because of the complete absence of faith in his heart. If any sentient beings and Sravakas do not believe that being "without Pure Mind" is the Buddha and Supreme Awakening, they can certainly be termed Icchantika.

All Bodhisattvas have confidence in the Buddhadharma, whether it is the teaching of the Sravaka or the Bodhisattva Vehicles. All sentient beings have the same Dharma nature as the Buddhas and, therefore, may be termed Icchantika with good roots. In short, those who depend on hearing the Teaching to attain Awakening are termed Sravakas. Those who contemplate the twelve nidanas of dependent origination and thus win Awakening are termed Pratyekabuddhas. Most Dharma students are awakened by Dharma teaching but not awakened directly to Pure Mind. Practicing for many kalpas, they still do not attain Original Buddha. Just as a dog is distracted by a clod of earth thrown at him, so we forget Original Pure Mind. However, if one can attain silent and unspoken understanding, one knows that because the Pure Mind is Dharma it is, therefore, not necessary to seek Dharma.

Most people's Pure Minds are hindered by the Pure Mind-realms and only perceive the Buddha principle polluted by and mixed with phenomena. Thus, they are always trying to escape the Pure Mind-realms and calm the Pure Mind. To attain Pure Pure Mind, they attempt to eradicate phenomena and keep the principle, not realizing that the Pure Mind-realms are hindered by Pure Mind and that phenomena are hindered by the principle. Without Pure Mind, the realms are empty; when the principle is tranquil, so are phenomena. One should not turn the Pure Mind upside down for some personal use. People do not really want to realize the state of being "Without Pure Mind", fearing that if they fail at their attempts at cultivation a one-sided emptiness would result. Foolish people only try to wipe out phenomena but do not wipe out Pure Mind. The wise man wipes out the Pure Mind and does not bother with phenomena. The Pure Mind of the Bodhisattva is void, having abandoned all and grasping neither bliss nor merit.

There are three degrees of renunciation in this practice. The highest degree is the renunciation of body and Pure Mind through the perception of everything, inside and out, as void, there being nothing to obtain and nothing to grasp. Depending on the limits of his strength of belief and committment to practice, one makes the great renunciation of negative and positive, existence and non-existence. Following this realization of truth with practice and non-expectation of reward or personal benefit is the middle degree of renunciation. The superior degree of renunciation is compared to holding a torch in front of oneself, being neither deluded nor awakened. The middle renunciation is compared to holding the torch at one's side; it is sometimes light and sometimes dark. The lowest renunciation is similar to holding the torch at one's back, thus being unable to see a pit or trap in front of one. The Pure Mind of the Bodhisattva is void, having abandoned all things. Past-Pure Mind not grasping is past renunciation; present-Pure Mind not grasping is present renunciation; future-Pure Mind not grasping is future renunciation.

Since that time when the Tathagata bequeathed his Teaching to Venerable Mahakasyapa, the Pure Mind has been used to transmit Pure Mind, nothing apart from this being necessary. As a seal makes no impression on the sky, one leaves no written mark. As a seal makes an impression on paper, one leaves no Dharma. Therefore, using the Pure Mind to imprint Pure Mind, one still has only Pure Mind. Without both the negative and positive imprint, the unspoken understanding is difficult to attain. For this reason, many Dharma students study, but few accomplish the path. However, no-Pure Mind is Pure Mind and no-attainment is Attainment.

The Tathagata has a threefold body. The Dharmakaya propagates the void-nature Dharma. The Dharmakaya preaches the Dharma beyond words and form. With really no Dharma to expound, it teaches the Dharma of emptiness as self-nature. The Nirmanakaya propagates the six paramitas and the myriad Dharma practices. The Sambhogakaya expounds Dharma according to the various conditions and capacities of all sentient beings.

The one essence is one Pure Mind. The six sense-organs with their six sense-objects and resultant six sense-consciousnesses are, altogether, called the eighteen realms. If one perceives these eighteen realms as empty and reduces them to one essence, that essence is Pure Mind. All Dharma students know this theoretically, but cannot divest themselves of views based on the duality and analysis of this essence and the grasping of the six senses. Being bound by these dharmas, they cannot silently understand Original Pure Mind.

The Tathagata appeared in the world to teach the Supreme Vehicle. However, because sentient beings were unable to believe in, and even slandered, the Teaching, they remained immersed and drowning in a sea of suffering. Therefore, the Tathagata utilized the expedient Teaching of the Three Vehicles to help them. Some disciples attained deep realization, some shallow; but since few or none had awakened to Buddha's Original Dharma, one sutra states: "They still do not manifest the Dharma of One Pure Mind." This special teaching of Pure Mind is a Dharma without words. The Ch'an School relies not on texts but, instead, on the special transmission received by the Venerable Mahakasyapa i.e., silent understanding and sudden attainment of the Great Awakening with arrival at the Ultimate Tao.

Once a bhiksu asked his master: "What is Tao and how is it practiced?" The master responded: "What is this Tao and what do you want to practice?" The bhiksu asked: "Is Tao receptive of the students who come for instruction in cultivation?" "That is for people of dull capacity; the Tao cannot be practiced," said the master. "If this is for people of dull capacity, what is the Dharma for people of superior ability?" asked the bhiksu. The master answered: "If one is of genuine superior ability, there is none for him to follow. Even seeking himself is impossible, so how can he grasp Dharma?" The bhiksu exclaimed, "If that is so, there is nothing to seek!" The master retorted, "Then save your mental energy." "But this would be tantamount to the annihilation view, and one could say nothing." said the bhiksu. "Who is it that says nothing? Who is he? Try to search for him, " said the master. "If this is the case, why seek who it is that says nothing'?" asked the bhiksu. The master answered: "If you do not seek, that is alright. Who asked you about annihilation? You see the void in front of you, so why do you think you have destroyed it?" "Could this Dharma be voidness?" asked the bhiksu. "Does this voidness tell you the difference between morning and night? I'm just speaking expediently to you because you are giving rise to thoughts and holding views about what I say," said the master. The bhiksu then asked: "One should not hold views?" The master answered: "I'm not obstructing you, but you should understand your view as emotion. When emotion arises, wisdom is concealed." The bhiksu asked: I'm just talking to you, so why call it superfluous?" The master said: " you do not understand what others say, so where is the superfluity?" The bhiksu said: Now you have talked for quite some time, all of which seemed to be for the sake of resisting the enemy of words, while giving no instruction at all in the Dharma." The master replied: "Just realize the Dharma without inverted view. Your questions are inverted! What true' Dharma do you want?" The bhiksu then observed: "So, my questions are inverted? How about the master's answers?" The master replied:" You should take something to illumine your face; do not meddle with others." The bhiksu exclaimed: "Just like a foolish dog! When he sees something move, he barks at shadows and sounds." The master said: "The Dhyana School, mutually receiving all sentient beings from the distant past until now, never taught people to hold views, but only stated, Learn Tao'." These words are designed to convert and receive the average person, but the Tao cannot be learned. If one hold some view of learning, then one is, indeed, deluded by the Tao. The Tao is nothing but this Mahayana Pure Mind. This Pure Mind is nowhere, neither inside, outside, nor somewhere in between. So primarily, one should not hold any view. The cessation of the dualistic view of like' is Tao. If like' is cut off, the Pure Mind is nowhere. The Original Tao is without name, but because worldly people do not comprehend, they are deluded by perverted views. All Buddhas appear in the world to explain and teach this Dharma. Since people are unable to understand it directly, the Buddhas utilize expedient methods to teach the Tao. One should not cling to names and create views. For example, when fishing, if one catches a fish, one should forget about the bamboo fish-trap. When one attains the other shore, one should then give up the raft."

At the very moment when one understands the Tao and recognizes the Pure Mind, one is then free of body and Pure Mind. One who reaches the ultimate source is called a Sramana. The fruit of a Sramana is the cessation of false thinking. This fruit cannot be attained through worldly learning. Using the Pure Mind to seek Pure Mind and depending on others for insight, how can one reach or acquire the Tao? The ancient cultivators were possessed of wisdom. Just by hearing a few words of Dharma, they suddenly attained the state beyond study and thinking. Today, people only want to seek worldly learning, mistakenly believing that more knowledge leads to better practice. They do not know that more and more learning leads only to obstacles in their cultivation. Giving a baby more and more cream to eat, who knows if he digests it or not? Likewise, the Teaching of the Three Vehicles is comparable to eating a lot without proper digestion. All study without proper digestion is poison. These things exist in the realm of production and annihilation, while in the Bhutatathata the state of absolute Thusness or Suchness, i.e., things as they are in reality, devoid of the usual distortion by klesa there is nothing whatsoever. Attaining the Bhutatathata and the Unconditioned means wiping out all previous views and remaining empty without false discrimination.

What is the Tathagata store? It is Emptiness, the kingly Dharma, appearing in the world to refute all relative things. Therefore, the sutra states: "There really was no Dharma by means of which the Tathagata attained Supreme Awakening." These words are only to be expediently used for wiping out one's perverted views. Without the inside-and-outside concept of perverted views, there is nothing whatsoever to depend on or to grasp. This is truly the reality of the unhindered one. All the teaching of the Three Vehicles is merely medicine for weak patients; all the various teachings are merely expedients to suit the temporary needs of sentient beings. However, one should not become confused by this Teaching. If one does not give rise to views or grasp words, there is no Dharma. Why? Because there is no fixed Dharma for the Tathagata to expound. My Dhyana school never talks about this matter. The Teaching's purpose is to stop false thinking; it is not meant to serve the ends of thinking, pondering and intellectual analysis.

A bhiksu once declared to his master: "You have said that, above all, the Pure Mind is Buddha, but I don't know which Pure Mind is the Buddha." " How many Pure Minds do you have?" questioned the master. "Is the worldly Pure Mind or the holy Pure Mind the Buddha?" asked the Bhiksu. The master then asked: " Exactly where do you find the worldly and the holy Pure Minds?" The bhiksu observed: " The Three Vehicles constantly speak of worldly and holy, so how can you say they don't exist?" The master replied: "Worldly and holy are very clearly explained in the Three Vehicles. You do not understand and grasp them as objects. Wouldn't it be incorrect to think of emptiness as really existing? Merely wipe out the worldly-and-holy view. There is no Buddha outside of the Pure Mind. The Patriarch came from the West solely to point out that people's Pure Minds are Buddha. You do not recognize this and actively pursue the Buddha. You do not recognize this and actively pursue the Buddha outside, thus deluding your own Pure Mind. For this reason, I talk about the Pure Mind as Buddha. Actually, giving rise to a single thought, one falls into heterodox paths. Since time without beginning, there is no differentiation or discrimination, Voidness is the Unconditioned Awakening."

The bhiksu queried: "In what theory do you say is'?" The master replied: "What theory do you seek? If you have some theory, that is a differentiating Pure Mind." The bhiksu asked further: "You said earlier that since time without beginning there is no differentiation. What theory is this?" The master answered: "Because of your seeking, you realize a difference. Without seeking, where is the difference?" The bhiksu asked: "If non-different, why do you say it is'?" The master replied: "If you do not have the worldly-and-holy view, who can tell you it is'? If it is' is not, it truly is'! When Pure Mind is not Pure Mind', then the Pure Mind and it is' all disappear. Where do you want to seek?" The bhiksu queried: "If the false can be an obstacle to the Pure Mind, how does one drive away the false?" The master answered: "The false arising and ceasing -- that is the false. Originally, the false has no root but arises from discrimination, If one has no perverted view of worldly versus holy, then automatically there is no false. With nothing to grasp and nothing to drive out, abandoning everything -- just there and then is the Buddha." The bhiksu then asked: "If there is already no grasping, then what is transmitted?" The master answered: "The Pure Mind is used to transmit Pure Mind." The bhiksu asked: "If the Pure Mind can be mutually transmitted, how can one then be said to be without Pure Mind?" The master responded: "Just nothing-to-obtain is the real transmission of Pure Mind. If one really understands, then the Pure Mind is no-Pure Mind and no-Dharma." The bhiksu asked: "If there is no-Pure Mind and no-Dharma, where is the transmission?" The master replied: When you hear the phrase transmission of Pure Mind' do you think there is something to obtain? The Patriarch has said, When you see the Pure Mind nature, that is the state beyond discrimination.' The complete Pure Mind is just nothing attained. Where is there attainment'? Knowing is not present. What do you think about that?" The bhiksu asked: "Only voidness in front of me without the Pure Mind's sphere! Without the Pure Mind's sphere, wouldn't one then see the Pure Mind? The master responded: "What Pure Mind do you want to see in this sphere? If you see something, it is only a reflection from the Pure Mind's sphere? Like a person looking at his face in a mirror thinking he clearly sees his face and eye-brows but, in reality, seeing only an image or a reflection, even so is any reflection from the Pure Mind's sphere. But what has all this got to do with you?" The bhiksu asked: "If not by reflection, how can one see the Pure Mind?" The master replied: "If one wants to point out the cause, one must continually refer to that which the cause is dependent upon. This is a never-ending process, for there is no end to the dependent origination of things. Relax your hold, for there is nothing to obtain. Talking continuously of thousands and thousands of things is just labor expended in vain."

"If one understands this, then even with reflection is there still nothing to obtain?" asked the bhiksu. "If there is nothing to obtain, then reflection is not necessary," said the master. "Don't depend on talk from a dream to open your eyes. Nothing-to-seek' is the primary Dharma. This is better than studying and learning a hundred different things. With nothing to obtain, one has finished the task," continued the master. The bhiksu queried: "What is ordinary truth?" The master replied: "Why do you persist in creating clinging vines? Originally, truth is clear and bright. It is not necessary to have questions and answers."

In summary, then, it is to be noted that this without-Pure Mind state is wisdom and detachment. Walking, standing, sitting, reclining, talking and all of one's other everyday actions are done without attachment and are thus transformed into non-action.

In this Dharma-ending age, many Dharma students grasp form and sound in their cultivation. If only they were able to make their Pure Minds as void as a withered, dead tree or like a stone or cold ashes, they might realize a bit of this Dharma. Otherwise, they might as well try to force information from the King of Hell. Being without the dualistic conception of existence and non-existence, like the sun shining in the sky, wouldn't they save energy?

Therefore, being with no place to dwell is the way of all Buddha activity. The Pure Mind that does not abide anywhere is the Perfect Awakening. Without understanding the Unconditioned Truth, even with much learning and diligent practice, one still does not recognize one's own Pure Mind. Therefore, all one's actions are nonsense, and one is a member of the Deva Mara's family. The Ch'an master Chi-Kung observed: "Buddha is one's own Pure Mind! Why do you search in words and letters?" "If you do not meet a teacher with this transcendental understanding, then you must take the Dharma medicine of Mahayana. Walking, standing, sitting and lying over a long period of time, one may realize the without-Pure Mind state if the right combination of causes fosters it. Because one lacks the capacity for sudden Awakening, one must study the Tao of Dhyana for 3, 5, or 10 years. There is no special arrangement or negotiation for achieving Buddhadharma. However, this Teaching of the Tathagata exists as an expedient for the purpose of transforming all beings. For example, one shows a yellow leaf to a crying baby and pretends that it is gold. This is not really true, but it stops the crying of the baby. If a teaching says that there is truly something to obtain, then it is not the Teaching of my sect, nor would I be a member of such an heretical sect. The sutra states: "There really was no Dharma by means of which the Tathagata attained Supreme Awakening." This is the truth of the non-heretical sect, with which I identify.

If one realizes the originally clear and bright Pure Mind, then both Buddha and Mara, as dualistic conceptions, are wrong. In this Pure Mind there is no square or round, no big or small, no short or long. It is passionless and non-active. Neither deluded nor awakened, it is clarity and emptiness. Human beings and Buddha in worlds as numerous as the sands of the Ganges appear as bubbles in the ocean. Nothing is better than "without-Pure Mind". Since time without beginning, all Buddhas and the

Dharmakaya are not different, neither increasing nor decreasing. For this reason, if one really comprehends the importance of such an insight, one should cultivate diligently until the end of one's life. Since the outbreath does not guarantee the inbreath, everybody should wake up!!

A bhiksu asked the master: "Since the Sixth Patriarch did not study the sutras, how could he possibly receive the transmission of the yellow robe and become Patriarch? Venerable Shen-Hsiu was the leader of five hundred monks and a Dharma teacher able to expound on thirty-two sutras and sastras. Why wasn't the Patriarch's robe transmitted to hem?" The master said:" The Venerable Shen-Hsiu still had a discriminating Pure Mind. His Dharma was action-oriented because he practiced and attained that which has form. The Sixth Patriarch, in contrast, was suddenly awakened and tacitly understood. Therefore, the Fifth Patriarch secretly transmitted to him the profound truth of the Tathagata's Teaching."

The Dharma Transmission Gatha of Sakyamuni Buddha states: "Original Dharma is no-Dharma; without Dharma is true Dharma. In transmitting the Dharma that is no-Dharma, has there ever been a Dharma?" If one accepts this right view, then one can practice with ease; such a one can truly be called one who has left home. When the Venerable Wai-Ming chased the Sixth Patriarch to Ta Yu Mountain, the Patriarch asked him: "What do you want by coming here? Do you seek the robe or the Dharma?" "I come for the Dharma, not for the robe," answered the Venerable Wai-Ming. The Sixth Patriarch then asked him: "Without thinking of good or evil, what is the original face of the Venerable Wai-Ming?" Venerable Wai-Ming was suddenly awakened and prostrated himself at the feet of the Patriarch, declaring: "Only a person who drinks the water knows whether it is cool or warm. My following the Fifth Patriarch for thirty years was just labor expended in vain." The Sixth Patriarch responded: "Yes! Now you know that the intention of the Patriarch's coming from the West was just to point to the Pure Mind directly. Beholding the Buddha Nature within oneself is the Perfect Awakening, for it never depends on words."

Once the Venerable Ananda asked the Venerable Mahakasyapa: "Besides handing down the robe, what else does the World Honored One transmit?" Venerable Mahakasyapa shouted, "Ananda!" "Yes!" answered Venerable Ananda. "Turn the flag-pole in front of the door upside down," commanded Venerable Mahakasyapa. This is an excellent example of the upholding and maintaining of the Patriarch's purpose. The foremost listener among the Buddha's disciples was Venerable Ananda, the Buddha's attendant for thirty years. However, his only reasons for listening to the Dharma had been to acquire vast erudition. Therefore, the Buddha scolded him thus: "Learning the Tao for one day is far superior to acquiring knowledge for a thousand." If Dharma students do not learn the Tao, even the digestion of one drop of water is difficult.

A bhiksu asked the master: "How does one practice without grade or degree?" The master replied: "Taking one's meal every day, one never chews a grain of rice. Walking every day, one never steps upon the ground." Without the discrimination between self and others, one lives in the world, not deluded by anything at all. This is a genuinely free person whose thinking is beyond name and form. Transcending the three periods of thought, he understands that the previous period has not passed, the present period does not stay, and that the future period will not come. Sitting properly and peacefully, not bound by the world this alone is called liberation! Everybody should strive diligently. Out of thousands and thousands of Dharma students in the Dhyana School, only three or five attain the fruit. If we do not care about our practice, misfortune could easily arise in the future. All of us should practice diligently and finish the task of liberation in this life. Who can or wants to bear misfortune for endless kalpas?

The Wan-Ling Record

Once, I asked the master that: "There are a few hundred monks dwelling on that mountain. How many of them have acquired your Dharma?" The master responded: "To know how many of them have acquired it is impossible because the Tao is expressed and comprehended only by Pure Mind, not by words. All thoughts and words are used only as expedients to teach innocent children."

Question: "What is the Buddha?" The master responded: "The Pure Mind is Buddha; no-Pure Mind is the Tao. Just be without Pure Mind and stop your thinking. Just be of that Pure Mind where there is no existence or non-existence, no long and no short, no self and no others, neither negative nor positive, and neither within nor without. Just know, above all, that non-differentiating Pure Mind is the Buddha, that Buddha is the Pure Mind and that the Pure Mind is voidness. Therefore, the real Dharmakaya is just voidness. It is not necessary to seek anything whatsoever, and all who do continue to seek for something only prolong their suffering in samsara. Even if they were to practice the Six Paramitas for as many numberless kalpas as there are sandgrains in the Ganges River, they would still not reach the Supreme Stage. And why not? Just because such practice depends on primary and secondary causes, and when these causes separate, the practitioner of this path will still have only reached a stage of impermanence. Therefore, even the Sambhogakaya and the Nirmanakaya are not the real Buddha. Also, the one who spreads Dharma is not the real Buddha. In reality, therefore, everybody should recognize that only one's own Pure Mind is the Original Buddha."

Question: "The holy without-Pure Mind' is Buddha, but might the worldly without-Pure Mind' sink into emptiness?" The master answered: "Hold neither a concept of holy nor of worldly; think neither of emptiness nor tranquillity in the Dharma. Since originally there is no non-existent Dharma, it is, therefore, not necessary to have a view of existence as such. Furthermore, concepts of existence and non-existence are all perverted views just like the illusion created by a film spread over diseased eyes. Analogously, the perceptions of seeing and hearing, just like the film that creates the illusion for diseased eyes, cause the errors and delusions of all sentient beings. Being without motive, desire or view, and without compromise, is the way of the Patriarch. In addition, being without motive is the principle that allows the flourishing of Buddha. In contrast, discriminating view, firmly grasped, encourages the thriving of the army of Mara."

Question: "If the Pure Mind is already the original Buddha, should we still need to practice the Six Paramitas and all such methods?" The master said: "We are enlightened only by Pure Mind, no matter whether we follow the Six Paramitas or other methods. All such methods and teaching are used only as expedients to help save all sentient beings. The goal is to realize Bodhi, liberation and Dharmakaya; even the four Phalas (Fruitions) and the ten stages of a Bodhisattvas progress are nothing but expedient teaching surely not ends in themselves to help sentient beings realize the Buddha Pure Mind. Since, in reality, the Pure Mind is Buddha, the first and only teaching necessary for saving sentient beings is THE PURE MIND IS BUDDHA'." If we were without concepts of birth and death as well as suffering and affliction, it would not then be necessary to have the Dharma of Bodhi. So all the Dharma ever spoken by Buddha was and is expediently designed to liberate the Pure Minds of all sentient beings. However, if all beings are without Pure Mind, it is not necessary to have any Dharma at all. The Buddha and the Patriarchs never talk about anything other than One Pure Mind, which is also called the One Vehicle. Therefore, even if you seek in the ten directions, you will find no other vehicle that is the Truth except this realization of One Pure Mind. So, in the Assembly that has this Right View, there are no leaves or branches only the One Vehicle.

However, it is extremely difficult for most beings to believe in or to grasp the profound meaning of this Dharma. Bodhidharma came to the two countries of Liang and Wei, just in order to spread the Venerable Wai-Kuo's esoteric belief in the Dharma and the understanding that one's own Pure Mind is Buddha. Without-body' and without-Pure Mind' is the great Tao! Since all sentient beings have fundamentally the same nature, everybody should be able to believe deeply. Pure Mind and self-nature are not different. One's self-nature is Pure Mind. One's Pure Mind is self-nature. It is frequently said that the recognition and realization of this identification of Pure Mind and self-nature is beyond comprehension."

Question: "Does the Buddha really save or rescue all sentient beings?" The master said: "There are really no sentient beings to be saved by Tathagata. Since there is, in reality, neither self nor non-self, how then can there be a Buddha to save or sentient beings to be saved?"

Question: "There are thirty-two Laksanas, that traditionally purport to save all sentient beings, so how can we say that there are no sentient being?" The master said: "Everything with form is unreal. If all form is seen as unreal, then the Taghagata will be perceived, Buddha, sentient beings and the infinite variety of forms all are generated by your false view, whereby you do not understand the Original Pure Mind. If you retain a view even of Buddha as real, then even Buddha is an obstacle! If you grasp a view of sentient beings as real, then sentient beings are also obstacles. If you hold a view that labels phenomena as worldly, holy, pure, dirty, etc., this is also an obstacle to enlightenment. Because of these obstacles in your Pure Mind, you transmigrate along the six illusory paths, becoming fixed to the wheel of transmigration, just as a monkey picks up one object and lets go of another in never-ending, habitual, monotonous repetition.

The important thing is to learn the Truth; for without learning that there is really no holy, no pure, no dirty, no big, no small, etc., but only emptiness and non-action and that this alone is ONE PURE MIND and that, always, any adornment is only an expedient to learn the truth, one only clings to illusion. Furthermore, even if you learn by heart the Three Vehicles and the twelve divisions of the Mahayana canon, you must abandon it all. Thus the Vimalakirti Sutra states that just as a person confined in bed by illness only lies in one bed, so there is only one Dharma that does not obstruct Dharma namely, the No-Dharma Dharma. This Dharma view alone can penetrate the three physical, mental and worldly realms, and it alone constitutes the supramundane Buddha.

Thus, just as one prostrates oneself, grasping at nothing, so this view is not at all heretical, for since the Pure Mind is no different from the Dharma? the Pure Mind being non-action and the Dharma being non-action? then everything is created by the Pure Mind. If the Pure Mind is empty, then all Dharma is emptiness, and all things are identical including space in the ten directions with the One Pure Mind. Because you hold to a discriminating view, you, therefore, have different names, forms and things, just as all the Devas take a meal from a one-jewelled container, but the color and the taste of the food depend upon their stages of bliss and morality. Thus, there was really no Dharma by means of which all the Buddhas in the ten directions attained what is called Supreme Enlightenment'. Without differentiation of form or luster, there is neither victory nor defeat; and if there is no victory or defeat, then sentient beings have no form."

Question: "If there never really has been form in the Pure Mind, then how can we correctly say that it is possible to save all sentient beings by means of the thirty-two Laksanas and the eighty notable physical characteristics?" The master responded: "The thirty-two Laksanas are form. The Sutra has said that everything with form is unreal. The eighty notable physical characteristics are appearance. So the Diamond Sutra said: He who seeks me by outward appearance and seeks me in sound treads the heterodox path and cannot perceive the Tathagata'."

Question: "Are the natures of Buddha and of sentient beings the same or different?" the master replied: "Their natures have no such characteristics as same' and different'. Suppose that a hypothetical three-vehicles teaching discriminated between Buddha Nature and sentient-beings nature. Thereupon would follow the view of cause and effect, and form this we could then say that their natures have such characteristics as same' and different'. However, suppose the Buddha and the Patriarchs never talked in this manner, but only pointed to the One Pure Mind. Then there could be no such same' and different', no cause and effect and, except as an expedient teaching, no two or three. In reality, therefore, there is only One Vehicle!"

Question: "Can the immeasurable body of a Bodhisattva be seen or not be seen?" The master answered: "There is really nothing to see. Why not? Just because the immeasurable body of a Bodhisattva is the Tathagata. So, again, there is nothing to see. Just do not hold any view of the Buddha and you will never go to the Buddha extreme; just do not hold a view about sentient beings and you will never go to the sentient-beings extreme; just do not hold any view about existence and you will never go to existence extreme; do not hold a view about non-existence extreme; do not hold any view about worldly characteristics and you will never go to the worldly-characteristics extreme; do not hold any view about holy characteristics and you will never go to the holy-characteristics extreme. Thus the state of merely being without any view whatsoever is already the Immeasurable Body. If you have something to see, you are a heretic. While heretics like to hold all different kinds of views, Bodhisattvas are not moved by any view whatsoever. Tathagata' means the suchness of all phenomena, the undifferentiated whole of all dharmas.

Therefore, the Maitreya and all the holy saints and sages are also suchness, having neither birth nor death and neither characteristics nor view. The real and true expression of Buddha is the Complete View. However, if you do not hold the view of the Complete View, you will never go to the Complete-View extreme. Remember that the body of Buddha is only non-form and non-action, ever crystallizing or materializing into phenomena, just as in the great space of the void nothing is lacking and nothing is in excess. Do not discern self versus others, if to discriminate in such a way would become illusory knowledge i.e., consciousness. So sink into the ocean of complete Perfection Consciousness, flowing, returning and drifting about alone. Merely learn how to be quietly enlightened and liberated. Regarding the view that desires victory and does not desire defeat I can only ask, What use is such a view?' I have just advised you that no matter what the usual way of acting or perceiving is, don't let your Pure Mind run wild. If you just cease holding any view whatsoever, then it is not necessary to search for truth. In this sense, then, both Buddha and Deva Mara are evil. So Manjusri said: If anyone gives rise to the transient, dualistic view of transcendence and calls it reality, he should be banished to the two iron-enclosing mountains at the very edge of the world.' Manjusri represents the wisdom of reality, while Samantabhadra represents the knowledge of relative truth, for there is only One Pure Mind. Even the Pure Mind itself is neither the nature of Buddha nor of sentient beings. Even if you abruptly have a vision of the Buddha, it is also, simultaneously, a vision of sentient beings. The view that holds to the duality of existence and non-existence and of permanent and impermanent is like being limited by the two iron-enclosing mountains, because understanding and liberation are obstructed by any and all views. To point out that the Original Pure Mind of all sentient beings is Buddha was the only purpose of the Patriarch who came from the West. Thus suddenly, rather than gradually, pointing to Original Pure Mind, the Patriarch showed that it was neither light nor dark and that without light there is no dark and that without dark there is no light. Consequently, it followed that there is no ignorance and also no ending of ignorance. As one enters the door of Dhyana, he should have this awareness and understanding. This discernment of reality is the Dharma which is no other than the awareness of Buddha as no Buddha and the Sangha as the Sangha of non-action and the realization of the Precious Three as One Body. If you seek to understand Dharma better, don't grasp the Sangha. You should realize that there is nothing to seek. Also, do not grasp the Buddha or the Dharma, for, again, there is nothing at all to seek. Don't grasp the Buddha in your seeking, for there is no Buddha. Don't grasp the Dharma in your seeking, for there is no Dharma. Don't grasp the Sangha in your seeking, for there is no Sangha. Such is the true and correct Dharma!"

Question: "Master, you spread Dharma now, so how can you say that there is no Sangha and no Dharma?" The master answered: "If you think that I have Dharma to spread, that means you perceive the Tathagata by sound. If you really have seen the Tathagata, that means you also perceive a place. The true Dharma is no-Dharma! The true Dharma is Pure Mind! So be aware that in the Dharma of Pure Mind Transmission, Dharma has, indeed, never been Dharma. Without the view of Dharma and Pure Mind', we would understand immediately that all Pure Mind is

Dharma. At this instant we would set up the Bodhimandala. Remember, there is really nothing to obtain, for the Bodhimandala is without any view whatsoever. To the enlightened ones, the Dharma is voidness and nothingness. Then where has it ever been defiled by any dust? Such is the Bhutatathata in its purity. If you comprehend this truth intuitively, you will have joy and freedom beyond comparison."

Question: "You say that originally there is nothingness. Doesn't this view assume that nothingness' is'?" The master replied: "Nothingness also is not is'. Bodhi is nowhere and also has no such view."

Question: "What is Buddha?" The master answered: "Your Pure Mind is Buddha. Buddha and Pure Mind are not different. If the Pure Mind were to depart, nothing else would be Buddha."

Question: "If one's own Pure Mind is Buddha, how can it be transmitted by the Patriarch who came from the West?" The master responded: "The patriarch who came from the West only transmitted the Buddha Pure Mind and directly pointed out that your Original Pure Mind is Buddha. Original Pure Mind itself is no different from the so-called Patriarch. If you comprehend this meaning deeply, suddenly you transcend the Three Vehicles and all the stages of a Bodhisattva's progress and realize that, since all is Buddha originally, it is not necessary to practice."

Questions: "If suddenly all Buddhas were to appear from all the ten directions of space, what Dharma would be preached by those Buddhas?" The master replied: "All Buddhas appearing from the ten directions of space would only spread the Dharma of One Pure Mind. Therefore, the World Honored One handed down just this esoteric Dharma to Mahakasyapa. The Dharma of One Pure Mind consists of utter voidness and the universal Dharmakaya, which alone is called The Truth of All Buddhas.' One cannot seek this Dharma in subjective and objective duality; neither can it be found by searching out books and concepts, nor can it be perceived in time or space. It can only be tacitly understood. This is the doorway to understanding the non-action Dharma. If you want to comprehend, just be without Pure Mind and you will suddenly be enlightened; for if you intend or plan to learn about or desire to get something, you will find yourself very far away from the truth. However, if you have no discrimination, do not grasp thought and abandon all views, then the Pure Mind, as firm and hard as a piece of wood or stone, will have a chance to realize the Tao."

Question: "Now, there really are many false thoughts, so how can you say there are none?" The master replied: "False thoughts have no self-nature, for they arise from your discriminating Pure Mind. If you recognize that the Pure Mind is Buddha, then the Pure Mind is not false nor does any thought arise that views the Pure Mind as false. Thus, if you do not raise any thought or start any thinking, then naturally there is no false thought; however, when the Pure Mind stirs, all sorts of things are created; but when the Pure Mind is annihilated, all sorts of things vanish."

Question: "When false thought stirs, where is the Buddha?" The master replied: "When you perceive false thought stirring, that very perception is the Buddha. If there is no false thought, there is no Buddha. Why not? Just because if you have a view of Buddha, you will think that there really is a Buddha to be attained. If you have a view of sentient beings, you will think there really are sentient beings to be delivered. Such is the totality of your false thought. However, if you are without any thought or view at all, where then is the Buddha? So this is why Manjusri said, To have any view of Buddha whatsoever is like being limited and obstructed by the two iron-enclosing mountains'."

Question: "At the moment of perception of and upon reaching Enlightenment, where is the Buddha?" The master said: "From where does the question come and from where does perception arise? Conversation and silence, movement and tranquillity, sound and form are all Buddha's affair, so where else can you seek a Buddha? You should not seek to put a head on a head or add a mouth to a mouth. Just let go of any discriminating view, and a mountain is a mountain, water is water, Sangha is Sangha, laymen are laymen; and these mountains, rivers, the earth, the sun, the moon and all the planets are absolutely nothing outside of your own Pure Mind.

Even the three kinds of thousands of great chiliocosms are all your own self, nor are they anything at all outside your own Pure Mind. It follows then that the green mountains and blue water and the multitudinous eyes of the infinite would are just voidness that is very clear and bright. Moreover, if you have the no-view' of things, then all sounds and forms are the wisdom-eyes of Buddha. The Dharma that phenomena are real does not raise a solitary thing that depends on a created realm. Even so, for sentient beings the Buddha used many different kinds of wisdom. However, Buddha spoke all day and said nothing; and sentient beings listened from morning to night but heard nothing. In this sense it can be asserted that Buddha Sakyamuni spoke the Dharma for forty-nine years but never spoke a single word."

Question: " If it is really thus, then where is Bodhi?" The master replied: "Bodhi is nowhere! Even Buddha has never attained Bodhi, while all sentient beings have never lost it. It is neither gotten by the body nor sought by the Pure Mind. All sentient beings are, indeed, the form of Bodhi."

Question: "How is it possible to develop the Supreme-Enlightenment Pure Mind?" The master said: "Bodhi means nothing to attain. Even now, just as you allow a thought to arise, you get nothing. Thus, realizing that there is absolutely nothing to attain is the Bodhi Pure Mind. The realization that there is nowhere to abide and nothing to attain is the Bodhi. Therefore, Sakyamuni Buddha said, Since there was really no Dharma by means of which the Tathagata attained Supreme Enlightenment, so Dipamkara Buddha predicted about me in my last lifetime, "In your next lifetime, you will be a Buddha named Sakyamuni".' It is very clear, then that originally all sentient beings are Bodhi, so there is no Bodhi to again attain. Thus, you have just now heard how to develop Bodhi Pure Mind. Do you think there really have a Pure Mind to develop? Do you think that you really is a Buddha to attain? If you practice with this view or in this way, even throughout the three Asankhyeya kalpas, you would only have attained the Sambhogakaya and the Nirmanakaya. What have these got to do with your Original Buddha Pure Mind? Furthermore, to seek the form of Buddha Pure Mind outside your own Pure Mind is illusion, for that whatever you find is not your Original Buddha Pure Mind."

Question: "If originally all is Buddha, how can there be four forms of birth, six conditions of sentient existence and all kinds of different forms?" The master answered: "The universal body of all Buddhas, without increasing or decreasing, represents everywhere the perfect combination. All sentient beings are Buddha, just as when a large bead of mercury disperses into many places but every smaller bead remains round like the original and just as all parts are contained, in potential, within the original if it does not disperse. One is all and all is one! Take a house as a further example. We abandon the house of a donkey in order to enter the house of a person. In turn, we abandon the body of a person to obtain the body of a heavenly being. Until you enter the houses of Sravaka, Pratyeka-Buddha, Bodhisattva and Buddha, you continue to accept, reject and discriminate among various places and bodies, thus experiencing difference in name and form and suffering. But where is there and differentiation at all in our Original Nature?"

Question: "How is it possible to spread Dharma and to perform the acts of great compassion of all the Buddhas?" The master answered: "That compassion of Buddha without immediate causal connection is the Great Compassion. Your not seeing a Buddha to be attained is Great Compassion. Your not seeing any sentient being to release from suffering is great pity. To spread Dharma, neither speak nor indicate; to listen to Dharma, hear nothing and desire to attain nothing. If as an illusionary person you spread Dharma to another illusionary person, or if you think that you understand the Dharma as correct even if you've heard it from a virtuous friend, or if you let the thought arise that you desire to attain great learning and compassion these conditions definitely are not your Enlightened Pure Mind. Finally, by grasping such views, you work without achieving anything at all in the end."

Question: "What is unadulterated progress?" The master said: "Your not allowing any view whatsoever of body and Pure Mind to arise is the very highest and strongest unadulterated progress. Allowing just one tiny thought to arise is to seek outside; then, like Kaliraja, you become interested in travelling here and there to hunt. However, the Pure Mind that does not search outside itself is like Ksantyrsi. Being without any Pure Mind-and-body view whatsoever is the way of the Buddha."

Question: "If we practice Dharma without discrimination, how do we know that it is the correct Dharma?" The master said: "To be without discriminating Pure Mind is the correct Dharma. Now when you conceive of right or wrong or even allow a single thought to arise, the idea of place arises; on the other hand, without a single thought arising, ideas of place and Pure Mind both vanish. In reality, there is nothing to seek and nothing to search for."

Question: "How is it possible to leave the three realms?" The master answered: "To be without a view either of good or evil is to leave the three realms. The Tathagata appeared in the world to refute the three kinds of existence. Therefore, if you are without any Pure Mind at all, then there are, suddenly, no three realms. To illustrate: If a molecule is separated into a hundred parts and ninety-nine parts are destroyed, with only one part remaining, the existence of this one remaining part, like the tiniest discriminating thought, makes impossible the victory of the Great Vehicle. Not until this last little bit of discrimination also vanishes can the Mahayana Dharma be truly victorious."

The master said: "The Pure Mind is Buddha. All Buddhas and all sentient beings have the same Buddha-Nature and one Pure Mind.

Therefore, Bodhidharma came from the West only to transmit the One-Pure Mind Doctrine. However, since the Pure Mind of all sentient beings is the same as original Buddha-Nature, there is no need to practice; for if one recognizes one's own Pure Mind and sees one's own Nature, there is nothing at all to seek outside oneself. But how is one to recognize one's own Pure Mind? Just that Pure Mind itself that wants to perceive the Pure Mind that is your own Pure Mind, which is as void as Original Pure Mind and is without words and function. However, we cannot say that up to now we have been talking about nothing but existence."

The master said: "The real nature of Pure Mind is without a head and without a tail. This is called expedient wisdom and is used to convert and deliver sentient beings, depending upon their capacity. If there is no conversion of sentient beings, we cannot say whether there is existence or non-existence. Therefore, one should understand as follows: Just to settle in voidness that is the way of all Buddhas. The Sutra said: One should develop a Pure Mind which does not abide in anything whatsoever.' All sentient beings have birth and death in endless transmigration because their Pure Mind-sense is intractable, always taking the path of the six senses and existence, thus grasping the wheel of life and death a condition that causes them perpetual suffering.

The Vimalakirti Sutra says: "It is very difficult to convert people because their Pure Minds are as intractable as monkeys.' They use many different methods to guard against conversion; and only gradually, after a long time, might they bring their Pure Minds under control. Therefore, when the Pure Mind stirs, all sorts of things are created; and when the Pure Mind is annihilated, all sorts of things are destroyed. In this manner, everything human beings, Devas, the six ways of sentient existence is created by the Pure Mind. If you wish to understand the truth or achieve the reality of no-Pure Mind, just stop all accessory conditions; i.e., suddenly and absolutely do not allow false thoughts and discriminatory ideas to arise. Without others, there is no self, no greed, no hate, no love, no abhorrence; neither is there victory or defeat. So just eliminate all delusions, and what remains is the Original Bright Nature Bodhi and Dharma. If you do not understand this, then even though you study extensively and practice diligently and even though you lead a simple life, but never come to recognize your own Pure Mind, you will finally only bear the fruit of evil action, perhaps becoming a deva-mara, a heretic, or a god of water or land. So what benefit is there at all in such practice! Master Chi Kung said, The Buddha-Nature is your own Pure Mind, so how can you search for it or find it through words and concepts?' Just recognize your own Pure Mind and stop thinking; then the false thoughts and all the troubles of the world automatically disappear. The Vimalakirti Sutra says: Just as a person confined in bed by illness who is resting to get well, do not allow any thought to arise. Just as a person lying in bed with an illness trying to cure himself, stop all activities that aggravate the illness. When false thoughts stop, Bodhi appears.' Now, if your Pure Mind is in great confusion, even if you arrive at the stage of the Three Vehicles and practice all the stages of a Bodhisattva's progress, you will still only remain hovering between the worldly and holy views. One should realize that everything is impermanent, that all power declines; just as an arrow shot up into the sky, expending the energy of the thrust, falls to earth, so human beings continuously revolve through the various states of transmigration, birth and death. If we do not understand the Dharma and practice, and instead only continue suffering and working in ignorance, achieving nothing, isn't this a great error?"

The Master Chi Kung said: "If you do not study with a teacher of images of supramundane reality, then it would be useless to take the medicine of Mahayana Dharma. Rather, while walking, standing, sitting, lying, etc., just learn being without-Pure Mind' and being without discrimination or dependence on anything. Also, learn neither to stay not to grasp. Then you will be prosperous and happy, as you wish, always, even though you might appear to others to be merely a fool. Nobody in the whole world will recognize you, but then you will not need them to recognize you. Your Pure Mind will become like an unpolished stone with no crack nothing whatsoever can pierce your Pure Mind. To stand firmly without grasping corresponds somewhat to this state. Passing right through the region of the three sense realms, one is suddenly in supramundane Reality. Not to grasp even a tiny spark of the Pure Mind is passionless wisdom. Neither create the karma of human beings and devas nor create the karma of hell. Do not allow any thought whatsoever to arise, and you will be at the end of all conditioned Pure Mind. At this stage, then, the body and Pure Mind are free yet not non-reborn, but reborn according to one's own wishes. So the Sutra said: The Bodhisattva assumes a body at his own will.' If you do not comprehend the Pure Mind or if you grasp any form, this only creates karma that belongs to Deva Nara. Even becoming involved in Buddhist rituals and practice such as Pure Land can all, if clung to , be obstructions to the realization of Buddha. Because of these obstructions in your Pure Mind and being bound to conditions of discipline brought about by cause and effect, there is no freedom to go from or to stay in any or all of the various realms at will.

Therefore, the Dharma of Bodhi was originally non-existent, but all the Tathagata's teaching is used as skillful means for the transformation of all sentient beings. Just as the golden-yellow leaves, used expediently to stop the crying of a baby, are not real gold, so there is a Dharma called Supreme Enlightenment. Now, if you already understand this teaching, there is no need at all to practice diligently. Just eliminate your old karma and never create new misfortune. Thus your Pure Mind will ever be very bright and clear. So abandon all of your previous views. The Vimalakirti Sutra says: Eliminate everything!' The Lotus Sutra says: Try to shovel out the dung from your Pure Mind that has been piling up for the last twenty years or so. Just eliminate the view of place and form from your Pure Mind, and automatically the dung of sophistry will be wiped out. Then and only then will you realize that the Tathagata Store is originally only voidness. So the Sutra says: All Buddhalands are truly void.' If you think that any Buddhas have attained Enlightenment by learning and practice, you will find no support for such a view.

If one holds to the subjective-objective view, he will feel proud when, after studying and practicing a little, he thinks he has tacitly understood and attained Enlightenment in the Ch'an method. So for this reason, if we see someone such as this who does not really understand anything at all, we scold him for his ignorance. If he gets some meaning from others, he is very happy and might feel superior to others, thus creating for himself even more unfortunate mental conditions. If one studies Ch'an with this focus, there is no possibility of profound understanding; for even if one is permitted to comprehend some small idea or theory, one merely obtains, as a result, some attribute of the Pure Mind but no insight into Ch'an or Tao. Therefore, the Bodhidharma sat facing the wall an example for people to totally reject all views. Thus, being without motive is the way of Buddha. Having any discrimination whatsoever is only achieving the stage of Deva Mara. For the ignorant person Buddha-Nature is never lost. For the enlightened person there is nothing to attain. In reality, Buddha Nature is originally neither confused nor enlightened. Remember that the endlessness of the ten directions of infinite space is originally one's own Pure Mind. Even though you have creative energy and physical and mental functions, still you are never separated from voidness. The void has in it neither the big nor the small. It is passionless, being neither active nor non-active. It is neither confused nor enlightened, and it is without any view whatsoever generated by phenomenal disturbances. It has neither sentient beings nor Buddhas. It depends on absolutely nothing, not even the tiniest mote or flash. It is fundamentally pure and bright and is identical with the patient endurance of the uncreated. The real Buddha has no mouth and no Dharma to state or spread. It is said that we hear the real Dharma without ears, but who hears? One should think well about this! There is really nothing to say about it!"

One day the master, preaching in the Dharma Hall to the assembly, said: "If you do not awaken soon rather than late, when the end of your life approaches there is no guarantee that you will not have some trouble." At that moment, some heretics in the hall were talking aloud about having achieved kung fu (a term for a certain level of attainment in meditation practice). One man was smiling sarcastically and said: "At the last moment I will still have my kung fu." The master responded thus: "I would like to know what you would say to yourself suddenly during your last breath to defend against being caught, once again, in the repetitive cycle of life and death. Try to think about it! In fact, you should have some plan or insight for these last moments, Tell me, where is there any inborn Maitreya and where do we have natural Sakyamuni? Some say that there is a heaven of gods and a hell of wild and hungry ghosts. If you saw a sick person, you might say to him, Just lie down and rest.' However, when you yourself get sick, you might not be able to focus, and you might be confused and afraid and unable to lie down, rest or even to take any medicine easily. Moreover, even if you could defend yourself with the very swords of hell and the boiling oil of the cooking pot, at that time you would have no assistance at all from any being with supernatural powers. So you should prepare a plan for yourself at the right time so you can use it in an emergency. Don't waste your energy. You should not prepare your plan too late and find yourself in a regretful state and bereft. If your Pure Mind is, at the last moment, in an hysterical flurry, how can you escape the disorder and dissolution of your body. The prospect is dark, and, lacking insight, you would be at a loss to know how to handle this situation. Alas! Alas! Commonly one learns about Samadhi only to speak platitudes about Ch'an and Tao or to shout at the Buddha and scold the Patriarch. However, during one's last breath, all is useless, all is in vain! If you have always cheated and lied you way through life, you will only cheat yourself on that final day. The hell of Avici already has imprisoned you, and you cannot escape at the last moment.

During this Dharma-ending age, when the Dharma has almost disappeared, there is a good opportunity and the perfect time for those monks who have taken a Great Vow to spread Dharma and to bear and transmit to future generations, for continued use, the wisdom-life of all Buddhas, not to let their Vow weaken or die. Now, we have quite a few wandering monks who desire to be responsible only for seeing and enjoying the brightness of the mountains and the beauty of the rivers. However, they do not know how much time they have left in this life, for if only one tiny outbreath does not return as an inbreath you are already on your way to the next life. Moreover, nobody knows what lies ahead or what he will have to face again in the next lifetime. Alas! So my advice to all of my brothers is to fulfill your promise during your period of good health and take advantage immediately of your good opportunity for Enlightenment. Do it now! Don't wait! This is the Universal Enlightenment and the Great Release, which average people are quite confused about. This confusion and obstruction to understanding is not difficult to conquer. However, if you do not have any ambition and determination to practice, but only talk, again and again, about how difficult it all is, you will not succeed. Rather, you should remember the origin of the wooden ladle that it began its life in a tree. Recalling this, you should change your way of thinking and turn to the Right Way. If you are really courageous, go seek a Kung-an!"

One monk asked Master Chao-Chou: "Does a dog have Buddha-Nature?" Chao-Chou replied: "None!" At once the monk just concentrated his Pure Mind exclusively on the word none'. For twenty-four hours of every day, while walking, staying, sitting and lying, he practiced. Day by day, even while eating and dressing, moving his bowels and urinating, his Pure Mind and mental energy were all focussed, at all times, towards profound and total concentration on the word none'. Gradually he understood the none (wu) was, indeed, just so. If you are suddenly enlightened regarding the nature of Buddha, you can never be fooled about truth by anyone in the world, no matter how clever he is. In this sense, then, you could say that Bodhidharma came from the West to make a lot of trouble out of nothing. Also you might say that when the World Honored One held up the golden flower, his performance was a complete failure. Furthermore, you can even say that Yama, the King of Hell, and even all the holy saints and sages are no different from you yourself. It doesn't matter whether you believe or not, for that which is real is beyond our comprehension. Why? Just because if there is really no problem or suffering in the world that is based on misconception and illusion, then you do not need to have any fear or desire anything whatsoever."

A Gatha

Abandon all trouble in the world --

This is the most extraordinary act.

As in an opera, grasp the rope

Only to swing on, progressing further.

If you don't feel penetrating cold

To the bone at least once,

How can you ever come to smell

The warm fragrance of plum flowers?

A Gatha by P'ei Hsiu

I heretofore acquired the Dharma of the Transmission of Pure Mind, as expressed in The Chung-Ling Record and in The Wan-Ling Record, from Ch'an Master Huang-po (Hsi-Yun). So thus I have come to write a gatha on The Transmission of Pure Mind:

The Pure Mind cannot be transmitted;

To tacitly understand is transmission.

The Pure Mind can perceive nothing at all,

But nothingness is true perception.

The tally is not the tally;

Also, nothing is not nothing.

Do not remain in Illusion City,

Or you'll mistake the pearl on your forehead;

Be aware, the word "pearl" is only an expedient,

For how can Illusion City have any form?

Only the Pure Mind is Buddha,

The Buddha without birth.

So know directly that "it is!"

Without seeking or acting.

For a Buddha to seek Buddha

Is just a waste of energy.

If you let a Dharma-view arise,

You'll only fall into Mara's realm.

Don't separate the worldly and the holy;

Then seeing and hearing will disappear.

Just like a clear mirror, be without Pure Mind,

And there is no competition with things.

Just like the bright void, be without thinking,

And you contain the ten thousand things.

The Three Vehicles are outside of the Dharma,

But to know this is rare in a kalpa's course.

When one attains such realization, then

He is the Hero Who Leaves the World.

Once I heard this gatha from a Mahasattva, who resided on the east side of the river and who was with the Master at Kao-An during that time when he was preaching the Dharma of the Transmission of Pure Mind to Prime Minister P'ei-Hsiu. It was about that time that P'ei-Hsiu wrote this gatha and recorded the teaching of the Master as clearly and brilliantly as if he were painting a picture, hoping that the deaf and the blind would suddenly be awakened. Since it would a great pity if P'ei-Hsiu's account of the Master's words was lost or destroyed, I have thus compiled and edited it in these Records. Complimentary Verses by the Southern Sect of Ch'an

The Year of Ching-Li Wu-Tzu

Master Tien Jen

The Precious Garland Ratnavali of Nagarjuna

Introduction

Often referred to as "the second Buddha" by Tibetan and East Asian Mahayana (Great Vehicle) traditions of Buddhism, Nagarjuna offered sharp criticisms of Brahminical and Buddhist substantialist philosophy, theory of knowledge, and approaches to practice. Nagarjuna's philosophy represents something of a watershed not only in the history of Indian philosophy but in the history of philosophy as a whole, as it calls into questions certain philosophical assumptions so easily resorted to in our attempt to understand the world.

Among these assumptions are the existence of stable substances, the linear and one-directional movement of causation, the atomic individuality of persons, the belief in a fixed identity or selfhood, and the strict separations between good and bad conduct and the blessed and fettered life. All such assumptions are called into fundamental question by Nagarjuna's unique perspective which is grounded in the insight of emptiness (sunyata), a concept which does not mean "non-existence" or "nihility" (abhava), but rather the lack of autonomous existence (nihsvabhava). Denial of autonomy according to Nagarjuna does not leave us with a sense of metaphysical or existential privation, a loss of some hoped-for independence and freedom, but instead offers us a sense of liberation through demonstrating the interconnectedness of all things, including human beings and the manner in which human life unfolds in the natural and social worlds.

Nagarjuna's central concept of the "emptiness (sunyata) of all things (dharmas)," which pointed to the incessantly changing and so never fixed nature of all phenomena, served as much as the terminological prop of subsequent Buddhist philosophical thinking as the vexation of opposed Vedic systems. The concept had fundamental implications for Indian philosophical models of causation, substance ontology, epistemology, conceptualizations of language, ethics and theories of world-liberating salvation, and proved seminal even for Buddhist philosophies in India, Tibet, China and Japan very different from Nagarjuna's own.

Indeed it would not be an overstatement to say that Nagarjuna's innovative concept of emptiness, though it was hermeneutically appropriated in many different ways by subsequent philosophers in both South and East Asia, was to profoundly influence the character of Buddhist thought.

Text

The Precious Garland of Advice for a King by the great master, the Superior Nagarjuna

Homage to all Buddhas and Bodhisattvas.

No. 1.

I bow down to the Omniscient,

Freed from all defects,

Adorned with all good qualities,

The sole friend of all beings.

No. 2.

O King, I will explain practices solely virtuous

To generate in you the doctrine,

For the practices will be established

In a vessel of the excellent doctrine.

No. 3.

In one who first practices high status

Definite goodness arises later,

For having attained high status,

One comes gradually to definite goodness.

No. 4.

High status is considered to be happiness,

Definite goodness is liberation.

The quintessence of their means

Is briefly faith and wisdom.

No. 5.

Due to having faith one relies on the practices,

Due to having wisdom one truly knows.

Of these two wisdom is the chief,

Faith is its prerequisite.

No. 6.

One who does not neglect the practices

Through desire, hatred, fear, or bewilderment

Is known as one of faith,

A superior vessel for definite goodness.

No. 7.

Having analyzed well

All deeds of body, speech, and mind,

Those who realize what benefit self and others

And always perform these are wise.

No. 8.

Not killing, not stealing,

Forsaking the mates of others,

Refraining completely from false,

Divisive, harsh, and senseless speech,

No. 9.

Thoroughly forsaking covetousness, harmful intent,

And the views of Nihilistic ones-

These are the ten gleaming paths of action;

Their opposites are dark.

No. 10.ab

Not drinking intoxicants, a good livelihood,

Non-harming, respectful giving,

No. 10.c

Honoring the honorable, and love-

No. 10.d

Practice in brief is that.

No. 11.

Practice is not done by just

Mortifying the body,

For one has not forsaken injuring others

And is not helping others.

No. 12.

Those not esteeming the great path of excellent doctrine

Bright with giving, ethics, and patience,

Afflict their bodies, taking

An aberrant path like a cow path [deceiving oneself and those following].

No. 13.

Their bodies embraced by the vicious snakes

Of the afflictive emotions, they enter for a long time

The dreadful jungle of cyclic existence

Among the trees of endless beings.

No. 14.

A short life comes through killing.

Much suffering comes through harming.

Poor resources, through stealing.

Enemies, through adultery.

No. 15.

From lying arises slander.

From divisiveness, a parting of friends.

From harshness, hearing the unpleasant.

From senselessness, one's speech is not respected.

No. 16.

Covetousness destroys one's wishes,

Harmful intent yields fright,

Wrong views lead to bad views,

And drink to confusion of the mind.

No. 17.

Through not giving comes poverty,

Through wrong livelihood, deception,

Through arrogance, a bad lineage,

Through jealousy, little beauty.

No. 18.ab

A bad color comes through anger,

Stupidity, from not questioning the wise.

No. 18.cd

These are effects for humans, But prior to all is a bad transmigration.

No. 19.

Opposite to the well-known

Fruits of these non-virtues

Is the arising of effects

Caused by all the virtues.

No. 20.

Desire, hatred, ignorance, and

The actions they generate are non-virtues.

Non-desire, non-hatred, non-ignorance,

And the actions they generate are virtues.

No. 21.

From non-virtues come all sufferings

And likewise all bad transmigrations,

From virtues, all happy transmigrations

And the pleasures of all lives.

No. 22.

Desisting from all non-virtues

And always engaging in virtues

With body, speech, and mind-

These are called the three forms of practice.

No. 23.

Through these practices one is freed from becoming

A hell-being, hungry ghost, or animal.

Reborn as a human or god one gains

Extensive happiness, fortune, and dominion.

No. 24.

Through the concentrations, immeasurables, and formlessnesses

One experiences the bliss of Brahma and so forth.

Thus in brief are the practices

For high status and their fruits.

No. 24.

Through the concentrations, immeasurables, and formlessnesses

One experiences the bliss of Brahma and so forth.

Thus in brief are the practices

For high status and their fruits.

No. 25.

The doctrines of definite goodness

Are said by the Conquerors

To be deep, subtle, and frightening

To the childish, who are not learned.

No. 26.

"I am not, I will not be.

I have not, I will not have,"

That frightens all the childish

And extinguishes fear in the wise.

No. 27.

By him who speaks only to help beings,

It was said that all beings

Have arisen from the conception of I

And are enveloped with the conception of mine.

No. 28.

"The I exists, the mine exists."

These are wrong as ultimates,

For the two are not established

By a thorough consciousness of reality just as it is.

No. 29.

The mental and physical aggregates arise

From the conception of I which is false in fact.

How could what is grown

From a false seed be true?

No. 30.

Having seen thus the aggregates as untrue,

The conception of I is abandoned,

And due to abandoning the conception of I

The aggregates arise no more.

No. 31.

Just as it is said

That an image of one's face is seen

Depending on a mirror

But does not really exist as a face,

No. 32.

So the conception of I exists

Dependent on the aggregates,

But like the image of one's face

The I does not at all really exist.

No. 33.

Just as without depending on a mirror

The image of one's face is not seen,

So too the conception of I does not exist

Without depending on the aggregates.

No. 34.

When the Superior Ananda

Heard what this means,

He attained the eye of doctrine

And repeatedly spoke of it to monastics.

No. 35.

As long as the aggregates are conceived,

So long thereby does the conception of I exist.

Further, when the conception of I exists,

There is action, and from it there also is birth.

No. 36.

With these three pathways mutually causing each other

Without a beginning, a middle, or an end,

This wheel of cyclic existence

Turns like the wheel of a firebrand.

No. 37.

Because this wheel is not obtained from self, other,

Or from both, in the past, the present, or the future,

The conception of I is overcome

And thereby action and rebirth.

No. 38.

One who sees how cause and effect

Are produced and destroyed

Does not regard the world

As really existent or really non-existent.

No. 39.

One who has heard thus the doctrine extinguishing

All suffering, but does not examine it

And fears the fearless state

Trembles due to ignorance.

No. 40.

That all these will not exist in nirvana

Does not frighten you.

Why does their non-existence

Explained here cause you fright?

No. 41.

"In liberation there is no self and are no aggregates."

If liberation is asserted thus,

Why is the removal here of the self

And of the aggregates not liked by you?

No. 42.ab

If nirvana is not a non-thing,

Just how could it have thingness?

No. 42.cd

The extinction of the misconception

Of things and non-things is called nirvana.

No. 43.

In brief the view of nihilism

Is that effects of actions do not exist.

Without merit and leading to a bad state,

It is regarded as a "wrong view."

No. 44.

In brief the view of existence

Is that effects of actions exist.

Meritorious and conducive to happy transmigrations

It is regarded as a "right view."

No. 45.

Because existence and non-existence are extinguished by wisdom,

There is a passage beyond meritorious and ill deeds.

This, say the excellent, is liberation from

Bad transmigrations and happy transmigrations.

No. 46.

Seeing production as caused

One passes beyond non-existence.

Seeing cessation as caused

One also does not assert existence.

No. 47.

Previously produced and simultaneously produced causes

Are non-causes; [thus] there are no causes in fact,

Because [such] production is not confirmed at all

As existing conventionally or in reality.

No. 48.

When this is, that arises,

Like short when there is long.

Due to the production of this, that is produced,

Like light from the production of a flame.

No. 49.

When there is long, there is short.

They do not exist through their own nature,

Just as due to the non-production

Of a flame, light also does not arise.

No. 50.

Having thus seen that effects arise

From causes, one asserts what appears

In the conventions of the world

And does not accept nihilism.

No. 51.

One who asserts, just as it is, cessation

That does not arise from conventions

Does not pass into a view of existence.

Thereby one not relying on duality is liberated.

No. 52.

A form seen from a distance

Is seen clearly by those nearby.

If a mirage were water,

Why is water not seen by those nearby?

No. 53.

The way this world is seen

As real by those afar

Is not so seen by those nearby

For whom it is signless like a mirage.

No. 54.

Just as a mirage is seemingly water

But not water and does not in fact exist as water,

So the aggregates are seemingly a self

But not a self and do not exist in fact.

No. 55.

Having thought a mirage to be water

And then having gone there,

Someone would just be stupid to surmise,

"That water does not exist."

No. 56.

One who conceives of the mirage-like world

That it does or does not exist

Is consequently ignorant.

When there is ignorance, one is not liberated.

No. 57.

A follower of non-existence goes to bad transmigrations,

And a follower of existence goes to happy transmigrations.

Through correct and true knowledge

One does not rely on dualism and becomes liberated.

No. 58.

If through correct and true knowledge

Such wise persons do not assert existence and non-existence

And thereby you think that they follow non-existence,

Why should they not be followers of existence?

No. 59.

If from refuting existence

Non-existence would accrue to them,

Why from refuting non-existence

Would existence not accrue to them?

No. 60.

They implicitly have no nihilistic thesis

And also have no nihilistic behavior

And due to relying on the path to enlightenment have no nihilistic thought.

Hence how can they be regarded as nihilistic ones?

No. 61.

Ask the Samkhyas, the followers of Kanada, Nirgranthas,

And the worldly proponents of a person and aggregates,

Whether they propound

What passes beyond "is" and "is not."

No. 62.

Thereby know that the ambrosia

Of the Buddhas' teaching is called profound,

An exclusive doctrine passing

Far beyond "is" and "is not."

No. 63.

How could the world exist in fact,

With a nature passed beyond the three times,

Not going when disintegrating, not coming,

And not staying even for an instant?

No. 64.

Because the coming, going, and staying

Of the world and nirvana do not exist

As [their own] reality, what difference

Is there in fact between the two?

No. 65.

If, due to the non-existence of staying,

Production and cessation do not exist as their own reality,

How could production, staying,

And ceasing exist in fact?

No. 66.

If always changing,

How are things non-momentary?

If not changing,

How can they be altered in fact?

No. 67.

Do they become momentary

Through partial or complete disintegration?

Because an inequality is not apprehended,

This momentariness cannot be admitted either way.

No. 68.

If momentary, then it becomes entirely non-existent;

Hence how could it be old?

Also if non-momentary, it is constant;

Hence how could it be old?

No. 69.

Just as a moment has an end, so a beginning

And a middle must be considered.

Thus due to this triple nature of a moment,

There is no momentary abiding of the world.

No. 70.

Also the beginning, middle, and end

Are to be analyzed like a moment.

Therefore beginning, middle, and end

Are also not produced from self or other.

No. 71.

Due to having many parts there is no unity,

There is not anything without parts.

Further, without one, there is not many.

Also, without existence there is no non-existence.

No. 72.

If it is thought that through disintegration or an antidote

An existent becomes non-existent,

Then how without an existent

Could there be disintegration or an antidote?

No. 73.

Hence, in fact there is no disappearance

Of the world through nirvana.

Asked whether the world has an end

The Conqueror remained silent.

No. 73.

Hence, in fact there is no disappearance

Of the world through nirvana.

Asked whether the world has an end

The Conqueror remained silent.

No. 74.

Because he did not teach this profound doctrine

To worldly beings who were not receptacles,

The All-Knowing is therefore known

By the wise to be omniscient.

No. 75.

Thus the doctrine of definite goodness

Was taught by the perfect Buddhas,

The seers of reality, as profound,

Unapprehendable, and baseless.

No. 76.

Frightened by this baseless doctrine,

Delighting in a base, not passing

Beyond existence and non-existence,

Unintelligent beings ruin themselves.

No. 77.ab

Afraid of the fearless abode,

Ruined, they ruin others.

No. 77.cd

O King, act in such a way

That the ruined do not ruin you.

No. 78.

O King, lest you be ruined

I will explain through the scriptures

The mode of the supramundane, just as it is,

The reality not partaking of dualism.

No. 79.

This profundity endowed with meanings drawn from scriptures

And beyond ill-deeds and meritorious deeds

Has not been tasted by those who fear the baseless-

The others-the Forders-and even by our own.

No. 80.

A person is not earth, not water,

Not fire, not wind, not space,

Not consciousness, and not all of them.

What person is there other than these?

No. 81.

Just as a person is not real

Due to being a composite of six constituents,

So each of the constituents also

Is not real due to being a composite.

No. 82.

The aggregates are not the self, they are not in it,

It is not in them, without them it is not,

It is not mixed with the aggregates like fire and fuel.

Therefore how could the self exist?

No. 83.

The three elements' are not earth, they are not in it,

It is not in them, without them it is not;

Since this also applies to each,

The elements, like the self, are false.

No. 84.

Earth, water, fire, and wind

Individually also do not inherently exist.

When any three are absent, an individual one does not exist.

When one is absent, the three also do not exist.

No. 85.

If when three are absent, an individual one does not exist

And if when one is absent, the three also do not exist,

Then each itself does not exist.

How could a composite be produced?

No. 86.

Otherwise, if each itself exists,

Why without fuel is there no fire?

Likewise why is there no water, wind, or earth

Without motility, obstructiveness, or cohesion?

No. 87.

If it is answered that fire is well known not to exist without fuel but the other three elements exist by way of their own entities,

How could your three exist in themselves

Without the others? It is impossible for the three

Not to accord with dependent-arising.

No. 88.

How could those-that themselves

Exist individually-be mutually dependent?

How could those-that do not themselves

Exist individually-be mutually dependent?

No. 89.

If it is the case that they do not themselves exist individually,

But where there is one, the other three exist,

Then if unmixed, they are not in one place,

And if mixed, they do not themselves exist individually.

No. 90.

The elements do not themselves exist individually,

So how could their own individual characters exist?

What do not themselves individually exist cannot predominate.

Their characters are regarded as conventionalities.

No. 91.

This mode of refutation is also to be applied

To colors, odors, tastes, and objects of touch;

Eye, consciousness, and form;

Ignorance, action, and birth;

No. 92.

Agent, object, and action,

Number, possession, cause and effect,

Time, short and long, and so forth,

Name and name-bearer as well.

No. 93.

Earth, water, fire, and wind,

Long and short, subtle and coarse,

As well as virtue and so forth are said by the Subduer

To be ceased in the consciousness of reality.

No. 94.

Earth, water, fire, and wind

Do not have a chance

In the face of that undemonstrable consciousness

Complete lord over the limitless.

No. 95.

Here long and short, subtle and coarse,

Virtue and non-virtue,

And here names and forms

All are ceased.

No. 96.

All those that earlier appeared to consciousness

Because of not knowing that[reality

Will later cease for consciousness in that way

Because of knowing that reality.

No. 97.

All these phenomena of beings

Are seen as fuel for the fire of consciousness.

They are pacified through being burned

By the light of true discrimination.

No. 98.

The reality is later ascertained

Of what was formerly imputed by ignorance.

When a thing is not found,

How can there be a non-thing?

No. 99.

Because the phenomena of forms

Are only names, space too is only a name.

Without the elements how could forms exist?

Therefore even name-only does not exist.

No. 100.

Feelings, discriminations, compositional factors,

And consciousnesses are to be considered

Like the elements and the self.

Thereby the six constituents are selfless.

The first chapter of the Precious Garland, An Indication of High Status and Definite Goodness, is finished.

No. 101.

Just as when a banana tree

With all its parts is torn apart, there is nothing,

So when a person having the [ix constituents

Is divided, it is the same.

No. 102.

Therefore the Conquerors said,

"All phenomena are selfless."

Since this is so, all six constituents

Have been delineated as selfless for you.

No. 103.

Thus neither self nor non-self

Are to be apprehended as real.

Therefore the Great Subduer rejected

Views of self and of non-self.

No. 104.

Sights, sounds, and so forth were said by the Subduer

Not to be true and not to be false.

If from one position its opposite arises,

Both do not exist in fact.

No. 105.

Thus ultimately this world

Is beyond truth and falsity.

Therefore the Subduer does not assert

That it really exists or does not.

No. 106.

Knowing that these in all ways do not exist,

How could the All-Knower say

They have limits or no limits,

Or have both or neither?

No. 107.

"Innumerable Buddhas have come,

And likewise will come and are here at present.

There are zillions of sentient beings,

And in addition the Buddhas intend to abide in the three times.

No. 108.

"The extinguishing of the world in the three

Times does not cause it to increase,

Then why was the All-Knower silent

About the limits of the world?"

No. 109.

That which is secret for a common being

Is the profound doctrine,

The world as like an illusion,

The ambrosia of the Buddhas' teaching.

No. 110.

Just as the production and disintegration

Of an illusory elephant are seen,

But the production and disintegration

Do not really exist,

No. 111.

So the production and disintegration

Of the illusion-like world are seen,

But the production and disintegration

Do not ultimately exist.

No. 112.

Just as an illusory elephant,

Being only a bewildering of consciousness,

Does not come from anywhere,

Nor go anywhere, nor really stay,

No. 113.

So the illusion-like world,

Being only a bewildering of consciousness,

Does not come from anywhere,

Nor go anywhere, nor really stay.

No. 114.

Thus it has a nature beyond the three times.

Other than as the imputation of a convention

What world is there in fact

Which would exist or not?

No. 115.

For this reason the Buddha,

Except for keeping silent, said nothing

About the fourfold format: having or

Not having a limit, both, or neither.

No. 116.

When the body, which is unclean,

Coarse, and an object of the senses,

pain Does not stay in the mind as having a nature of uncleanliness and

Although it is continually in view,

No. 117.

Then how could this doctrine

Which is most subtle, profound,

Baseless, and not manifest,

Easily appear to the mind?

No. 118.

Realizing that because of its profundity

This doctrine is difficult for beings to understand,

The Subduer, having become enlightened

At first turned away from teaching doctrine.

No. 119.

This doctrine wrongly understood

Causes the unwise to be ruined

Because they sink into the uncleanliness

Of nihilistic views.

No. 120.

Further, the stupid who fancy

Themselves wise, having a nature

Ruined by rejecting emptiness, go headfirst

To a terrible hell due to their wrong understanding.

No. 121.

Just as one comes to ruin

Through wrong eating but obtains

Long life, freedom from disease,

Strength, and pleasures through right eating,

No. 122.

So one comes to ruin

Through wrong understanding

But obtains bliss and highest enlightenment

Through right understanding.

No. 123.

Therefore having forsaken with respect to this doctrine of emptiness

Nihilistic views and rejection,

Be supremely intent on correct understanding

For the sake of achieving all aims.

No. 124.

If this doctrine is not understood thoroughly,

The conception of an I prevails,

Hence come virtuous and non-virtuous actions

Which give rise to good and bad rebirths.

No. 125.

Therefore, as long as the doctrine removing

The conception of I is not known,

Take heed of the practices

Of giving, ethics, and patience.

No. 126.

A Lord of the Earth who performs actions

With their prior, intermediary,

And final practices

Is not harmed here or in the future.

No. 127.

Through the practices there are fame and happiness here,

There is no fear now or at the point of death,

In the next life happiness flourishes,

Therefore always observe the practices.

No. 128.

The practices are the best policy,

It is through them that the world is pleased;

Neither here nor in the future is one cheated

By a world that has been pleased.

No. 129.

The world is displeased

By the policies of non-practice.

Due to the displeasure of the world

One is not pleased here or in the future.

No. 130.

How could those with senseless deviant minds

On a path to bad transmigrations,

Wretched, intent on deceiving others,

Have understood what is meaningful?

No. 131.

How could those intent on deceiving others

Be persons of policy?

Through it they themselves will be cheated

In many thousands of births.

No. 132.

Even if you seek to harm an enemy,

You should remove your own defects and cultivate good qualities.

Through that you will help yourself,

And the enemy will be displeased.

No. 133.

You should cause the assembling

Of the religious and the worldly

Through giving, speaking pleasantly,

Purposeful behavior, and concordant behavior.

No. 134.

Just as by themselves the true words

Of kings generate firm trust,

So their false words are the best means

To create distrust.

No. 135.

What is not deceitful is the truth;

It is not an intentional fabrication.

What is solely helpful to others is the truth.

The opposite is falsehood since it does not help.

No. 136.

Just as a single splendid charity

Conceals the faults of kings,

So avarice destroys

All their wealth.

No. 137.

In peace there is profundity.

From profundity the highest respect arises,

From respect come influence and command,

Therefore observe peace.

No. 138.

From wisdom one has a mind unshakable,

Non-reliance on others, firmness,

And is not deceived. Therefore,

O King, be intent on wisdom.

No. 139.

A lord of humanity having the four goodnesses-

Truth, generosity, peace, and wisdom-

Is praised by gods and humans

As are the four good practices themselves.

No. 140.

Wisdom and practice always grow

For one who keeps company

With those who speak advisedly,

Who are pure, and who have unstained wisdom and compassion.

No. 141.

Rare are helpful speakers,

Listeners are very rare,

But rarer still are those who act at once

On words that though unpleasant are beneficial.

No. 142.

Therefore having realized that though unpleasant

It is helpful, act on it quickly,

Just as to cure an illness one drinks

Dreadful medicine from one who cares.

No. 143.

Always considering the impermanence

Of life, health, and dominion,

You thereby will make intense effort

Solely at the practices.

No. 144.

Seeing that death is certain

And that, having died, you suffer from ill deeds,

You should not commit ill deeds

Though there might be temporary pleasure.

No. 145.

Sometimes no horror is seen

And sometimes it is.

If there is comfort in one,

Why do you have no fear for the other?

No. 146.

Intoxicants lead to worldly scorn,

Your affairs are ruined, wealth is wasted,

The unsuitable is done from delusion,

Therefore always avoid intoxicants.

No. 147.

Gambling causes avarice,

Unpleasantness, hatred, deception, cheating,

Wildness, lying, senseless talk, and harsh speech,

Therefore always avoid gambling.

No. 148.

Lust for a woman mostly comes

From thinking that her body is clean,

But there is nothing clean

In a woman's body in fact.

No. 149.

The mouth is a vessel of foul saliva

And scum between the teeth,

The nose a vessel of snot, slime, and mucus,

The eyes are vessels of tears and other excretions.

No. 150.

The abdomen and chest is a vessel

Of feces, urine, lungs, liver, and so forth.

Those who through obscuration do not see

A woman this way, lust for her body.

No. 151.

Just as some fools desire

An ornamented pot filled with what is unclean,

So ignorant, obscured

Worldly beings desire women.

No. 152.

If the world is greatly attached

Even to this ever-so-smelly body

Which should cause loss of attachment,

How can it be led to freedom from desire?

No. 153.

Just as pigs are greatly attached

To a site of excrement, urine, and vomit,

So some lustful ones desire

A site of excrement, urine, and vomit.

No. 154.

This city of a body with protruding holes

From which impurities emerge

Is called an object of pleasure

By beings who are stupid.

No. 155.

Once you yourself have seen the impurities

Of excrement, urine, and so forth,

How could you be attracted

To a body composed of those?

No. 156.

Why should you lust desirously for this

While recognizing it as an unclean form

Produced by a seed whose essence is impure,

A mixture of blood and semen?

No. 157.

One who lies on this impure mass

Covered by skin moistened

With those fluids, merely lies

On top of a woman's bladder,

No. 158.

If whether beautiful or ugly,

Whether old or young,

All female bodies are unclean,

From what attribute does your lust arise?

No. 159.

Just as it is not fit to desire

Filth although it has a good color,

Is very fresh, and has a nice shape,

So is it with a woman's body.

No. 160.

How could the nature of this putrid corpse,

A rotten mass covered outside by skin,

Not be seen when it looks

So very horrible?

No. 161.

"The skin is not foul,

It is like a garment."

Like a hide over a mass of impurities

How could it be clean?

No. 162.

A pot though beautiful outside,

Is reviled when filled with impurities.

Why is the body, filled with impurities

And foul by nature, not reviled?

No. 163.

If you revile against impurities,

Why not against this body

Which befouls clean scents,

Garlands, food, and drink?

No. 164.

Just as one's own or others' Impurities are reviled,

Why not revile against one's own

And others' unclean bodies?

No. 165.

Since your own body is

As unclean as a woman's,

Is it not suitable to part

From desire for self and other?

No. 165.

Since your own body is

As unclean as a woman's,

Is it not suitable to part

From desire for self and other?

No. 166.

If you yourself wash this body

Dripping from the nine wounds

And still do not think it unclean,

What use is religious instruction for you?

No. 167.

Whoever composes poetry

With metaphors elevating this body-

O how shameless! O how stupid!

How embarrassing before wise beings!

No. 168.

Moreover, these sentient beings-

Obscured by the darkness of ignorance-

Quarrel most over what they desire,

Like dogs for the sake of some dirty thing.

No. 169.

There is pleasure when a sore is scratched,

But to be without sores is more pleasurable still.

Just so, there are pleasures in worldly desires,

But to be without desires is more pleasurable still.

No. 170.

If you analyze thus, even though

You do not achieve freedom from desire,

Because your desire has lessened

You will not lust for women.

No. 171.

To hunt game is a horrible

Cause of short life,

Fear, suffering, and hell,

Therefore always steadfastly keep from killing.

No. 172.

Those who frighten embodied beings

When they encounter them are malevolent

Like a snake spitting poison,

Its body completely stained with impurity.

No. 173.

Just as farmers are gladdened

When a great rain-cloud gathers,

So those who gladden embodied beings

When encountering them are beneficent.

No. 174.

Thus observe the practices incessantly

And abandon those counter to them.

If you and the world wish to attain

Unparalleled enlightenment,

No. 175.

Its roots are the altruistic aspiration to enlightenment

Firm like the monarch of mountains,

Compassion reaching to all quarters,

And wisdom not relying on duality.

No. 176.

O great King, listen to how

Your body will be adorned

With the thirty-two signs

Of a great being.

No. 177.

Through proper honoring of stupas,

Honorable beings, Superiors, and the elderly

You will become a Universal Monarch,

Your glorious hands and feet marked with a design of wheels.

No. 178.

O King, always maintain firmly

What you have vowed about the practices,

You will then become a Bodhisattva

With feet that are very level.

No. 179.

Through giving, speaking pleasantly,

Purposeful behavior, and concordant behavior

You will have hands with glorious

Fingers joined by webs of light,

No. 180.

Through abundant giving

Of the best food and drink

Your glorious hands and feet will be soft;

Your hands, feet, shoulder blades,

And the nape of your neck will broaden,

So your body will be large and those seven areas broad.

No. 181.

Through never doing harm and freeing the condemned

Your body will be beautiful, straight, and large,

Very tall with long fingers

And broad backs of the heels.

No. 182.

Through spreading the vowed practices

You will have glory, a good color,

Your ankles will not be prominent,

Your body hairs will stand upwards.

No. 183.

Through your zest for knowledge, the arts,

And so forth, and through imparting them

You will have the calves of an antelope,

A sharp mind, and great wisdom.

No. 184.

If others seek your wealth and possessions,

Through the discipline of immediate giving

You will have broad arms and a pleasant appearance

And will become a leader of the world.

No. 185.

Through reconciling well

Friends who have become divided

You will become the best of those

Whose glorious secret organ retracts inside.

No. 186.

Through giving good houses

And nice comfortable carpets

Your color will be very soft

Like refined stainless gold.

No. 187.

Through giving the highest powers

And following a teacher properly

You will be adorned by each and every hair

And by a spiraling hair between the eyebrows.

No. 188.

Through speech that is pleasant and pleasing

And by acting upon the good speech of others

You will have curving shoulders

And a lion-like upper body.

No. 189.

Through nursing and curing the sick,

The area between your shoulders will be broad,

You will live in a natural state,

And all tastes will be the best.

No. 190.

Through initiating activities concordant

With the practices, your crown protrusion

Will stand out well, and your body will be

Symmetrical like a banana tree.

No. 191.

Through speaking true and soft words

Over a long time, O lord of humanity,

Your tongue will be long

And your voice that of Brahma.

No. 192.

Through speaking true words

Always and continuously

You will have cheeks like a lion,

Be glorious, and hard to overcome.

No. 193.

Through showing great respect,

Serving others, and doing what is fitting,

Your teeth will be very white,

Shining, and even.

No. 194.

Through using true and non-divisive

Speech over a long time

You will have forty glorious teeth

That are set evenly and are wondrous.

No. 195.

Through viewing beings with love

And without desire, hatred, or delusion

Your eyes will be bright and blue

With eyelashes like a bull.

No. 196.

Thus in brief know well

These thirty-two signs

Of a great lion of beings

Together with their causes.

No. 197.

The eighty beautiful features arise

From a concordant cause of love.

Fearing this text would be too long,

I will not, O my King, explain them.

No. 198.

All Universal Emperors

Are regarded as having these,

But their purity, beauty, and luster

Cannot match even a little those of a Buddha.

No. 199.

The auspicious signs and beautiful features

Of a Universal Emperor Are said to arise from the single cause

Of faith in the King of Subduers.

No. 200.abcd

But such virtue accumulated one-pointedly

For a hundred times ten million eons

Cannot produce even one

Of the hair-pores of a Buddha.

No. 200.efgh

Just as the brilliance of suns

Is slightly like that of fireflies,

So the signs of a Buddha are slightly like

Those of a Universal Emperor.

The second chapter of the Precious Garland, The Interwoven, is finished.

No. 201.

Great king, hear from the great scriptures

Of the Great Vehicle How the marks of a Buddha

Arise from inconceivable merit.

No. 202.

The merit giving rise to all

Solitary Realizers, to Learners, and Non-Learners,

And all the merit of the transient world

Is measureless like the universe itself.

No. 203.

Through such merit ten times extended

One hair-pore of a Buddha is achieved.

All the hair-pores of a Buddha

Arise in just the same way.

No. 204.

Through multiplying by a hundred

The merit which produces

All the hair-pores of a Buddha

One auspicious beauty is acquired.

No. 205.

O King, as much merit as is required

For one auspicious beautiful feature,

So much also is required

For each up to the eightieth.

No. 206.

Through multiplying a hundred-fold

The collection of merit which achieves

The eighty auspicious beautiful features

One mark of a great being arises.

No. 207.

Through multiplying a thousand-fold

The extensive merit that is the cause

Of achieving the thirty signs

The hair-treasure like a full moon arises.

No. 208.

Through multiplying a hundred thousand-fold

The merit for the hair-treasure

A Protector's crown-protrusion

Is produced, imperceptible as it actually is.

Through increasing ten million times

A hundred thousand the merit

For the crown-protrusion there comes

The excellence producing the euphony

Of a Buddha's speech and its sixty qualities.

No. 209.

Though such merit is measureless,

It is said for brevity to have a measure,

Just as [the merit of] the world is said

For brevity to be included in the ten directions.

No. 210.

When the causes of even the Form Body

Of a Buddha are as immeasurable

As the world, how then could the causes

Of the Truth Body be measured?

No. 211.

If the causes of all things are small

But they produce extensive effects,

The thought that the measureless causes of Buddhahood

Have measurable effects should be eliminated.

No. 212.

The Form Body of a Buddha

Arises from the collections of merit.

The Truth Body in brief, O King,

Arises from the collections of wisdom.

No. 213.

Thus these two collections

Are the causes of attaining Buddhahood,

So in sum always rely

Upon merit and wisdom.

No. 214.

Do not feel inadequate about this accumulation

Of merit to achieve enlightenment,

Since reasoning and scripture

Can restore one's spirits.

No. 215.

Just as in all directions

Space, earth, water, fire, and wind

Are without limit,

So suffering sentient beings are limitless.

No. 216.

Through their compassion

Bodhisattvas are determined to lead

These limitless sentient beings out of suffering

And establish them in Buddhahood.

No. 217.

[Hence] whether sleeping or not sleeping,

After thoroughly assuming such compassion

Those who remain steadfast-

Even though they might not be meticulous-

No. 218.

Always accumulate merit as limitless as all sentient beings

Since sentient beings are limitless.

Know then that since the causes are limitless,

Limitless Buddhahood is not hard to attain.

No. 219.

[Bodhisattvas] stay for a limitless time in the world;

For limitless embodied beings they seek

The limitless good qualities of enlightenment

And perform limitless virtuous actions.

No. 220.

Hence though enlightenment is limitless,

How could they not attain it

With these four limitless collections

Without being delayed for long?

No. 221. The limitless collection of merit

And the limitless collection of wisdom

Eradicate just quickly

Physical and mental sufferings.

No. 222.

The physical sufferings of bad transmigrations

Such as hunger and thirst arise from ill deeds;

Bodhisattvas do not commit ill deeds,

And due to meritorious deeds do not have

physical suffering in other lives.

No. 223.

The mental sufferings of desire, hatred, fear,

Lust, and so forth arise from obscuration.

Through knowing them to be baseless

They just quickly forsake mental suffering.

No. 224.

Since thus they are not greatly harmed

By physical and mental suffering,

Why should they be discouraged

Though they lead beings in all worlds?

No. 225.

It is hard to bear suffering even for a little,

What need is there to speak of doing so for long!

What could bring harm even over limitless time

To happy beings who have no suffering?

No. 226.

They have no physical suffering;

How could they have mental suffering?

Through their compassion they feel pain

For the world and so stay in it long.

No. 227.

Hence do not feel inadequate thinking,

"Buddhahood is far away."

Always strive at these collections

To remove defects and attain good qualities.

No. 228.

Realizing that desire, hatred, and obscuration

Are defects, forsake them completely.

Realizing that non-desire, non-hatred, and non-obscuration

Are good qualities, inculcate them with vigor.

No. 229.

Through desire one goes into a hungry ghost transmigration,

Through hatred one is impelled into a hell,

Through obscuration one mostly goes into an animal transmigration.

Through stopping these one becomes a god or a human.

No. 230.

Eliminating defects and acquiring good qualities

Are the practices of those seeking high status.

Thoroughly extinguishing conceptions through consciousness of reality

Is the practice of those seeking definite goodness.

No. 231.

You should respectfully and extensively construct

Images of Buddha, monuments, and temples

And provide residences,

Abundant riches, and so forth.

No. 232.

Please construct from all precious substances

Images of Buddha with fine proportions,

Well designed and sitting on lotuses,

Adorned with all precious substances.

No. 233.

You should sustain with all endeavor

The excellent doctrine and the communities

Of monastics, and decorate monuments

With gold and jeweled friezes.

No. 234.

Revere the monuments

With gold and silver flowers,

Diamonds, corals, pearls,

Emeralds, cat's eye gems, and sapphires.

No. 235.

To revere propounders of doctrine

Is to do what pleases them-

Offering goods and services

And relying firmly on the doctrine.

No. 236.

Listen to teachers with homage

And respect, serve, and pray to them.

Always respectfully revere

The other Bodhisattvas.

No. 237.

You should not respect, revere,

Or do homage to others, the Forders,

Because through that the ignorant

Would become enamored of the faulty.

No. 238.

You should make donations of pages and books

Of the word of the King of Subduers

And of the treatises they gave rise to,

Along with their prerequisites, pens and ink.

No. 239.

As ways to increase wisdom,

Wherever there is a school in the land

Provide for the livelihood of teachers

And give lands to them for their provision.

No. 240.

In order to alleviate the suffering

Of sentient beings-the old, young, and infirm-

You should establish through the estates that you control

Doctors and barbers throughout your country.

No. 241.

O One of Good Wisdom, please provide

Hostels, parks, dikes,

Ponds, rest-houses, water-vessels,

Beds, food, hay, and wood.

No. 242.

Please establish rest-houses

In all towns, at temples, and in all cities

And provide water-vessels

On all arid roadways.

No. 243.

Always care compassionately

For the sick, the unprotected, those stricken

With suffering, the lowly, and the poor

And take special care to nourish them.

No. 244.

Until you have given to monastics and beggars

Seasonally-appropriate food and drink,

As well as produce, grain, and fruit,

You should not partake of them.

No. 245.

At the sites of the water-vessels

Place shoes, umbrellas, water-filters,

Tweezers for removing thorns,

Needles, thread, and fans.

No. 246.

Within vessels place the three medicinal fruits,

The three fever medicines, butter,

Honey, eye medicines, and antidotes to poison,

And write out mantras and prescriptions.

No. 247.

At the sites of the vessels place

Salves for the body, feet, and head,

As well as wool, stools, gruel,

Jars for getting water cooking pots, axes, and so forth.

No. 248.

Please have small containers

In the shade filled with sesame,

Rice, grains, foods, molasses,

And suitable water.

No. 249.

At the openings of ant-hills

Please have trustworthy persons

Always put food, water,

Sugar, and piles of grain.

No. 250.

Before and after taking food

Always appropriately offer fare

To hungry ghosts, dogs,

Ants, birds, and so forth.

No. 251.

Provide extensive care

For the persecuted, the victims of crop failure,

The stricken, those suffering contagion,

And for beings in conquered areas.

No. 252.

Provide stricken farmers

With seeds and sustenance.

Eliminate high taxes levied by the previous monarch

Reduce the tax rate on harvests.

No. 253.

Protect the poor from the pain of wanting your wealth.

Set up no new tolls and reduce those that are heavy.

Also free traders from other areas from the afflictions

That come from waiting at your door.

No. 254.

Eliminate robbers and thieves

In your own and others' countries.

Please set prices fairly

And keep profits level even during scarcity.

No. 255.

You should know full well the counsel

That your ministers offer,

And should always enact it

If it nurses the world.

No. 256.

Just as you are intent on thinking

Of what could be done to help yourself,

So you should be intent on thinking

Of what could be done to help others.

No. 257.

If only for a moment make yourself

Available for the use of others

Just as earth, water, fire, wind, medicine,

And forests are available to all.

No. 258.

Even during their seventh step

Merit measureless as the sky

Is generated in Bodhisattvas

Whose attitude is to give all wealth away.

No. 259.

If you give to those so seeking

Girls of beauty well adorned,

You will thereby attain

Thorough retention of the excellent doctrine.

No. 260.

Formerly the Subduer provided

Along with every need and so forth

Eighty thousand girls

With all adornments.

No. 261.

Lovingly give to beggars

Various and glittering

Clothes, adornments, perfumes,

Garlands, and enjoyments.

No. 262.

If you provide facilities

For those most deprived who lack

The means to study the doctrine,

There is no greater gift than that.

No. 263.

Even give poison

To those whom it will help,

But do not give even the best food

To those whom it will not help.

No. 264.

Just as it is said that it will help

To cut off a finger bitten by a snake,

So the Subduer says that if it helps others,

One should even bring temporary discomfort.

No. 265.

You should respect most highly

The excellent doctrine and its proponents.

You should listen reverently to the doctrine

And also impart it to others.

No. 266.

Take no pleasure in worldly talk;

Take delight in what passes beyond the world.

Cause good qualities to grow in others

In the same way you wish them for yourself.

No. 267.

Please do not be satisfied with doctrine heard,

But retain and discriminate meanings.

Please always be intent

On offering presents to teachers.

No. 268.

Do not recite the books of worldly Nihilistic ones, and so forth.

Forsake debating in the interest of pride.

Do not praise your own good qualities.

Speak of the good qualities even of your foes.

No. 269.

When debating do not attack to the quick.

Do not talk about others

With bad intent. Individually

Analyze your own mistakes yourself.

No. 270.

You should root out completely from yourself

The faults the wise decry in others,

And through your influence

Also cause others to do the same.

No. 271.

Considering the harm others do to you

As created by your former deeds, do not anger.

Act such that further suffering will not be created

And your own faults will disappear.

No. 272.

Without hope of reward

Provide help to others.

Bear suffering alone,

And share your pleasures with beggars.

No. 273.

Do not be inflated

Even by the prosperity of gods.

Do not be depressed

Even by the poverty of hungry ghosts.

No. 274.

For your sake always speak the truth.

Even should it cause your death

Or ruin your governance,

Do not speak in any other way.

No. 275.

Always observe the discipline

Of actions just as it has been explained.

In that way, O glorious one, you will become

The best of authoritative beings upon the earth.

No. 276.

You should always analyze well

Everything before you act,

And through seeing things correctly as they are

Do not put full reliance on others.

No. 277.

(1) Through these practices your realm will be happy,

(2) A broad canopy of fame

Will rise in all directions,

And (3) your officials will respect you fully.

No. 278.

The causes of death are many,

Those of staying alive are few,

These too can become causes of death,

Therefore always perform the practices.

No. 279.

If you always perform thus the practices,

The mental happiness which arises

In the world and in yourself

Is most favorable.

No. 280.

(4) Through the practices you will sleep happily

And will awaken happily.

(5) Because your inner nature will be without defect,

Even your dreams will be happy.

No. 281.

(1) Intent on serving your parents,

Respectful to the principals of your lineage,

Using your resources well, patient, generous,

With kindly speech, without divisiveness, and truthful,

No. 282.

Through performing such discipline for one lifetime

You will become a monarch of gods

Whereupon even more so you will be a monarch of gods.

Therefore observe such practices.

No. 283.

(2) Even three times a day to offer

Three hundred cooking pots of food

Does not match a portion of the merit

In one instant of love.

No. 284.

Though through love you are not liberated

You will attain the eight good qualities of love-

Gods and humans will be friendly,

Even non-humans will protect you,

No. 285.

You will have mental pleasures and many physical pleasures,

Poison and weapons will not harm you,

Without striving you will attain your aims,

And be reborn in the world of Brahma.

No. 286.

(3) If you cause sentient beings to generate

The altruistic aspiration to enlightenment and make it firm,

You will always attain an altruistic aspiration to enlightenment

Firm like the monarch of mountains.

No. 287.

(4) Through faith you will not be without leisure,

(5) Through good ethics you will move in good transmigrations,

(6) Through becoming familiar with emptiness

You will attain detachment from all phenomena.

No. 288.

(7) Through not wavering you will attain mindfulness,

(8) Through thinking you will attain intelligence,

(9) Through respect you will be endowed with realization of meaning,

(10) Through guarding the doctrine you will become wise.

No. 289.

(11) Through making the hearing and the giving

Of the doctrine be unobstructed

You will company with Buddhas

And will quickly attain your wishes.

No. 290.

(12) Through non-attachment you will achieve the meaning of doctrines,

(13) Through not being miserly your resources will increase,

(14) Through not being proud you will become chief [of those respected],

(15) Through enduring the doctrine you will attain retention.

No. 291.

(16) Through giving the five essentials

As well as non-fright to the frightened

You will not be harmed by any demons

And will become the best of the mighty.

No. 292.

(17) Through offering series of lamps at monuments

And through offering lamps in dark places

As well as the oil for them

You will attain the divine eye.

No. 293.

(18) Through offering musical instruments and bells or the worship of monuments

And through offering drums and trumpets

You will attain the divine ear.

No. 294.

(19) Through not mentioning others' mistakes

And not talking of others' defective limbs

But protecting their minds

You will attain knowledge of others' minds.

No. 295.

(20) Through giving shoes and conveyances,

Through serving the feeble,

And through providing teachers with transport

You will attain the skill to create magical emanations.

No. 296.

(21) Through acting for the doctrine,

Remembering books of doctrine and their meaning,

And through stainless giving of the doctrine

You will attain memory of your continuum of lives.

No. 297.

(22) Through knowing thoroughly, correctly, and truly

That all phenomena lack inherent existence,

You will attain the sixth clairvoyance

The excellent extinction of all contamination.

No. 298.

(23) Through meditatively cultivating the wisdom of reality

Which is the same [for all phenomena] and is moistened with compassion

For the sake of liberating all sentient beings,

You will become a Conqueror endowed with all supreme aspects.

No. 299.

(24) Through multitudes of pure wishes

Your Buddha Land will be purified.

(25) Through offering gems to the Kings of Subduers

You will emit infinite light.

No. 300.

Therefore knowing the concordance

Of actions and their effects,

Always help beings in fact.

Just that will help yourself.

The third chapter of the Precious Garland, A Compendium of the Collections for Enlightenment, is finished.

No. 301.

Monarchs who do what is against the practices

And senseless are mostly praised

By their citizens, for it is hard to know

What will or will not be tolerated.

Hence it is hard to know

What is useful or not [to say].

No. 302.

If useful but unpleasant words

Are hard to speak to anyone else,

What could I, a monk, say to you,

A King who is a lord of the great earth?

No. 303.

But because of my affection for you

And from compassion for all beings,

I tell you without hesitation

That which is useful but unpleasant.

No. 304.

The Supramundane Victor said that students are to be told

The truth-gentle, meaningful, and salutary-

At the proper time and from compassion.

That is why you are being told all this.

No. 305.

O Steadfast One, when true words

Are spoken without belligerence,

They should be taken as fit to be heard,

Like water fit for bathing.

No. 306.

Realize that I am telling you

What is useful here and otherwise.

Act on it so as to help

Yourself and also others.

No. 307.

If you do not make contributions of the wealth

Obtained from former giving to the needy,

Through your ingratitude and attachment

You will not obtain wealth in the future.

No. 308.

Here in the world workers do not carry

Provisions for a journey unpaid,

But lowly beggars, without payment, carry to your future life

[What you give them] multiplied a hundred times.

No. 309.

Always be of exalted mind

And take delight in exalted deeds.

From exalted actions arise

All effects that are exalted.

No. 310.

Create foundations of doctrine, abodes

Of the Three Jewels-fraught with glory and fame-

That lowly kings have not even

Conceived in their minds.

No. 311.

O King, it is preferable not to create

Foundations of doctrine that do not stir

The hairs of wealthy kings

Because [those centers] will not become famous even after your death.

No. 312.

Through your great exaltation, use even all your wealth

Such that the exalted become free from pride,

The equal become delighted,

And the inclinations of the lowly are reversed.

No. 313.

Having let go of all possessions,

[At death] powerless you must go elsewhere,

But all that has been used for the doctrine

Precedes you [as good karma],

No. 314.

When all the possessions of a previous monarch

Come under the control of the successor,

Of what use are they then to the former monarch

For practice, happiness, or fame?

No. 315.

Through using wealth there is happiness here in this life,

Through giving there is happiness in the future,

From wasting it without using or giving it away,

There is only misery. How could there be happiness?

No. 316.

Because of lack of power while dying,

You will be unable to make donations by way of your ministers

Who will shamelessly lose affection for you

And will seek to please the new monarch.

No. 317.

Hence while in good health create foundations of doctrine

Immediately with all your wealth,

For you are living amidst the causes of death

Like a lamp standing in a breeze.

No. 318.

Also you should maintain other centers of doctrine

Established by the previous kings-

All the temples and so forth-

As they were before.

No. 319.

Please have them attended by those

Who are not harmful, are virtuous,

Keep their vows, are kind to visitors, truthful,

Patient, non-combative, and always diligent.

No. 320.

Cause the blind, the sick, the lowly,

The protectorless, the destitute,

And the crippled equally to obtain

Food and drink without interruption.

No. 321.

Provide all types of support

For practitioners who do not seek it

And even for those living

In the countries of other monarchs.

No. 322.

At all centers of the doctrine

Appoint attendants who are

Not negligent, not greedy, skillful,

Religious, and not harmful to anyone.

No. 323.

Appoint ministers who know good policy,

Who practice the doctrine, are civil,

Pure, harmonious, undaunted, of good lineage,

Of excellent ethics, and grateful.

No. 324.

Appoint generals who are generous,

Without attachments, brave, kindly,

Who use [the treasury] properly, are steadfast,

Always conscientious, and practice the doctrine.

No. 325.

As administrators appoint elders

Of religious disposition, pure, and able,

Who know what should be done, are skilled in the royal treatises,

Understand good policy, are unbiased, and are kindly.

No. 326.

Every month you should hear from them

About all the income and expenses,

And having heard, you yourself should tell them

All that should be done for the centers of doctrine and so forth.

No. 327.

If your realm exists for the doctrine

And not for fame or desire,

Then it will be extremely fruitful.

If not, its fruit will be misfortune.

No. 328.

O Lord of Humans, since in this world nowadays

Most are prone to wreak havoc on each other,

Listen to how your governance

And your practice should be.

No. 329.

Let there always be around you many persons

Old in experience, of good lineage,

Knowing good policy, who shrink from ill deeds,

Are agreeable, and know what should be done.

No. 330.

Even to those whom they have rightfully fined,

Bound, punished, and so forth,

You, being moistened with compassion,

Should always be caring.

No. 331.

O King, through compassion you should

Always generate just an attitude of altruism

Even for all those embodied beings

Who have committed awful ill deeds.

No. 332.

Especially generate compassion

For those whose ill deeds are horrible, the murderers.

Those of fallen nature are receptacles

Of compassion from those whose nature is magnanimous.

No. 333.

Free the weaker prisoners

After a day or five days.

Do not think the others

Are not to be freed under any conditions.

No. 334.

For each one whom you do not think to free

You will lose the [layperson's] vow.

Due to having lost the vow,

Faults will constantly be amassed.

No. 335.

As long as prisoners are not freed,

They should be made comfortable

With barbers, baths, food, drink,

Medicine, and clothing.

No. 336.

Just as deficient children are punished

Out of a wish to make them competent,

So punishment should be carried out with compassion,

Not through hatred nor desire for wealth.

No. 337.

Once you have analyzed and thoroughly recognized

The angry murderers,

Have them banished

Without killing or tormenting them.

No. 338.

In order to maintain control, oversee all the country

Through the eyes of agents.

Always conscientious and mindful,

Do what accords with the practices.

No. 339.

Continually honor in an exalted way

Those who are foundations of good qualities

With gifts, respect, and service,

And likewise honor all the rest.

No. 340.

The birds of the populace will alight upon

The royal tree providing the shade of patience,

Flourishing flowers of respect,

And large fruits of resplendent giving.

No. 341.

Monarchs whose nature is generosity

Are liked if they are strong,

Like a sweet hardened outside

With cardamom and pepper.

No. 342.

If you analyze with reason thus,

Your governance will not degenerate.

It will not be without principle

Nor become unreligious but be religious.

No. 343.

You did not bring your dominion with you from your former life

Nor will you take it to the next.

Since it was gained through religious practice,

You would be wrong to act against the practices.

No. 344.

O King, exert yourself

To avert a sequence

Of miserable supplies for the realm

Through [misuse of] royal resources.

No. 345.

O King, exert yourself

To increase the succession

Of the dominion's resources

Through [proper use of] royal resources.

No. 346.

Although Universal Monarchs rule

Over the four continents, their pleasures

Are regarded as only two-

The physical and the mental.

No. 347.

Physical feelings of pleasure

Are only a lessening of pain.

Mental pleasures are made of thought,

Created only by conceptuality.

No. 348.

All the wealth of worldly pleasures

Are just a lessening of suffering,

Or are only [creations of] thought,

Hence they are in fact not meaningful.

No. 349.

Just one by one there is enjoyment

Of continents, countries, towns, homes,

Conveyances, seats, clothing, beds,

Food, drink, elephants, horses, and women.

No. 350.

When the mind has any [one of these as its object],

Due to it there is said to be pleasure,

But since at that time no attention is paid to the others,

The others are not then in fact meaningful [causes of pleasure].

No. 351.

When [all] five senses, eye and so forth,

[Simultaneously] apprehend their objects,

A thought [of pleasure] does not refer [to all of them],

Therefore at that time they do not [all] give pleasure.

No. 352.

Whenever any of the [five] objects is known

[As pleasurable] by one of the [five] senses,

Then the remaining [objects] are not so known by the remaining [senses]

Since they then are not meaningful [causes of pleasure].

No. 353.

The mind apprehends an image of a past object

Which has been apprehended by the senses

And imagines and fancies

It to be pleasurable.

No. 354.

Also the one sense which here [in the world

Is said to] know one object

Is meaningless without an object,

And the object also is meaningless without it.

No. 355.

Just as a child is said to be born

In dependence on a father and a mother,

So a [visual] consciousness is said to arise

In dependence on an eye sense and on a form.

No. 356.

Past and future objects

And the senses are meaningless,

So too are present objects

Since they are not distinct from these two."

No. 357.

Just as due to error the eye perceives

A whirling firebrand as a wheel,

So the senses apprehend

Present objects [as if real].

No. 358.

The senses and their objects are regarded

As being composed of the elements.

Since the elements are meaningless individually,

These also are meaningless in fact.

No. 359.

If the elements are each different,

It follows that there could be fire without fuel.

If mixed, they would be characterless.

Such is also to be ascertained about the other elements.

No. 360.

Because the elements are thus meaningless in both these ways,

So too is a composite.

Because a composite is meaningless

So too are forms meaningless in fact.

No. 361.

Also because consciousnesses, feelings,

Discriminations, and compositional factors

Altogether and individually are without essential factuality,

[Pleasures] are not ultimately meaningful.

No. 362.

Just as lessening of pain

Is fancied to be pleasure in fact,

So destruction of pleasure

Is also fancied to be pain.

No. 363.

Thus attachment to meeting with pleasure

And attachment to separating from pain

Are to be abandoned because they do not inherently exist.

Thereby those who see thus are liberated.

No. 364.

What sees [reality]?

Conventionally it is said to be the mind

[For] without mental factors there is no mind

[And hence minds and mental factors] are meaningless,

due to which it is not asserted that they are simultaneous.

No. 365.

Knowing thus correctly, just as it is,

That transmigrating beings do not exist in fact,

One passes [from suffering] not subject [to rebirth and hence] without appropriating [rebirth],

Like a fire without its cause.

No. 366.

Bodhisattvas also who have seen it thus,

Seek perfect enlightenment with certainty.

They make the connection between lives

Until enlightenment only through their compassion.

No. 367.

Since the collections [of merit and wisdom] of Bodhisattvas

Were taught by the One Gone Thus in the Great Vehicle,

Those who are bewildered [about the full extent of the paths and fruits of the Great Vehicle]

Deride them out of antagonism.

No. 368.

Either through not knowing the good qualities [of altruism] and the defects [of mere self-concern],

Or identifying good qualities as defects,

Or through despising good qualities,

They deride the Great Vehicle.

No. 369.

Those who deride the Great Vehicle-

Knowing that to harm others is defective

And that to help others is a good quality-

Are said to despise good qualities.

No. 370.

Those who despise the Great Vehicle,

Source of all good qualities in that [it teaches] taking delight

Solely in the aims of others due to not looking to one's own,

Consequently burn themselves [in bad transmigrations],

No. 371.

One type with faith [in emptiness forsakes it]79 through misconception [of it as denying cause and effect].

Others who are angry [forsake emptiness] through despising it.

If even the faithful type is said [in sutra] to be burned,

What can be said about those who turn their backs on it through despising it!

No. 372.

Just as it is explained in medicine

That poison can removed by poison,

What contradiction is there in saying

That what is injurious [in the future]can be removed by suffering?

No. 373.

It is renowned [in Great Vehicle scriptures] that motivation determines practices

And that the mind is most important.

Hence how could even suffering not be helpful

For one who gives help with an altruistic motivation?

No. 374.

If even [in ordinary life] pain can bring future benefit,

What need is there to say that [accepting suffering]

Beneficial for one's own and others' happiness will help!

This practice is known as the policy of the ancients.

No. 375.

If through relinquishing small pleasures

There is extensive happiness later,

Seeing the greater happiness

The resolute should relinquish small pleasures.

No. 376.

If such things cannot be borne,

Then doctors giving distasteful medicines

Would disappear. It is not [reasonable]

To forsake [great pleasure for the small].

No. 377.

Sometimes what is thought harmful

Is regarded as helpful by the wise.

General rules and their exceptions

Are commended in all treatises.

No. 378.

Who with intelligence would deride

The explanation in the Great Vehicle

Of deeds motivated by compassion

And of stainless wisdom!

No. 379.

Feeling inadequate about its great extent and profound depth

Untrained beings-foes of themselves and others-

Nowadays deride the Great Vehicle

Because of bewilderment.

No. 380.

The Great Vehicle has a nature

Of giving, ethics, patience, effort,

Concentration, wisdom, and compassion.

Hence how could there be any bad explanations in it?

No. 381.

Others' aims are [achieved][83] through giving and ethics.

One's own are [achieved] through patience and effort.

Concentration and wisdom are causes of liberation.

These epitomize the sense of the Great Vehicle.

No. 382.

The aims of benefiting oneself and others and the meaning of liberation

As briefly taught by the Buddha [in the Hearers' Vehicle]

Are contained in the six perfections.

Therefore these [scriptures of the Great Vehicle] are the word of Buddha.

No. 383.

Those blind with ignorance cannot stand

This Great Vehicle where Buddhas taught

The great path of enlightenment

Consisting of merit and wisdom.

No. 384.

Conquerors are said to have inconceivable good qualities

Because the [causal] good qualities are inconceivable like the sky.

Therefore let this great nature of a Buddha

Explained in the Great Vehicle be allowed.

No. 385.

Even [Buddha's] ethics were beyond

The scope of Shariputra.

So why is the inconceivable great nature

Of a Buddha not accepted?

No. 386.

The absence of production taught in the Great Vehicle

And the extinction of the others are in fact the same emptiness

[Since they indicate] the non-existence of [inherently existent] production and the extinction [of inherent existence].

Therefore let [the Great Vehicle] be allowed [as Buddha's word].

No. 387.

If emptiness and the great nature of a Buddha

Are viewed in this way with reason,

How could what is taught in the Great Vehicle and the other

Be unequal for the wise?

No. 388.

What the One Gone Thus taught with a special intention

Is not easy to understand.

Therefore since he taught one as well as three vehicles,

You should protect yourself through neutrality.

No. 389.

There is no fault with neutrality, but there is fault

From despising it. How could there be virtue?

Therefore those who seek good for themselves

Should not despise the Great Vehicle.

No. 390.

Bodhisattvas' aspirational wishes, deeds, and dedications [of merit]

Were not described in the Hearers' Vehicle.

Therefore how could one become

A Bodhisattva through it?

No. 391.

[In the Hearers' Vehicle] Buddha did not explain

The foundations for a Bodhisattva's enlightenment.

What greater authority for this subject

Is there other than the Victor?

No. 392.

How could the fruit of Buddhahood be superior

[If achieved] through the path common to Hearers

Which has the foundations [of the Hearer enlightenment],

The meanings of the four noble truths, and the harmonies with enlightenment?

No. 393.

The subjects concerned with the Bodhisattva deeds

Were not mentioned in the [Hearers' Vehicle] sutras

But were explained in the Great Vehicle.

Hence the wise should accept it [as Buddha's word].

No. 394.

Just as a grammarian [first] has students

Read a model of the alphabet,

So Buddha taught trainees

The doctrines that they could bear.

No. 395.

To some he taught doctrines

To turn them away from ill-deeds;

To some, for the sake of achieving merit;

To some, doctrines based on duality;

No. 396.

To some, doctrines based on non-duality;

To some what is profound and frightening to the fearful-

Having an essence of emptiness and compassion-

The means of achieving [unsurpassed] enlightenment.

No. 397.

Therefore the wise should extinguish

Any belligerence toward the Great Vehicle

And generate special faith

For the sake of achieving perfect enlightenment.

No. 398.

Through faith in the Great Vehicle

And through practicing what is explained in it

The highest enlightenment is attained

And, along the way, even all [worldly] pleasures.

No. 399.

At that time [when you are a ruler] you should internalize

Firmly the practices of giving, ethics, and patience,

Which were especially taught for householders

And which have an essence of compassion.

No. 400.

However, if from the unrighteousness of the world

It is difficult to rule religiously,

Then it is right for you to become a monastic

For the sake of practice and grandeur.

The fourth chapter of the Precious Garland,

An Indication of Royal Policy, is finished.

No. 401.

Then having become a monastic

You should first be intent on the training [in ethics].

You should endeavor at the discipline of individual liberation,

At hearing frequently, and delineating their meaning.

No. 402.

Then, you should forsake

These which are called assorted faults.

With vigor you should definitely realize

Those renowned as the fifty-seven.

No. 403.

(1) Belligerence is a disturbance of mind.

(2) Enmity is a [tight] hanging onto that.

(3) Concealment is a hiding of ill-deeds [when confronted].

(4) Malevolence is to cling to ill-deeds.

No. 404.

(5) Dissimulation is deceptiveness.

(6) Deceit is crookedness of mind.

(7) Jealousy is to be bothered by others' good qualities.

(8) Miserliness is a fear of giving.

No. 405.

(9) Non-shame and (10) non-embarrassment

Are insensibility concerning oneself and others [respectively].

(11) Inflatedness is not to pay respect.

(12) Faulty exertion is to be polluted by belligerence.

No. 406.

(13) Arrogance is haughtiness [due to wealth, and so forth].

(14) Non-conscientiousness is non-application at virtues.

(15) Pride has seven forms

Each of which I will explain.

No. 406.

(13) Arrogance is haughtiness [due to wealth, and so forth].

(14) Non-conscientiousness is non-application at virtues.

(15) Pride has seven forms

Each of which I will explain.

No. 407.

Fancying that one is lower than the lowly,

Or equal with the equal,

Or greater than or equal to the lowly-

All are called the pride of selfhood.

No. 408.

Boasting that one is equal to those

Who by some good quality are superior to oneself

Is called exceeding pride.

Fancying that one is superior to the superior,

No. 409.

Thinking that one is higher than the very high,

Is pride beyond pride;

Like sores on an abscess

It is very vicious.

No. 410.

Conceiving an I through obscuration

In the five empty [aggregates]

Which are called the appropriation

Is said to be the pride of thinking I.

No. 411.

Thinking one has won fruits [of the spiritual path]

Not yet attained is the pride of conceit.

Praising oneself for faulty deeds

Is known by the wise as erroneous pride.

No. 412.

Deriding oneself, thinking

"I am useless," is called

The pride of inferiority.

Such is a brief description of the seven prides.

No. 413.

(16) Hypocrisy is to control the senses

For the sake of goods and respect.

(17) Flattery is to speak pleasant phrases

For the sake of goods and respect.

No. 414.

(18) Indirect acquisition is to praise

Another's wealth in order to acquire it.

(19) Pressured acquisition is manifest derision

Of others in order to acquire goods.

No. 415.

(20) Desiring profit from profit

Is to praise previous acquisitions.

(21) Repeating faults is to recite again and again

The mistakes made by others.

No. 416.

(22) Non-collectedness is inconsiderate irritation

Arisen from illness.

(23) Clinging is the attachment

Of the lazy to their bad possessions.

No. 417.

(24) Discrimination of differences is discrimination

Impeded by desire, hatred, or obscuration.

(25) Not looking into the mind is explained

As not applying it to anything.

No. 418.

(26) Degeneration of respect and reverence for deeds

Concordant with the practices occurs through laziness.

(27) A bad person is regarded as being a spiritual guide

[Pretending] to have the ways of the

Supramundane Victor.

No. 419.

(28) Yearning is a small entanglement

Arising from lustful desire.

(29) Obsession, a great entanglement

Arising from desire.

No. 420.

(30) Avarice is an attitude

Of clinging to one's own property,

(31) Inopportune avarice is attachment

To the property of others.

No. 421.

(32) Irreligious lust is desirous praise

Of women who ought to be avoided.

(32) Hypocrisy is to pretend that one possesses

Good qualities that one lacks, while desiring ill deeds.

No. 422.

(34) Great desire is extreme greed

Gone beyond the fortune of knowing satisfaction.

(35) Desire for advantage is to want to be known

By whatever way as having superior good qualities.

No. 423.

(36) Non-endurance is an inability

To bear injury and suffering.

(37) Impropriety is not to respect the activities

Of a teacher or spiritual guide.

No. 424.

(38) Not heeding advice is to not respect

Counsel concordant with practice.

(39) Intention to meet with relatives

Is sentimental attachment to one's kin.

No. 425.

(40) Attachment to objects is to relate

Their good qualities in order to acquire them.

(41) Fancying immortality is to be

Unaffected by concern over death.

No. 426.

(42) Conceptuality concerned with approbation

Is the thought that-no matter what-

Others will take one as a spiritual guide

Due to possessing good qualities.

No. 427.

(43,44) Conceptuality concerned with attachment to others

Is an intention to help or not help others

Due to being affected by desire

Or an intent to harm.

No. 428.

(45) Dislike is a mind that is unsteady.

(46) Desiring union is a dirtied mind.

(47) Indifference is a laziness with a sense of inadequacy

Coming from a listless body.

No. 429.

(48) Distortion is for the afflictive emotions

To influence body and color.

(49) Not wishing for food is explained

As physical sluggishness due to over-eating.

No. 430.

(50) A very dejected mind is taught

To be fearful faintheartedness.

(51) Longing for desires is to desire

And seek after the five attributes.

No. 431.

(52) Harmful intent arises from nine causes

Of intending to injure others-

Having senseless qualms concerning oneself, friends, and foes

In the past, present, and future.

No. 432.

(53) Sluggishness is non-activity

Due to heaviness of mind and body.

(54) Drowsiness is sleepiness.

(55) Excitement is strong disquiet of body and mind.

No. 433.

(56) Contrition is regret for bad deeds

Which arises afterwards from grief about them.

(57) Doubt is to be of two minds

About the [four] truths, the Three Jewels, and so forth.

No. 434.ab

[Householder] Bodhisattvas abandon those.

Those diligent in [monastic] vows abandon more.

No. 434.cd

Freed from these defects

Good qualities are easily observed.

No. 435.

Briefly the good qualities

Observed by Bodhisattvas are

Giving, ethics, patience, effort,

Concentration, wisdom, compassion, and so forth.

No. 436.

Giving is to give away one's wealth.

Ethics is to help others.

Patience is to have forsaken anger.

Effort is enthusiasm for virtues.

No. 437.

Concentration is unafflicted one-pointedness.

Wisdom is ascertainment of the meaning of the truths.

Compassion is a mind having the one savor

Of mercy for all sentient beings.

No. 438.

From giving there arises wealth, from ethics happiness,

From patience a good appearance, from [effort in] virtue brilliance,

From concentration peace, from wisdom liberation,

From compassion all aims are achieved.

No. 439.

From the simultaneous perfection

Of all those seven is attained

The sphere of inconceivable wisdom,

The protectorship of the world.

No. 440.

Just as eight grounds of Hearers

Are described in the Hearers' Vehicle,

So ten grounds of Bodhisattvas

Are described in the Great Vehicle.

No. 441.

The first of these is the Very Joyful

Because those Bodhisattvas are rejoicing

From having forsaken the three entwinements

And being born into the lineage of Ones Gone Thus.

No. 442.

Through the maturation of those [good qualities]

The perfection of giving becomes supreme.

They vibrate a hundred worlds

And become Great Lords of Jambudvlpa.

No. 443.

The second is called the Stainless

Because all ten [virtuous] actions

Of body, speech, and mind are stainless

And they naturally abide in those [deeds of ethics].

No. 444.

Through the maturation of those [good qualities]

The perfection of ethics becomes supreme.

They become Universal Monarchs helping beings,

Masters of the glorious [four continents] and of the seven precious objects.

No. 445.

The third ground is called the Luminous

Because the pacifying light of wisdom arises.

The concentrations and clairvoyances are generated,

And desire and hatred are completely extinguished.

No. 446.

Through the maturation of those [good qualities]

They practice supremely the deeds of patience

And become a great wise monarch of the gods.

They put an end to desire.

No. 447.

The fourth is called the Radiant

Because the light of true wisdom arises.

They cultivate supremely

All the harmonies with enlightenment.

No. 448.

Through the maturation of those [good qualities]

They become monarchs of the gods in [the heaven]

Without Combat. [effort]

They are skilled in quelling the arising of the view

That the transitory collection [is inherently existent I and mine].

No. 449.

The fifth is called the Extremely Difficult to Overcome

Because all evil ones find it extremely hard to conquer them.

They become skilled in knowing

The subtle meanings of the noble truths and so forth.

No. 450.

Through the maturation of those [good qualities]

They become monarchs of the gods abiding in the Joyous Land, [concentration]

They overcome the foundations of all Borders

Afflictive emotions and views.

No. 451.

The sixth is called the Approaching

Because they are approaching the good qualities of a Buddha.

Through familiarity with calm abiding and special insight

They attain cessation and hence are advanced [in wisdom].

No. 452.

Through the maturation of those [good qualities]

They become monarchs of the gods [in the land] of Liking Emanation. [wisdom]

Hearers cannot surpass them.

They pacify those with the pride of superiority.

No. 453.

The seventh is the Gone Afar

Because the number [of good qualities] has increased.

Moment by moment they [can] enter

The equipoise of cessation.

No. 454.

Through the maturation of those [good qualities]

They become masters of the gods [in the land] of Control over Others' Emanations. [means]

They become great leaders of teachers

Who know direct realization of the [four] noble truths.

No. 455.

The eighth is the Immovable, the youthful ground.

Through non-conceptuality they are immovable,

And the spheres of activity

Of their body, speech, and mind are inconceivable.

No. 456.

Through the maturation of those [good qualities]

They become a Brahma, master of a thousand worlds. [prayers]

Foe Destroyers, Solitary Realizers, and so forth

Cannot surpass them in positing the meaning [of doctrines].

No. 457.

The ninth ground is called Excellent Intelligence.

Like a regent they have attained

Correct individual realization

And therefore have good intelligence.

No. 458.

Through the maturation of those [good qualities]

They become a Brahma, master of a million worlds. [forces]

Foe Destroyers and so forth cannot surpass them

In [responding to] questions in the thoughts of sentient beings.

No. 459.

The tenth is the Cloud of Doctrine

Because the rain of holy doctrine falls.

The Bodhisattva is bestowed empowerment

With light rays by the Buddhas.

No. 460.

Through the maturation of those [good qualities]

They become master of the gods of Pure Abode. [awareness]

They are supreme great lords,

Master of the sphere of infinite wisdom.

No. 461.

Thus those ten grounds are renowned

As the ten Bodhisattva grounds.

The ground of Buddhahood is different.

Being in all ways inconceivable,

No. 461.

Thus those ten grounds are renowned

As the ten Bodhisattva grounds.

The ground of Buddhahood is different.

Being in all ways inconceivable,

No. 462.

Its great extent is merely said

To be endowed with the ten powers.

Each power is immeasurable too

Like [the limitless number of] all transmigrators.

No. 462.

Its great extent is merely said

To be endowed with the ten powers.

Each power is immeasurable too

Like [the limitless number of] all transmigrators.

No. 463.

The limitlessness of a Buddha's [good qualities]

Is said to be like the limitlessness

Of space, earth, water, fire,

And wind in all directions.

No. 464.

If the causes are [reduced] to a mere [measure]

And not seen to be limitless,

One will not believe the limitlessness

[Of the good qualities] of the Buddhas.

No. 465.

Therefore in the presence of an image

Or monument or something else

Say these twenty stanzas

Three times every day:

No. 466.

Going for refuge with all forms of respect

To the Buddhas, excellent Doctrine,

Supreme Community, and Bodhisattvas,

I bow down to all that are worthy of honor.

No. 467.

I will turn away from all ill deeds

And thoroughly take up all meritorious actions.

I will admire all the merits

Of all embodied beings.

No. 468. With bowed head and joined palms I petition the perfect Buddhas

To turn the wheel of doctrine and remain

As long as transmigrating beings remain.

No. 469.

Through the merit of having done thus

And through the merit that I did earlier and will do

May all sentient beings aspire

To the highest enlightenment.

No. 470.

May all sentient beings have all the stainless faculties,

Release from all conditions of non-leisure,

Freedom of action,

And endowment with good livelihood.

No. 471.

Also may all embodied beings

Have jewels in their hands,

And may all the limitless necessities of life remain

Unconsumed as long as there is cyclic existence.

No. 472.

May all women at all times

Become supreme persons. a

May all embodied beings have

The intelligence [of wisdom] and the legs [of ethics].

No. 473.

May embodied beings have a pleasant complexion,

Good physique, great splendor,

A pleasing appearance, freedom from disease,

Strength, and long life.

No. 474.

May all be skilled in the means [to extinguish suffering]

And have liberation from all suffering,

Inclination to the Three Jewels,

And the great wealth of Buddha's doctrine.

No. 475.

May they be adorned with love, compassion, joy,

Even-mindedness [devoid of] the afflictive emotions,

Giving, ethics, patience, effort,

Concentration, and wisdom.

No. 476.

Completing the two collections [of merit and wisdom],

May they have the brilliant marks and beautiful features [even while on the path],

And may they cross without interruption

The ten inconceivable grounds.

No. 477.

May I also be adorned completely

With those and all other good qualities,

Be freed from all defects,

And have superior love for all sentient beings.

No. 478.

May I perfect all the virtues

For which all sentient beings hope,

And may I always relieve

The sufferings of all embodied beings.

No. 479.

May those beings in all worlds

Who are distressed through fear

Become entirely fearless

Even through merely hearing my name.

No. 480.

Through seeing or thinking of me or only hearing my name

May beings attain great joy,

Naturalness free from error,

Definiteness toward complete enlightenment,

No. 481.

And the five clairvoyances a

Throughout their continuum of lives.

May I always in all ways bring

Help and happiness to all sentient beings.

No. 482.

May I always without harm

Simultaneously stop

All beings in all worlds

Who wish to commit ill deeds.

No. 483.

May I always be an object of enjoyment

For all sentient beings according to their wish

And without interference, as are the earth,

Water, fire, wind, herbs, and wild forests.

No. 484.

May I be as dear to sentient beings as their own life,

And may they be even more dear to me.

May their ill deeds fructify for me,

And all my virtues fructify for them.

No. 485.

As long as any sentient being

Anywhere has not been liberated,

May I remain [in the world] for the sake of that being

Though I have attained highest enlightenment.

No. 486.

If the merit of saying this

Had form, it would never fit

Into realms of worlds as numerous

As the sand grains of the Ganges.

No. 487.

The Supramundane Victor said so,

And the reasoning is this:

[The limitlessness of the merit of] wishing to help limitless realms

Of sentient beings is like [the limitlessness of those beings].

No. 488.

These practices that I have explained

Briefly to you in this way

Should be as dear to you

As your body always is.

No. 489.

Those who feel a dearness for the practices

Have in fact a dearness for their body.

If dearness [for the body] helps it,

The practices will do just that.

No. 490.

Therefore pay heed to the practices as you do to yourself.

Pay heed to achievement as you do to the practices.

Pay heed to wisdom as you do to achievement.

Pay heed to the wise as you do to wisdom.

No. 491.

Those who have qualms that it would be bad for themselves

[If they relied] on one who has purity, love, and intelligence

As well as helpful and appropriate speech,

Cause their own interests to be destroyed.

No. 492.

You should know in brief

The qualifications of spiritual guides.

If you are taught by those knowing contentment

And having compassion and ethics,

No. 493.ab

As well as wisdom that can drive out your afflictive emotions,

You should realize [what they teach] and respect them.

No. 493.cd

You will attain the supreme achievement

By following this excellent system:

No. 494.

Speak the truth, speak gently to sentient beings.

Be of pleasant nature, compelling.

Be politic, do not wish to defame,

Be independent, and speak well.

No. 495.

Be well-disciplined, contained, generous,

Magnificent, of peaceful mind,

Not excitable, not procrastinating,

Not deceitful, but amiable.

No. 496.

Be gentle like a full moon.

Be lustrous like the sun in autumn.

Be deep like the ocean.

Be firm like Mount Meru.

No. 497.

Freed from all defects

And adorned with all good qualities,

Become a sustenance for all sentient beings

And become omniscient.

No. 498.

These doctrines were not just taught

Only for monarchs

But were taught with a wish to help

Other sentient beings as befits them.

No. 499.

O King, it would be right for you

Each day to think about this advice

So that you and others may achieve

Complete and perfect enlightenment.

No. 500.

For the sake of enlightenment aspirants should always apply themselves

To ethics, supreme respect for teachers, patience, non-jealousy, non-miserliness,

Endowment with the wealth of altruism without hope for reward, helping the destitute,

Remaining with supreme people, leaving the non-supreme, and thoroughly maintaining the doctrine.

The fifth chapter of the Precious Garland, An Indication of the Bodhisattva Deeds, is finished.

Here ends the Precious Garland of Advice for a King by the great master, the Superior Nagarjuna.

Self-Realisation of Noble Wisdom (The Lankavatara Sutra)

Introduction

A Mahayana sutra that discusses the Consciousness-Only doctrine, especially the alaya-consciousness, and the inherent potential for Buddhahood. The Sanskrit text of the Lankavatara Sutra is thought to have been composed around C.E. 400. It represents the integration of two doctrines—that of the matrix of the Thus Come One and the Consciousness-Only doctrine—and asserts that all people possess the matrix of the Thus Come One, or the potential for Buddhahood.

It equates the matrix of the Thus Come One with the alaya-consciousness. The sutra takes the form of a discourse by Shakyamuni Buddha on Mount Lanka, the actual location of which is unknown. Some scholars identify Lankawith Sri Lanka, while others place it in southern or central India. In addition to the Sanskrit manuscript and two Tibetan translations, there are three extant Chinese versions: (1) one translated in 443 by Gunabhadra, a monk from central India; (2) another, in 513 by Bodhiruchi, a monk from northern India; and (3) a third produced between 700 and 704 by Shikshananda, a monk of Khotan in Central Asia. A fourth, actually the earliest version, translated in the early fifth century by Dharmaraksha, a monk from central India, is lost. An important text for the early Ch'an school in China, the Lankavatara Sutra was related to the development of the Zen school during the T'ang dynasty (618-907). Many commentaries on the sutra were produced during the T'ang, Sung (960-1279), and Ming (1368-1644) dynasties

Chapter I: Discrimination

Thus have I heard. The Blessed Lord once appeared in the Castle of Lanka which is on the summit of Mt. Malaya in the midst of the great Ocean. A great many Bodhisattvas-Mahasattvas had miraculously assembled from all the Buddha-lands, and a large number of bhikshus were gathered there. The Bodhisattvas-Mahasattvas with Mahamati at their head were all perfect masters of the various Samadhis, the tenfold Self-mastery, the ten Powers, and the six Psychic Faculties. Having been annointed by the Buddha's own hands, they all well understood the significance of the objective world; they all knew how to apply the various means, teachings and diciplinary measures according to the various mentalities abd behaviours of beings; they were all thoroughly versed in the five Dharmas. The three Svabhas, the eight Vijnanas, and the twofold Egolessness.

The Blessed Lord, knowing the mental agitations going on in the minds of those assembled (like the surface of the ocean stirred into waves by the passing winds), and his great heart moved by compassion, smiled and said: In the days of old the Tathagatas of the past who were Arhats and fully-enlightened Ones came to the Castle of Lanka on Mount Malaya and discoursed on the Truth of Noble Wisdom that is beyond the reasoning knowledge of the philosophers as well as being beyond the understanding of ordinary diciples and masters; and which is realisable only within the inmost conciousness; for your sakes, I too, would discourse on the same Truth. All that is seen in the world is devoid of effort and action because all things in the world are like a dream, or like an image miraculously projected. This is not comprehended by the philosophers and the ignorant, but those who thus see things see them truthfully. Those who see things otherwise walk in discrimination and, as they depend upon discrimination, they cling to dualism. The world as seem by discrimination is like seeing one's own image reflected in a mirror, or one's shadow, or the moon reflected in water, or an echo heard in a valley. People grasping their own shadows of discrimination become attached to this thing and that thing and failing to abandom dualism they go on forever discriminating and thus never attain tranquility. By tranquility is meant Oneness, and Oneness gives birth to the highest Samadhi which is gained by entering into the realm of Noble Wisdom that is realisable only within one's inmost conciousness.

Then all Bodhisattvas-Mahasattvas rose from their seats and respectfully paid homage and Mahamati the Bodhisattva-Mahasattva sustained by the power of the Buddhas drew his upper garment over one shoulder, knelt and pressing his hands together, praised him in the following verses:

As though reviewest the world with thy perfect intelligence and compassion, it must seem to thee like an ethereal flower of which one cannot say: it is born, it is destroyed, for the terms beings and non-being do not apply to it.

As though reviewest the world with thy perfect intelleigence and compassion, it must seem to thee like a dream of which it cannot be said: it is permanent or it is destructible, for the being and non-being do not apply to it.

As though reviewest all things by the perfect intelligence and compassion, they must seem to thee like visions beyond the reach of the human mind, as being and non-being do noy apply to them.

With thy perfect intelligence and compassion which are beyond all limit, thou comprehendest the egolessness of things and persons, and art free and clear from the hindraces of passion and learning and egoism.

Thou dost not vanish into Nirvana, nor does Nirvana abide in thee, for Nirvana trancends all duality of knowing and known, of being and non-being.

Those who see thee thus, serene and beyond conception, will be enmancipated from attachment, will be cleansed of all defilments, both in this world and in the spiritual world beyond.

In this world whose nature is like a dream, there is place for praise and blame, but in the ultimate Reality of Dharmakaya which is far beyond the senses and the discriminating mind, what is there to praise? O Thou most Wise!

Then said Mahamati the Bodhisattva-Mahasattva: O Blessed Lord, Sugata, Arhat and Fully-Enlightened One, pray tell us about the realisation of Noble Wisdom which is beyond the path and usage of philosophers; which is devoid of all predicates such as being and non-being, oneness and otherness, bothness and non-bothness, existence and non-existence, enternity and non-eternity; which has nothing to do with individuality and generality, nor false-imagination, nor any illusion arising from the mind itself; but which manifests itself as the Truth of Highest Reality. By which, going uo continuously by the stages of purification, one enters at last upon the stage of Tathagatahood, whereby, by the power of his original vows unattended by any striving, one will radiate its influence to infinite worlds, like a gem reflecting its variegated colors, whereby I and other Bodhisattvas-Mahasattvas will be enabled to bring all beings to the same perfection of virtue.

Said the Blessed Lord: Well done, well done, Mahamati! And again, well done, indeed! It is because of your compassion for the world, because of the benefit it will bring upon many people both human kind and celestial, that you have presented yourself before us to make this request. Therefore, Mahamati, listen well and truly reflect upon what I shall say, for I will instruct you.

Then Mahamati and the other Bodhisattva-Mahasattvas gave devout attention to the teaching of the Blessed Lord.

Mahamati, since the ignorant and simple-minded, not knowing that the world is only something seen of the mind itself, cling to the multitudiousness of external objects, cling to the notions of beings and non-being, oness and otherness, bothness and non-bothness, existence and non-existencem enternity and non-eternity, and think that they have a self-nature of their own, and all of which rises from the discriminations of the mind and is perpetuated by habit-energy, and from which they are given over to false imagination. It is all like a mirage in which springs of water are seen as if they were real. They are thus imagined by animals who, made thirsty by the heat of the season, run after them. Animals not knowing that the springs are an hallucination of their own minds, do not realise that there are no such springs. In the same way, Mahamati, the ignorant and simple-minded, their minds burning with the fires of greed, anger and folly, finding delight in a world of multitudinous forms, their thoughts obsessed with ideas of birth, growth and destruction, not well understanding what is meant by existence and non-existence, and being impressed by erroneous discriminations and speculations since beginningless time, fall into the habit of grasping this and that and thereby becoming attached to them.

It is like the city of the Gandharvas which the unwitting take to be a real city though it is not so in fact. The city appears as in a vision owing to their attachment to the memory of a city preserved in the mind as a seed; the city can thus be said to be both existent and non-existent. In the same way, clinging to the memory of erroneous speculations and doctrines accumulated since beginningless time, the hold fast to such ideas as oneness and otherness, being and non-being, and their thoughts are not at all clear as to what after all is only seen of the mind. It is like a man dreaming in his sleep of a country that seems to be filled with various men, women, elephants, horses, cars, pedestrians, villages, towns, hamlets, cows, buffalos, masions, woods, mountains, rivers and lakes, and who moves about in that city until he is awakened. As he lies half awake, he recalls the city of his dreams and reviews his experiences there; what do you think, Mahamati, is this dreamer who is letting his mind dwell upon the various unrealities he has seen in his dream,- is he to be considered wise or foolish? In the same way, the ignorant and simple-minded who are favorably influenced by the erroneous views of the philosophers do not recognise that the views that are influencing them are only dream-like ideas originating in the mind itself, and consenquently they are held fast by their notions of oneness and otherness, of being and non-being. It is like a painter's canvas on which the ignorant imagine they see the elevations and depressions of mountains and valleys.

In the same way there are people today being brought up under the influence of similar erroneous views of oneness and otherness, of bothness and not-bothness, whose mentality is being conditioned by the habit-energy of these false-imaginings and who later on will declare those who hold the true doctrine of no-birth, to be nihilist abd by so doing will bring themselves abd others to ruin. By the natural law of cause and effect these followers of pernicious views uproot meritorious causes that otherwise would lead unstained purity. They are to be shunned by those whose desires are for more excellent things.

It is like the dim-eyed ones who seeing the hairnet exclaim to one another: "It is wonderful! Look, Honorable sirs, it is wonderful!" But the hairnet has never existed; in fact; it is neither an entity, nor a non-entity, for it has both been seen and has not been seen. In the same manner those whose minds have been addicted to the discriminations of the errouneous views cherished by the philosophers which are given over to the unrealistic views of being and non-being, will contradict the good Dharma and will end in the destruction of themselves and others.

It is like a wheel of fire made by a revolving firebrand which is no wheel but which is imagined to be one by the ignorant. Nor is it a not-a-wheel because it has not been seen by some. By the same reasoning, those who are in the habit of listening to the discriminations and views of the philosophers will regard things born as non-existent and those destroyed by causation as existent. It is like a mirror relfecting colors abd images as determined by conditions but without any partiality. It is like the echo of the wind that gives the sound of a human voice. It is like a mirage of moving water seen in a desert. In the same way the discriminating mind of the ignorant which has been heated by false-imaginations and speculations is stirred into mirage-like waves by the winds of birth, growth and destruction. It is like the magician Pisaca, who by means of his spells makes a wooden image or a dead body to throb with life, through it has no power of its own. In the same way the ignorant and the simple-minded, committing themselves to erroneous philospical views become thoroghly devoted to the ideas of oneness and otherness, but their confidence is not well grounded. For this reason, Mahamati, you and other Bodhisattvas-Mahasattvas should cast off all discriminations leading to the notions of birth, abiding, and destruction, of oneness and otherness, of bothness and not-bothness, of being and non-being and thus getting free of the bondage of habit-energy become able to attain reality realisable wihtin yourselves of Noble Wisdom.

Then said Mahamati to the Blessed Lord: Why is it that the ignorant are given up to discrimination and the wise are not?

The Blessed Lord replied: it is because the ignorant cling to names, signs and ideas; as their minds move along these channels they feed on multiplicities of objects and fall into the notion of and ego-soul and what belongs to it; they make discriminations of good and bad among appearances and cling to the agreeable. As they thus cling there is a reversion to ignorance, and karma born of greed, anger and folly, is accumulated. As the accumulation of karma goes on they become imprisoned in a cocoon of discrimination and are thenceforth unable to free themselves from the round of birth and death.

Because of folly they do not understand that all things are like maya, like the reflection of the moon in water, that there is no self-substance to be imagined as an ego-soul and its belongings, and that all their definite ideas rise from their false discriminations of what exists only as it is seen of the mind itself. They do not realise that things have nothing to do with qualify and qualifying, nor with the course of birth, abiding and destruction, and instead they assert that they are born of a creator, of time, of atoms, of some celestial spirit. It is because the ignorant are given up to discrimination that they move along with the stream of appearances, but it is not so with the wise.

Chapter II: False-Imaginations and Knowledge of Appearances

Then Mahamati the Bodhisattva-Mahasattva spoke to the Blessed Lord, saying: You speak of the erroneous views of the philosophers, will you please tell us of them, that we may be on our guard against them?

The Blessed Lord replied, saying: Mahamati, the error in these teachings that are generally held by the philosophers lies in this: they do not recognise that the objective world rises from the mind itself; they do not understand that the whole mind-system also arises from the mind itself; but depending upon these manifestations of the mind as being real they go on discriminating them, like the simple-minded ones that they are, cherishing the dualism of this and that, of being and non-being, ignorant to the fact that there is but one common Essence.

One the contrary my teaching is based upon recognition that the objective world, like a vision, is a manifestation of the mind itself; it teaches the cessation of ignorance, desire, deed and casualty; it teaches the cessation of suffering that arises from the discriminations of the triple world.

There are some Brahman scholars who, assuming something out of nothing, assert that there is substance bound up with causation which abides in time, and that the elements that make up personality and its environment have their genesis and continuation in causation and after thus existing, pass away. Then there are other scholars who hold a destructive and nihilistic view concerning such subjects as continuation, activity, breaking-up, existence, Nirvana, the Path, karma, fruition and Truth. Why? Because they have not attained an intuitive understanding of Truth itself and therefore they have no clear insight into the fundamentals of things. They are like a jar broken into pieces which is no longer able to fuction as a jar; they are like a burnt seed which is no longer capable of sprouting. But the elements that make up personality and its environment which they regard as subject to change are really incapable of uninterrupted transformations. Their views are based upon erroneous discriminations of the objective world; they are not based upon true conceptions.

Again, if it is true that something comes out of nothing and there is the rise of the mind-system by reason of the combinations of the three effect-producing causes, we could say the same of any non-existing thing: for instance, that a tortoise could grow hair, or sand produce oil. This proposition is of no avail; it ends up in affirming nothing. It follows that the deed, work and cause of which they speak is of no use, and so also is their reference to being and non-being, if they argue that there is a combination of the three effect-producing causes, they must do it on the principle of cause and effect, that is, that something comes out of something and not out of nothing. As long a world of relativity is asserted, there is an ever recurring chain of causation which cannot be denied under any circunstance, therefore we cannot talk of anything comming to and end or of cessation. As long as these scholars remain on their philosophical ground their demostration must conform to logic and their textbooks, and the memory habit of erroneous intellection will ever cling to them. To make the matter worse, the simple-minded ones, poisoned by these erroneous view, will declare this incorrect way of thinking taught by the ignorant, to be the same as that presented by the All-knowing One.

But the way of instruction presented by the Tathagatas is not based on claims and refutations by means of words and logic. There are four forms of assertion that can be made concerning things not in existence, namely, claims made about individual marks that are not in existence; about objects that are not in existence, about a cause that is non-existent; and about philosophical views that are erroneous. By refutation is meant that one, because of ignorance, has not examined properly the error that lies at the base of these claims.

The assertion about individual marks that really have no existence, concerns the distinctive marks as percived by the eye, ear, nose, etc., as indicating individuality and generality in the elements that make up personality and its external world; and then, taking these marks for reality and getting attached to them, to ge into the habit or affirming that things are just so and not otherwise.

The assertion about objects that are non-existent is an assertion that rises from attachment to these associated marks of individuality and generality. Objects in themselves are neither in existence nor in non-existence and are quite devoid of the alternative of being and non-being; and should only be thought of as one thinks of the horns of a hare, a horse, or a camel, which never existed. Objects are discriminated by the ignorant who are addicted to assertion and negation, because their intelligence has not been acute enough to penetrate into the truth that there is nothing but what is seen of the mind itself.

The assertion of a cause that is non-existent assumes the causeless birth of the first element of the mind-system which later comes to have only a maya-like non-existence. That is to say, there are philosophers who assert that an originally unborn mind-system begins to fuction under the conditions of eye, form, light and memory, which functioning goes on for a time and then ceases. This is a example of a cause that is non-existent.

The assertion of philosophical views concerning the elements that make up personality and its environing world that are non-existent, assume the existence of an ego, a being, a soul, a living being, a "nourisher", or a spirit. This is an example of philosophical views that are not true. It is this combination of discrimination of imaginary marks of individuality, grouping them and giving them a name and becoming attached to them as objects, by reason of habit-energy that has been accumulated since beginningless time, that one builds up erroneous views whose only basis is false-imaginations. For this reason Bodhisattvas should avoid all discussions relating the claims and negations whose only basis is words and logic.

Word-discrimination goes on by the coordination of brain, chest, nose, throat, palate, lips, tongue, teeth and lips. Words are neither different nor not-different from discrimination. Words rise from discrimination as their cause; if words were different from discrimination they could not have discriminationfor their cause; then again, if words are not different, they could not carry and express meaning. Words, therefore, are produced by causation and are mutually conditioning and shifting and, just like things, are subject to birth and destruction.

There are four kinds of word discrimination, all of which are to be avoided because they are alike unreal. First there are words indicating individual marks which rise from discriminating forms and signs as being real in themselves and, then, becoming attached to them. There are memory-words which rise from the unreal surroundings which come before the mind when it recalls some previous experience. Then there are words growing out of attachment to the erroneous distinctions and speculations of the mental processes. And finally, there are words growing out of inherited prejudices as seeds of habit-energy accumulated since beginingless time, or which had their origing in some long forgotten clinging to false-imagination and erroneous speculation.

Then there are words where there are no corresponding objects, as for instance, the hare's horns, a barren woman's child, etc.,- there are no such things but we have the words, just the same. Words are an artificial creation; there are Buddha-lands where there are no words. In some Buddha-lands ideas are indicated by looking steadily, in other gestures, in still others by a frown, by a movement of the eyes, by laughing, by yawning, by the clearing of the throat, or by trembling. For instance, in the Buddha-land of the Tathagata Samantabhadra, Bodhisattvas, by a dhyana transcending words and ideas, attain recognition of all things as un-born and they, also, experience various most excellent Samadhis that transcend words. Even in this world such specialised beings as ants and bees carry on their activities very well without recourse to words. No, Mahamati, the validity of things is independent of the validity of words.

Moreover, there are other things that belong to words, namely, the syllable-body of words, the name-body of words, and the sentence-body of words. By the syllable-body is meant that by which words and sentences are set up or indicated: there is a reason for some syllables, some are mnemonic, and some are choosen arbitrarily. By name-body is meant the object depending upon which name-words obtains its significance, or in other words, name-body is the "substance" of a name-word. By sentence-body is meant the completion of the meaning by expressing the word more fully in a sentence. The name for this sentence-body is suggested by the footprints left in the road by elephants, horses, people, deer, catlle, goats, etc. But neither words nor sentences can exactly express meanings, for words are only sweet sounds that are arbitrarily chosen to represent things, they are not the things themselves, which in turn are only manifestations of mind. Discrimination of meaning is based upon false-imagination that these sweet sounds which we call words and which are dependent upon whatever subjects they are supposed to stand for, and which subjects are supposed to be self-existent, all of which is based on error. Diciples should be on their guard against the seductions of words and sentences and their illusive meanings, for by them the ignorant and the dull-witted become entangled and helpless as an elephant floundering about in the deep mud.

Words and sentences are produced by the law of causation and are mutually conditioning,- they cannot express highest Reality. Moreover, in highest Reality there are no differentiations to be discriminated and there is nothing to be predicated in regards to it. Highest Reality is an exalted state of bliss, it is not a state of word-discrimination and it cannot be entered into by mere statements concerning it. The Tathagatas have a better way of teaching, namely, through self-realisation of Noble Wisdom.

Mahamati asked the Blessed Lord: Pray tell us about the causation of all things whereby I and other Bodhisattvas may see into the nature of causation and may no more discriminate it as to the gradual or simultaneous rising of all things?

The Blessed Lord replied: There are two factors of causation by reason fo which all things come into seeming existence: external and internal factors. The external factors are a lump of clay, a stick, a wheel, a thread, water, a worker, and his labor, the combination of all which produces a jar. As with a jar which is made froma lump of clay, or a piece of cloth made from thread, or matting made from fragant grass, or a sprout growing out of a seed, or fresh butter made sour milk by a man churning it; so it is with all things which appear one after another in continuous succesion. As regards the inner factors of causation, they are of such kinds as ignorance, desire, purpose, all of which enter into the idea of causation. Born of these two factors there is a manifestation of personality and the individual things that make up its environment, but they are not indivual and distinctive things: they are only so discriminated by the ignorant.

Causation may be divided into six elements: indifference-cause, manifesting-cause, possibility-cause, agency-cause, objective-cause, manifesting-cause. Indifference-cause means that if there is no discrimination present, there is no power of combination present and so no combination takes place, or of present there is dissolution. Dependance-cause means that the elements must be present. Possibility-cause means that when a cause is to become effective there must be a suitable meeting of conditions both internal and external. Agency-cause means that there must be a principle vested with supreme authority like a sovereing king present and asserting itself. Objectivity-cause means that to be a part of the objective world the mind-system must be in existence and must be keeping up its continuous activity. Manifesting-cause means that as the discriminating faculty of the mind-system becomes busy individual marks will be revealed as forms are revealed by the light of a lamp.

All causes are thus seen to be the outcome of discrimination carried on by the ignorant and simple-minded, and there is, therefore, no such thing as gradual or simultaneous rising of existence. If such a thing as the gradual rising of existence is asserted, it can be dissaproved showing that there is no basic susbtance to hold the individual signs together which makes gradual rising impossible. If smultaneous rising of existence is asserted, there would ne no distinction between cause and effect and there will be nothing to characterise a cause as such. While a child is not yet born, the term father has no significance. Logicians argue that there is that which is born and that which gives birth by the mutual fuctioning of such casual factors as cause, substance, continuity, acceleration, etc., and so they conclude that there is a gradual rising of existence; but this gradual rising does not obtain except by reason of attachment to the notion of a self-nature.

When ideas of body, property and abode are seen, discriminated and cherished in what after all is nothing but what is conceived of the mind itself, and external world is perceived under the aspect of individuality and generality which, however, are not realities and, therefore, neither a gradual nor a simultaneous rising of things is possible. It is only when the mind-system comes into activity and discriminates the manifestations of mind that existence can be said to come into view. For these reasons, Mahamati, you must get rid of notions of graduation and simultaneity in the combination of casual activities.

Mahamati said: Blessed Lord; To what kind of discrimination and to what kind of thoughts should the term, false-imaginations, be applied?

The Blessed Lord replied: So long as people do no understand the true nature of the objective world, they fall into the dualistic view of things. They imagine the multiplicity of external objects to be real and become attached to them and are nourished by their habit-energy. Because of this system of mentation-mind and what belongs to it-is discriminated and is thought of as real; this leads to the assertion of an ego-soul and its belongings, and thus the mind-system goes on fuctioning. Depending upon and attaching itself to the dualistic habit of mind, they accept the views of the philosophers founded upon these erroneous distinctions, of being and non-being, existence, and non-existence, and there evolves what we call, false-imaginations. But Mahamati, discrimination does not evolve nor is it put away because, when all that is seen is truly recognized to be nothing but the manifestation of mind, how can discrimination as regards being and non-being evolve? It is for the sake of the ignorant who are addicted to the discriminations of the multiplicity of things which are of their own mind, that it is said by me that discrimination takes rise owing to attachment to the aspect of multiplicity which is characteristic of objects. How otherwise the ignorant and simple-minded recognize that there is nothing but what is seen of the mind itself, and how otherwise can they gain an insight into the true nature of mind and be able to free themselves from wrong conceptions of cause and effect? How otherwise can they gain a clear conception of the Bodhisattva stages, and attain and "turning-about" in the deepest seat of their consciousness, and finally attain an inner self-realization of Noble Wisdom which transcends the five Dharmas, the three Self-natures, and the whole idea of a discriminated Reality? For this reason it is said by me that discrimination takes rise from the mind becoming attached to the multiplicities of things which in themselves are not real, and that emancipation comes from throughly understanding the meaning of Reality as it truly is. False-imaginations rise from the consideration of appearances; things are discriminated as to form, signs and shape; as to having color, warmth, humidity, mobility or rigidity. False-imagination consists in becoming attached to these appearances and their names. By attachment to objects is meant, the getting attached to inner and outer things as if they were real. By attachment to names is meant, the recognition in these inner and outer things of the characteristic marks of individuation and generality, and to regard them definitely belonging to the names of the objects. False-imagination teaches that because all things are bound up with causes and conditions of habit-energy that has been accumulating since beginingless time by not recognizing that the external world is of mind itself, all things are comprehensible under the aspects of individuality and genereality. By reason of clinging to these false-imaginations there is multitudinousness of appearances which are imagined to be real but which are only imaginary. To illustrate: when a magician depending on grass, wood, shrubs and creepers, exercises his art, many shapes and beings take form that are only magically created; sometimes they even make figures that have bodies and that move and act like human beings; they are variously and fancifully discriminated but there is no reality in them; everyone but children and the simple-minded know that they are not real. Likewise based upon the notion of relativity false-imagination perceives a variety of appearances which the discriminating mind proceeds to objectify and name and become attached to, and memory and habit-energy perpetuate. Here is all that is necessary to constitute the self-nature of false-imagination. The various features of false imaginations can be distinguished as follows: as regards to words, meaning, individual marks, property, self-nature, cause, philosphical views, reasoning, birth, no-birth, dependence, bondage and emancipation.

Discrimination of words is the becoming attached to various sounds carrying familiar meanings. Discrimination of meaning comes when one imagines that words rise depending upon whatever subjects they express, and which subjects are regarded as self-existent. Discrimination of individual marks is to imagine that whatever is denoted in words concerning the multiplicities of individual marks (which in themselves are like a mirage) is true, and clinging tenaciously to them, to discriminate all things according to such categories as warmth, fluidity, motility, and solidity. Discrimination of property is to desire a state of wealth, such as gold, silver, and various precious stones. Discrimination of self-nature is to make discriminations according to the views of the philosophers in reference to the self-nature of all things which they imagine and stoutly maintain to be true, saying: "This is just what it is and it cannot be otherwise." Discrimination of cause is to distinguish the notion of causation in reference to being and non-being and to imagine that there are such things as "cause-signs".

Discrimination of philosophical views means considering different views relating to the notions of beings and non-being, oneness and otherness, bothness and not-bothness, existence and non-existence, all of which are erroneous, and becoming attached to particular views. Discrimination of reasoning means the teaching whose reasoning is based on the grasping of the notion and ego-substance and what belongs to it. Discrimination of birth means getting attached to the notion that things come into existence and pass out of existence by reason of causation. Discrimination of no-birth is to see that causeless substances which were not, come into existence by reason of causation.

Discrimination of dependence means the mutual dependence of gold and the filaments made of it. Discriminations of bondage and imagination is like imagining that there is something bound because something binding, as in the case of a man who ties a knot and then loosens one. These are the various features of false-imagination to which all the ignorant and simple-minded cling. Those attached to the notions of relativity are attached to the notions of the multitudinousness of things which arises from false-imagination. It is like seeing varieties of objects depending on maya, but these varieties thus revealing themselves are discriminated by the ignorant as something other than maya itself, according to their way of thinking. Now the truth is, maya and varieties of objects are neither different nor not different; if they were different, varieties of objects objects would have no maya for their characteristic; if they were not different there would be no distiction between them. But as there is a distinction these two-maya and variety of objects-are neither different nor not different, for the very good reason: they are one thing.

Mahamati said to the Blessed Lord: Is error an entity or not? The Blessed Lord replied: Error has no character in it making for attachment; if error had such a character no liberation would be possible from its attachment to existence, and the chain of origination would only be understood in the sense of creation as upheld by the philosophers. Error is like maya, also, and as maya is incapable from producing other maya, so error in itself cannot produce error; it is discrimination and attachment that produce evil thoughts and faults. Moreover, maya has no power of discrimination in itself; it only rises when invoked by the charm of a magician. Error has in itself no habit-energy; habit-energy only rises from discrimination and attachment. Error in itself has no faults; faults are due to the confused discriminations fondly cherished by the ignorant concerning ego-soul and its mind. The wise have nothing to do either with maya or error.

Maya, however, is not an unreality because it only has the appearance of reality; all things have the nature of maya. It is not because all things are imagined and clung to because of the multitudinousness of individual signs, that they are like maya; it is because they are alike unreal and as quickly appearing and disappearning. Being attached to erroneous thoughts they confuse and contradict themselves and others. As they do not clearly grasp the fact that the world is no more than mind itself, they imagine and cling to causation, work, birth and individual signs, and their thoughts are characterized by error and false-imaginations. The teaching that all things are characterized by the self-nature of maya and a dream is meant to make the ignorant and simple-minded cast aside the idea of self-nature in anything.

False-imagination teaches that such things as light and shade, long and short, black and white are different and are to be discriminated; but they are not independent of each other; they are only different aspects of the same thing, they are terms of relation and not of reality. Conditions of existence are not of a mutually exclusive character; in essence things are not two but one. Even Nirvana and Samsara's world of life and death are aspects of the same thing, for there is no Nirvana expect where is Samsara, and Samsara except where is Nirvana. All duality is falsely imagined.

Mahamati, you and all Bodhisattvas should dicipline yourselves in the realisation and patience acceptance of the truths of the emptiness, un-bornness, no self-natureness, and the non-duality of all things. This teaching is found in all the sutras of all the Buddhas and is presented to meet the varied dispositions of beings, but it is not the Truth itself. These teachings are only a finger pointing towards Noble Wisdom. They are like a mirage with its springs of water which the deer take to be real and chase after. So with the teachings in all the sutras: They are intended for the consideration and guidance of the discriminating minds of all people, but they are not the Truth itself, which can only be self-realised within one's deepest consciousness.

Mahamati, you and akk the Bodhisattvas must seek for this inner self-realisation of Noble Wisdom, and not be captivated by word-teachings.

Chapter III: Right Knowledge or Knowledge of Relations

Then Mahamati said: Pray tell us, Blessed Lord, about the being and the non-being of all things?

The Blessed Lord replied: People of this world are dependent in their thinking on one of two things: on the notion of being whereby they take pleasure in realism, or in the notion of non-being whereby they take pleasure in nihilism; in either case they imagine enmancipation where there is no enmancipation. Those who are dependent upon notions of being, regard the world as rising from a causation that is really existent, and that this actually existing and becoming world does not take its rise from a causation that is non-existent. This is the realistic view as held by some people. Then there are other people who are dependent on the notion of the non-being of all things. These people admit the existence of greed, anger and folly, and at the same time they deny the existence of things that produce greed, anger and folly. This is not rational, for greed, anger and folly are no more to be taken hold as real; they neither have substance nor individual marks. Where there is a state of bondage, there is binding and means for binding; but where there is enmancipation, as in the case of Buddhas, Bodhisattvas, masters and diciples, who have ceased to believe in both being and non-being, there is neither bondage, binding nor means for binding.

It is better to cherish the notion of an ego-substance than to entertain the notion of emptiness derived from the view of being and non-being, for those who so believe fail to understand the fundamental fact that the external world is nothing but a manifestation of mind. Because they see things as transient, as rising from cause and passing away from cause, now dividing, now combining into the elements which make up the aggregates of personality and its external world and now passing away, they are doomed to suffer every moment from the changes that follow one after another, and finally are doomed to ruin.

Then Mahamati asked the Blessed Lord, saying: Tell us, Blessed Lord, how all things can be empty, un-born, and have no self-nature, so that we may awakened and quickly realise highest enlightenment?

The Blessed Lord replied: What is emptiness, indeed! It is a term whose very self-nature is false-imagination, but because of one's attachment to false-imagination we are obliged to talk of emptiness, no-birth, and no self-nature. There are seven kind of emptiness: emptiness of mutuality which is non-existent; emptiness of individual marks; emptiness of self-nature; emptiness of no-work, emptiness of work; emptiness of all things in the sense that they are unpredictable, and emptiness in its highest sense of Ultimate Reality.

By emptiness of of mutuality which is non-existent is meant that when a thing is missing here, one speaks of it being empty here. For instance: in the lecture hall of Mrigarama there are no elephants present, nor bulls, nor sheep; but as to monks there are many present. We can rightly speak of the hall being empty as far as animals are concerned. It is not asserted that the hall is empty of its own characteristics, or that the monks are empty of that which makes their monkhood, nor that in some other place there are no elephants, bulls, nor sheep to be found. In this case we are speaking of things in their aspect of individuality and generality, but from the point of view of mutuality some things do not exist somewhere. This is the lowest form of emptiness and is to be sedulously put away.

By emptiness of individual marks is meant that all things have no distinguising marks of individuality and generality. Because mutual relations and interactions things are superficially discriminated but when they are further and more carefully investigated and analysed they are seen to be non-existent and nothing as to individuality and generality can be predicated of them. Thus when individual marks can no longer be seen, ideas of self, otherness and bothness, no longer hold good. So it must be said that all things are empty of self-marks.

By emptiness of self-nature is meant that all things in their self-nature are un-born; therefore, it is said that things are empty as to self-nature. By emptiness of no-work is meant that the aggregate of elements that makes up personality and its external world is Nirvana itself and from the beginning there is no activity in them; therefore, one speaks of the emptiness of no-work. By emptiness of work is meant that the aggregates being devoid of an ego and its belongings, go on fuctioning automatically as there is mutual conjuction of causes and conditions; thus one speaks of the emptiness of work. By emptiness of all things in the sense that they are unpredictable is meant that, as the very self-nature of false-imagination is inexpressible, so all things are unpredictable, and, therefore, are empty in that sense. By emptiness in the highest sense of the emptiness of Ultimate Reality is meant that the in the attainment of inner self-realisation of Noble Wisdom there is no trace of habit-energy generated by erroneous conceptions; thus one speaks of the highest emptiness of Ultimate Reality.

When things are examined by right knowledge there are no signs obtainable which could characterise them with marks of individuality and generality, therefore, they are said to have no self-nature. Because these signs of individuality and generality are both seen as existing and yet are known to be non-existent, are seen as going out and yet are known not to be going out, they are never annihilated. Why is this true? For this reason; because individual signs that should make up the self-nature of all things are non-existent. Again in their self-nature things are both eternal and non-eternal. Things are not eternal because the marks of individuality appear and disappear, that is, the marks of self-nature are characterise by non-eternality. On the other hand, because things are un-born and are only mind-made, they are in a deep sense eternal. That is, things are eternal because of their very non-eternality.

Further, besides understanding the emptiness of all things both in regard to substance and self-nature, it is necessary for Bodhisattvas to clearly understand that all things are un-born. It is not asserted that things arc not born in a superficial sense, but that in a deep sense they are not born of themselves. All that can be said, is this, that relatively speaking, there is a constant stream of becoming, a momentary and uninterrupted change from from one state of appearance to another. When it is recognised that the world as it presents itself is no more than a manifestation of mind, then birth is seen as no-birth, and all existing objects, concerning which discrimination asserts that they are and are not, are non-existent and, therefore, un-born; being devoid of agent and action things are un-born.

If things are not born of being and non-being, but are simply manifestations of mind itself, they have no reality, no self-nature:- they are like the horns of a hare, a horse, a donkey, a camel. But the ignorant and simple-minded, who are given over to their false and erroneous imaginings, discriminate things where they are not. To the ignorant the characteristic marks of the self-nature of body-property-and-abode seem to be fundamental and rooted in the very nature of mind itself, so they discriminate their multitudinousness and become attach to them.

There are two kinds of attachment: attachment to objects as having a self-nature, and attachment to words as having self-nature. The first takes place by not knowing that the external world is only a manifestation of mind itself; and the second arises from one's clinging to words and names by reason of habit-energy. In the teaching of no-birth, causation is out of place because, seeing that all things are like maya and a dream, one does not discriminate individual signs. That all things are un-born and have no self-nature because they are like maya is asserted to meet the thesis of the philosophers that birth is by causation. They foster the notion that the birth of all things is derived from the concept of being and non-being, and fail to regard it as it truly is,- as caused by attachments to the multitudinousness which arises from discriminations of the mind itself.

Those who believe in the birth of something that has never been in existence and, comming into existence, vanishes away, are obliged to assert that things come to exist and vanish away by causation – such people find no foothold in my teachings. When it is realised that there is nothing born, and nothing passes away, then there is no way to admit being and non-being, and the mind becomes quiescent.

Then Mahamati said to the Blessed Lord: The philosophers declare that the world rises from casual agencies according to the law of causation; they state that their cause is unborn and is not annihilated. They mention nine primary elements: Ishvara the Creator, the Creation, atoms, etc., which being elementary are unborn and not to be annihilated. The Blessed Lord, while teaching that all things are un-born and that there is no annihilation, also declares that the world takes its rise from ignorance, discrimination, attachment, deed, etc., working according to the law of causation. Though the two sects of elements may differ in form and name, there does not appear to be any essential difference between the two positions. If there is anything that is distinctive and superior in the Blessed Lord's teaching, pray tell us, Blessed Lord, what is it?

The Blessed Lord replied: My teaching of no-birth and no-annihilation is not like that of the philosophers, nor is it like their doctrine of birth and impermacency. That to which the philosophers ascribe the charateristic of no-birth and no-annihilation is the self-nature of all things, which causes them to fall into the dualism of being and non-being. My teaching transcends the whole conception of being and non-being; it has nothing to do with birth, abiding and destruction; nor with existence and non-existence. I teach that the multitudinouesness of objects have no reality in themselves but are only seen of mind and, therefore, are of the nature of maya and a dream. I teach the non-existence of things because they carry no signs of any inherent self-nature. It is true that in one sense they are seen and discriminated by the senses as individualised objects; but in another sense, because of the absence of any characteristic marks of self-nature, they are not seen but are only imagined. In one sense they are graspable, but in another sense, they are not graspable.

When it is clearly understood that there is nothing in the world but what is seen of the mind itself, discrimination no more rises, and the wise are established in their true abode which is the realm of quietude. The ignorant discriminate and work trying to adjust themselves to external conditions, and are constantly perturbed in mind; unrealities are imagined and discriminated, while realities and no seen and ignored. It is not so with the wise. To illustrate: What the ignorant see is like the magically-created city of the Gandharvas, where children are shown, street and houses, and phantom merchants, and people going in and comming out. This with its streets and houses and people going in and comming out, are not thought of as being born or annihilated, because in their case there is no question as to their existence or non-existence. In like manner, I teach, that there is nothing made nor un-made; that there is nothing that has connection with birth and destruction except as the ignorant cherish falsely imagined notions as to the reality of the external world. When objects are not seen and judged as they truly are in themselves, there is discrimination and clinging to the notions of being and non-being, and individualised self-nature, and as long as these notions of individuality and self-nature persist, the philosophers are bound to explain the external world by a law of causation. This position rises the question of a first cause which the philosophers meet by asserting that their first cause, Ishvara and the primal elements, are un-born and un-annihilate; which position is without evidence and is irrational.

Ignorant people and worldly philophers cherish a kind of no-birth, but it is not the no-birth which I teach. I teach the un-bornness of the un-born essence of all things which teaching is established in the minds of the wise by their self-realisation of Noble Wisdom. A ladle, clay, a vessel, a wheel, or seeds, or elements – these are external conditions; ignorance, discrimination, attachment, habit, karma, - these are inner conditions. When this entire universe is regarded as concatenation and as nothing else but concetenation, then the mind, but its patient acceptance of the truth that all things are un-born, gains tranquility.

Chapter IV: Perfect Knowledge or Knowledge of the Real

Then Mahamati asked the Blessed Lord: Pray tell us, Blessed Lord, about the five Dharmas, so that we may fully understand perfect knowledge?

The Blessed Lord replied: The five Dharmas are: appearance, name, discrimination, right-knowledge, and Reality. By appearance is meant that which reveals itself to the senses and to the discriminating-mind and is perviced as form, sound, odour, taste, and touch. Out of these appearances ideas are formed, such as clay, water, jar, etc., by which one says: this is such and such a thing and no other,- this is name. When appearances are constrasted and names compared, as when we say: this is an elephant, this is horse, a cart, a pedestrian, a man, a woman, or, this is mind and what belongs to it, - the things thus named are said to be discriminated. As these discriminations come to be seen as mutually conditioning, as empty of self-substance, as un-born, and thus come to be seen as they truly are, that is, as manifestations of the mind itself, - this is right-knowledge. By it the wise cease to regard appearances and names as realities.

When appearances and names are put away and all discrimination ceases, that which remains is the true and essential nature of things and, as nothing can be predicated as to the nature of essence, it is called the "Suchness" of Reality. This universal, undifferentiated, inscrutable, "Suchness" is the only Reality but it is variously characterised by Truth, Mind-essence, Transcendental Intelligence, Noble Wisdom, etc. This Dharma of the imagelessness of the Essence-nature of Ultimate Reality is the Dharma which has been proclaimed by all the Buddhas, and when all things are understood in full agreement with it, one is in possesion of Perfect Knowledge, and is on his way to the attainment of the Transcendental Inteeligence of the Tathagatas.

Then Mahamati said to the Blessed Lord: Are the three self-natures, of things, ideas, and Reality, to be considered as included in the Five Dharmas, or as having their own characteristics complete in themselves.

The Blessed Lord replied: The three self-natures, the eightfold mind-system, and the twofold egolessness are all included in the Five Dharmas. The self-natures of things, of ideas, and of the sixfold mind-system, correspond with the Dharma of appearance, name and discrimination; the self-nature of Universal Mind and Reality corresponds to the Dharmas of right-knowledge and "Suchness".

By becoming attached to what is seen of the mind itself, there is an activity awakened which is perpetuated by habit-energy that becomes manifest in the mind-system, from the activities of the mind-system there rises the notion of an ego-soul and its belongings; the discrimintations, attachments, and notion of an ego-soul, rising simultaneously like the sun and its rays of light.

By the egolessness of things is meant that the elements that make up the aggregates of personality and its objective world being characterised by the nature of maya and destitute of anything that can be called self-substance, are therefore un-born and have no self-nature. How can things be said to have an ego-soul? By the egolessness of persons is meant is that in the aggregates that make up personality there is no ego-substance, nor anything that is like an ego-susbtance nor that belongs to it. The mind-system, which is the most characteristic mark of personality, originated in ignorance, discrimination, desire and deed; and its activities are perpetuated by perceiving, grasping and becoming attached to objects as if they were real. The memory of these discriminations, desires, attachments and deeds is stored in Universal Mind since beginningless time, ad is still being accumulated where it conditions the appearance of personality and its environment and brings about constant change and destruction from moment to moment. The manifestations are like a river, a seed, a lamp, a cloud, the wind; Universal mind in its voraciousness to store up everything, is like a monkey never at rest, like a fly ever in search of food and without partiality, like a fire that is never satisfied, like a water-lifting machine that goes on rolling. Universal mind as defiled by habit-energy is like a magician that causes phantom things and people to appear and move about. A throrough understanding of these things is necessary to an understanding of the egolessness of persons.

There are four kinds of Knowledge: Appearance-knowledge, relative-knowledge, perfect-knowledge, and Transcendental Intelligence. Appearance-knowledge belongs to the ignorant and simple-minded who are addicted to the notion of being and non-being, and who are frightened at the thought of being un-born. It is produced by the concordance of the triple combination and attaches itself to the multiplicities of objects; it is characterised by attainability and accumulation; it is subject to birth and destruction. Appearance-knowledge belongs to word-mongers who revel in discriminations, claims and negations.

Relative-knowledge belongs to the mind-world of the philosophers. It rises from the mind's ability to arrange, combine and analyse these relations by its powers of discursive logic and imagination, by reason of which it is able to peer into the meaning and significance of things.

Perfect-knowledge belongs to the world of the Bodhisattvas who recognise that all things are but manifestations of mind; who clearly understand the emptiness, the un-borness, the egolessness of all things; and who have entered into an understanding of the Five Dharmas, the twofold egolessness, and into the truth of imagelessness. Perfect-knowledge differentiates the Bodhisattva stages, and is the pathway and entrance into the exalted state of self-realisation of Noble Wisdom.

Perfect-knowledge (jnana) belongs to the Bodhisattvas who are entirely free from the dualism of being and non-being, no-birth and no-annihilation, all claims and negations, and who, by reason of self-realisation, have gained an insight into the truth of egolessness and imagelessness. They no longer discriminate the world as subject to causation: they regard the causation that rules the world as something like the fabled city of the Gandharvas. To them the world is like a vision and a dream, it is like the birth and death of a barren-woman's child; to them there is nothing evolving and nothing disappearing.

The wise who cherish Perfect-knowledge, may be divided into three classes, disciples, masters and Arhats. Common disciples are separated fro masters as common disciples continue to cherish the notion of individuality and generality; masters rise from common disciples when, forsaking the erros of individuality and generality, they still cling to the notion of an ego-soul by reasons of which they go off by themselves into retirement and solitude. Arhats rise when the error of all discrimination is realised. Error being discriminated by the wise turns into Truth by virtue of the "turning-about" that takes place within the deepest consciousness. Mind, thus emancipated, enters into perfect self-realisation of Noble Wisdom.

But, Mahamati, if you assert that there is such a thing as Noble Wisdom, it no longer holds good, because anything of which something is asserted thereby partakes of the nature of being and is thus characterised with the quality of birth. The very assertion: "All things are un-born" destroys the truthfulness of it. The same is true of the statements: "All things are empty", and "All things have no self-nature",- both are untenable when put in the form of claims. But when it is pointed out that all things are like a dream and a vision, it means that in one way they are perceived, and in another way they are not perceived; that is, in ignorance they are perceived but in Perfect-knowledge they are not perceived. All claims and negations being thought-constructions are un-born. Even the assertion that Universal Mind and Noble Wisdom are Ultimate Reality, is thought construction and, therefore, is un-born. As "things" there is no Universal Mind, there is no Noble Wisdom, there is no Ultimate Reality. The insight of the wise who move about in the realm of imagelessness and its solitude is pure. That is, for the wise all "things" are wiped away even the state of imagelessness ceases to exist.

Chapter V: The System of the Mind

Then Mahamati said to the Blessed Lord: Pray tell us, Blessed Lord, what is meant by mind (citta)?

The Blessed Lord replied: All things of this world, be they seemingly good or bad, faulty or faultless, effect-producing or not effect-producing, receptive or non-receptive, may be divided into two classes: evil out-flowings and the non out-flowing good. The five grasping elements that make up the aggregates of personality, namely, form, sensation, perception, discrimination, and consciousness, and that are imagined to be good and bad, have their rise in the habit-energy of the mind-system,- they are the evil out-flowings of life. The spiritual attainments and the joys of the Samadhis and the fruitage of the Samapatis that come the wise throgh their self-realisation of Noble Wisdom and that culminate in their return and participation in the relations of the triple world are called the non out-flowing good.

The mind-system which is the source of the evil out-flowings consists of the five sense-organs and their accompanying sense-minds (vijnanas) all of which are unified in the discriminating-mind (manovijnana). There is an unending succesion of sense-concepts flowing into this discriminating or thinking-mind which combines them and discriminates them and passes judgement upon them as to their goodness or badness. Then follows aversion to or desire for them and attachment and deed; thus the entire system moves on continuously and closely bound together. But it fails to see and understand that what it sees and discriminates and grasps is only a manifestation of its own activity and has no other basis, and so the mind goes on erroneously perceiving and discriminating differences of forms and qualities, not remaining still even for a minute.

In the mind-system there are three modes of activity distinguishable: the sense-minds fuctioning while remaining in their original nature, the sense-minds as producing effects, and the sense-minds as evolving. By normal fuctioning the sense-minds grasp appropiate elements of their external world, by which sensation and perception arise at once and by degrees in every sense-organ and every sense-mind, in the pores of the skin, and even in the atoms that make up the body, by which the whole field is apprehended like a mirror reflecting objects, and not realising that the external world itself is only a manifestation of mind. The second mode of activity produces effects by which these sensations react on the discriminating mind to produce perceptions, attractions, aversions, grasping, deed andhabit. The third mode of activity has to do with the growth, development and passing of the mind-system, that is, the mind-system is in subjection to its own habit-energy accumulated from beginningless time time, as for instance: the "eyeness" in the eye that predisposes it to grasp and become attached to multiple forms and appearances. In this way the activities of the evolving mind-system by reason of its habit-energy stirs up waves of objectivity in the face of Universal Mind which in turn conditions the activities and evolvement of the mind-system.

Appearances, perception, attraction, grasping, deed, habit, reaction, condition one another incessantly, and the fuctioning sense-minds, the discriminating-mind and Universal Mind are thus bound up together. Thus, by reason of discrimination of that which by nature maya-like and unreal false-imagination and erroneous reasoning takes place, action follows and its habit-energy accumulates thereby defiling the pure face of Universal Mind, and as a result the mind-system comes into fuctioning and the physical body has its genesis. But the discriminating-mind has not thought that by its discriminations and attachments it is conditioning the whole body and so the sense-minds and discriminating-mind go on mutually related and mutually conditioned in a most intimate manner and building up a world of representations out of the activities of its own imagination. As a mirror reflects forms, the percieving senses percieve appearances which the discriminating-mind gathers together and proceeds to discriminate, to name and become attached to. Between these two fuctions there is no gap, nevertheless, they are mutually conditioning. The percieving sense grasp that for which they have an affinity, and there is a transformation takes place in their structure by reason of which the mind proceeds to combine, discriminate, apprise, and act; then follows habit-energy and the establishing of the mind and its continuance.

The discriminating-mine because of its capacity to discriminate, judge, select and reason about, is also called the thinking-mind, or intellectual-mind. There are three divisions of its mental activity: mentation which fuctions in connection with attachment to objects and ideas, mentation that fuctions in connection with general ideas, and mentation that examines into the validity of these general ideas. The mentation which fuctions in connection with attachment to objects and ideas derived from discrimination, discriminates the mind from its mental processes and accepts the ideas from it as being realand becomes attached to them. A variety of false judgements are thus arrived at as to being, multiplicity, individuality, value, etc., a strong grasping takes place which is perpetuated by habit-energy and thus discrimination goes on asserting itself.

These mental processes give rise to general conceptions of warmth, fluidity, motility, and solidity, as characterising the objects of discimination, while the tenacious holding to these general ideas gives rise to proposition, reason, definition, and illustration, all of which lead to the claims of relative knowledge and the establishment of confidence in birth, self-nature, and an ego-soul.

By mentation as an examining fuction is meant the intellectual act of examining into these general conclusions as to their validity, significance, and truthfulness. This is the faculty that leads to understanding, right-knowledge and points the way to self-realisation.

Then Mahamati said to the Blessed Lord: Pray tell us, Blessed Lord, what relation ego-personality bears to the mind-system?

The Blessed Lord replied: To explain it, it is first necessary to speak of the self-nature of the five grasping aggregates that make up personality, although as i have already shown they are empty, un-born, and without self-nature. These five grasping aggregates are: form, sensation, perception, discrimination, consciousness. Of these, form belongs to what is made of the so-called primary elements, whatever they may be. The four remainding aggregates are without form and ought not to be reckoned as four, because they merge imperceptibly into one another. They are like space which cannot be numbered; it is only due to imagination that they are discriminated and likened to space. Because things are endowed with appearances of being, characteristic-marks, percievableness, abode, work, one can say that they are born of effect-producing causes, but this cannot be said of these four intangible aggregates for they are without any form of marks. These four mental aggregates that make up personality are beyond calculability, they are beyond the four propositions, they are not to be predicated as existing or as not existing, but together they constitute what is known as mortal-mind. They are even more maya-like and dream-like than are things, nevertheless, as discriminating mortal-mind they obstruct the self-realisation of Noble Wisdom. But it is only by the ignorant that they are enumerated and thought of as an ego-personality; the wise do not do so. This discrimination of the five aggregates that make up personality and that serve as a basis for an ego-soul and ground for its desires and self-interests must be given up, and in its place the truth of imagelessness and solitude should be established.

Then said Mahamati to the Blessed Lord: Pray tell us, Blessed Lord, about Universal Mind and its relation to the lower mind-system?

The Blessed Lord replied: The sense-minds and their centralised discriminating-mind are related to the external world which is a manifestation of itself and is given over to pervceiving, discriminating, and grasping its maya-like appearances. Universal Mind (Alaya-vijnana) transncends all individuation and limits. Universal Mind is thoroughly pure in its essential nature, subsisting unchanged and free from faults of impermanence, undisturbed by egoism, unruffled by distinctions, desires and aversions. Universal Mind is like a great ocean, its surface rufflled by waves and surges but its depths remaining forever unmoved. In itself it is devoid of personality and all that belongs to it, but by reason of the defilments upon its face it is like an actor a plays a variety of parts, among which a mutual fuctioning takes place and the mind-system arises. The principle of intellection becomes divided and mind, the fuctions of mind, the evil out-flowings of mind, take on individuation. The sevenfold gradation of mind appcars: namely, intuitive self-realisation, thinking-desiring-discriminating, seeing, hearing, tasting, smelling, touching, and all their interactions and reactions take their rise.

The discriminating-mind is the cause of the sense-minds and is their support and with them is kept fuctioning as it describes and becomes attached to a world of objects, and then, by means of its habit-energy, it defiles the face of Universal Mind. Thus Universal Mind becomes the storage and clearing house of all the accumulated products of mentation and action since beginningless time.

Between Universal Mind and the individual discriminating-mind is the intuitive-mind (manas) which is dependent upon Universal Mind for its cause and support and enters into relation with both. It partakes of the universality of Universal Mind, shares its purity, and like it, is above form and momentariness. It is through the intuitive-mind that the good non out-flowing emerge, are manifested and are realised. Fortunate it is that intuition is not momentary for if the enlightenment which comes by intuition were momentary the wise would loose their "wiseness" which the do not. But the intuitive-mind enters into relations with the lower mind-system, shares its experiences and reflects upon its activities.

Intuitive-mind is one with Universal Mind by reason of its participation in Transcendendal Intelligence (Arya-jnana), and is one with the mind-system by its comprehension of differentiated knowledge (vijnana). Intuitive-mind has no body of its own nor any marks by which it can be differentiated. Universal Mind is its cause and support but it is evolved along with the notion of an ego and what belongs to it, to which it clings and upon which it reflects. Through intuitive-mind, by the faculty of intuition which is a mingling of both indentity and percieving, the inconceivable wisdom of Universal Mind is revealed and made realisable. Like Universal Mind it can not be the source of error.

Then said Mahamati to the Blessed Lord: Pray tell us, Blessed Lord, what is meant by the cessation of the mind-system?

The Blessed Lord replied: The five sense-fuctions and their discriminating and thinking fuction have their risings and complete ending from moment to moment. They are born with discrimination as cause, with form and appearance and objectivity closely linked together as condition. The will-to-live is the mother, ignorance is the father. By setting up names and forms greed is multiplied and thus the mind goes on mutually conditioning and being conditioned. By becoming attached to names and forms, not realising that they have no more basis than the activities of the mind itself, error rises, false-imagination as to pleasure and pain rises, and the way to emancipation is blocked. The lower system of sense-minds and the discriminating-mind do not really suffer pleasure and pain – they only imagine they do. Pleasrue and pain are the deceptive reactions of mortal-mind as it grasps an imaginary objective world.

There are two ways in which the ceasing of the mind-system may take place: as regards form, and as regards continuation. The sense-organs fuction as regards form by the interaction of form, contact and grasping; and they cease to fuction when this contact is broken. As regards continuation,- when these interactions of form, contact and grasping cease, there is no more continuation of the seeing, hearing and other sense fuctions; with the ceasing of these sense fuctions, the discriminations, graspings and attachments of the discriminating-mind cease; and with their ceasing act and eed and they habit-energy cease, and there is no more accumulation of karma-defilment on the face of Universal Mind.

If the evolving mortal-mind were of the same nature as Universal Mind the cessation of the lower mind-system would mean the cessation of Universal Mind, but they are different for Universal Mind is not the cause of mortal-mind. There is no cessation of Universal Mind in its pure and essence-nature. What ceases to fuction is not Universal Mind in its essence-nature, but is the cessation of the effect-producing defilments upon its face that have been caused by the accumulation of the habit-energy of the activities of the discriminating and thinking mortal-mind. There is no cessation of Divine Mind which, in itself, is the abode of Reality and the Womb of Truth.

By the cessation of the sense-minds is meant, not the cessation of their percieving fuctions, but the cessation of their discriminating and naming activities which are centralised in the discriminating mortal-mind. By the cessation of the mind-system as a whole is meant, the cessation of discrimination, the clearing away of the various attachments, and, therefore, the clearing away of the defilments of habit-energy in the face of Universal Mind which have been accumulating since beginningless time by reason of these discriminations, attachments, erroneous reasonings, and following acts. The cessation of the continuation aspect of the mind-system, namely, the discriminating mortal-mind the entire world of maya and desire disappears. Getting rid of the discriminating mortal-mind is Nirvana.

But the cessation of the discriminating-mind can not take place until there has been a "turning-about" in the deepest seat of consciousness. The mental habit of looking outward by the discriminating-mind upon an external objective world must be given up, and a new habit of realising Truth within the intuitive-mind by becoming one with the Truth itself must be established. Until this intuitive self-realisation of Noble Wisdom is attained. The evolving mind-system will go on. But when an insight into the five Dharmas, the three self-natures, and the twofold egolessness is attained, then the way will be opened for this "turning-about" to take place. With the ending of pleasure and pain, of conflicting ideas, of the disturbing interests of egoism, a state of tranqulisation will be attained in which the truths of emancipation will be fully understood and there will be no further evil out-flowings of the mind-system to interfere with the perfect self-realisation of Noble Wisdom.

Chapter VI: The Transcendence of Intelligence

Then said Mahamati: Pray tell us, Blessed Lord, what constitutes Transcendental Intelligence?

The Blessed Lord replied: Transcendental Intelligence is the inner state of self-realisation of Noble Wisdom. It is realised suddenly and intuitively as the "turning-about" takes place in the deepest seat of consciousness; it neither enters nor goes out – it is like the moon seen in water. Transcendental Intelligence is not subject to birth nor destruction; it has nothing to do with combination nor concordance; it is devoid of attachment and accumulation; it transcends all dualistic concepts.

When Transcendental Intelligence is considered, four things must be kept in mind: words, meanings, teachings and Noble Wisdom (Arya-prajna). Words are employed to express meanings but they are dependent upon discriminations and memory as cause, and upon the employment of sounds and letters by which a mutual transference of meaning is possible. Words are only symbols and may and may not clearly and fully express the meaning intended and, moreover, words may be understood quite differently from what was intended by the speaker. Words are neither different nor not different from meaning and meaning stands in the same relation to words.

If meaning is different from words it could not be made manifest by means of words; but meaning is illumined by words as things are by a lamp. Words are just like a man carrying a lamp to look for his property, by which he can say: this is my property. Just so, by means of words and speech originating in discrimination, the Bodhisattva can enter into the meaning of the teachings of the Tathagatas and through the meaning he can enter the exalted state of self-realisation of Noble Wisdom, which, in itself, is free from word discrimination. But if a man becomes attached to the literal meaning of words and holds fast to the illusion that words and meaning are in agreement, especially such things as Nirvana which is un-born and un-dying, or as to distinctions of the Vehicles, the five Dharmas, the three self-natures, the he will fail to understand the true meaning and will become entangled in claims and refutations. Just as varieties of objects are seen and discriminated in dreams and in visions, so ideas and statements are discriminated erroneously and error goes on multiplying.

The ignorant and simple-minded declare that meaning is not otherwise than words, that as words are, so is meaning. They think that as meaning has no body of its own that it cannot be different from words and, therefore, declare meaning to be indentical to words. In this they are ignorant of the nature of words, which are subject to birth and death, whereas meaning is not; words are dependent upon letters and meaning is not; meaning is apart from existence and non-existence, it has no substratum, it is un-born. The Tathagatas do not teach a Dharma that is dependent upon letters. Anyone who teaches a doctrine that is dependent upon letters and words is a mere prattler, because Truth is beyond letters and words and books.

This does not mean that letters and books never declare what is in conformity with meaning and truth, but it means that words and books are dependent upon discriminations, while meaning and truth are not; moreover, words and books are subject to the interpretation of individual minds, while meaning and truth are not. But if Truth is not expressed in words and books, the scriptures which contains the meaning of Truth would disappear, and when the scriptures there will be no more disciples and masters and Bodhisattvas and Buddhas, and there will ne nothing to teach. But no one must become attached to the words of the scriptures because even the canonical texts sometimes deviate from their straightfoward course owing to the imperfect fuctioning of sentient minds. Religious discourses are given by myself and other Tathagatas in response to the varying needs and faiths of all manner of being, in order to free them from dependance upon the thinking fuction of the mind-system, but they are not given to take the place of self-realisation of Noble Wisdom. When there is recognition that there is nothing in the world but what is seen of the mind itself, all dualistic discriminations will be discarded and the truth of imagelessness will be understood, and will be seen to be in conformity with the meaning rather than with words and letters.

The ignorant and simple-minded being fascinated with their self-imaginations and erroneous reasonings, keep on dancing and leap about, but are unable to understand the discourse by words about the truth of self-realisation, much less are they able to understand the Truth itself. Clinging to the external world, they cling to the study of books which are a means only, and do not know properly how to ascertain the truth of self-realisation, which is Truth unspoiled by the four propositions. Self-realisation is an exalted state of inner attainment which transcends all dualistic thinking and which is above the mind-system with its logic, reasoning, theorising, and illustrations. The Tathagatas discourse to the ignorant, but sustain Bodhisattvas as they seek self-realisation of Noble Wisdom.

Therefore, let every disciple take good heed not to become attached to words as being in perfect conformity with meaning, because Truth is not in the letters. When a man with his finger-tip points to something to somebody, the finger-tip may be mistaken for the thing pointed at; in the like manner the ignorant and simple-minded, like children, are unable even to the day of their death to abandon the idea that the finger-tip of words where there is meaning itself. They cannot realise Ultimate Reality because of their intent clinging to words where intended to be no more than a pointing finger. Words and their discrimination bind one to the dreary round of rebirths into the world of birth-and-death.; meaning stands alone and is a guide to Nirvana. Meaning is attained by much learning, and much learning is attained by becoming conversant with the meaning and not with words; therefore, let seekers for truth reverently apporach those who are wise and avoid the sticklers for particular words.

As for teachings: there are priests and popular preachers who are given to ritual and ceremony and who are skilled in the various incantations and in the art of eloquence; they should not be honored nor reverently attended upon, for what one gains from them is emotional excitement and worldly enjoyment; it is not the Dharma. Such preachers, by their clever manipulation of words and phrases and various reasonings and incantations, being the mere prattle of a child, as far as one can make out and not at all in accordance with truth nor in unision with meaning, only serves to awaken sentient and emotion, while it stupefies the mind. As he himself does not understand the meaning of all things, he only confuses the minds of his hearers with his dualistic views. Not understanding himself, that there is nothing but what is seen of the mind, and himself attached to the notion of self-nature in external things, and unable to know one path from another, he has no deliverance to offer others. Thus these priests and popular preachers who are clever in various incantations and skilled in the art of eloquence, themselves never being emancipated from such calamities as birth, old age, disease, sorrow, lamentation, pain and despair, lead the ignorant to bewilderment by means of their various words, phrases, examples, and conclusions.

Then there are the materialistic philosophers. No respect nor service is to be shown to them because their teaching, though they may be explained using hundred of thousands of words and phrases, do not go beyond the concerns of this world and this body and in the end they lead to suffering. As the materialistic recognise no truth existing by itself, they are split up into many schools, each which clings to its own way of reasoning.

But there is that which does not belong to materialism and which is not reached by the knowledge of the philosophers who cling to false-imaginations and erroneous reasonings because they fail to see that, fundamentally, there is no reality in external objects. When it is recognised that there is nothing beyond what is seen of the mind itself, the discrimination of being and non-being ceases and, as there is thus no external world of object of perception, nothing remains but the solitude of Reality. This does not belong to the materialistic philosophers, it is the domain of the Tathagatas. If such things are imagined as the comming and going of the mind-system, vanishing and appearing, solicitation, attachment, intenses affection, a philosphic hypothesis, a theory, an abode, a sense-concept, atomic attraction, organism, growth, thirst, grasping,- these things belong to materialism, they are not mine.

These are things that are the object of worldly interest, to be sensed, handled and tasted; these are the things that appear in the elements that make up the aggregates of personality where, owing to the procreative force of lust, there arise all kinds of disaster, birth, sorrow, lamentation, pain, despair, disease, old age, death. All these things concerns worldly interests and enjoyment; they lie along the path of the philosophers, which is not the path of the Dharma. When true egolessness of things and persons is understood , discrimination ceases to assert itself; the lower mind-system ceases to fuction; the various Bodhisattva stages are followed one after another; the Bodhisattva is able to utter his ten inexhaustible vows and is anointed by all the Buddhas. The Bodhisattva becomes master of himself and of all things by virtue of a life of spontaneous and radiant effortlessness. Thus the Dharma, which is Transcendental Intelligence, transcends all discriminations, all false-reasonings, all philosophical systems, all dualism.

Then Mahamati said to the Blessed Lord: In the Scriptures mention is made of the Womb of Tathagatahood and it is taught that that which is born of it is by nature bright and pure, originally unspotted and endowed with the thirty-two marks of excellence. As it is described it is a precious gem but wrapped in a dirty garment soiled by greed, anger, folly and false-imagination. We are taught that this Buddha-nature immanent in everyone is eternal, unchanging, auspicious. It is not this which is born of the Womb of Tathagatahood the same as the soul-substance that is taught by the philosophers? The Divine Atman as taught by them is also claimed to be eternal, inscrutable, unchanging, imperishable. It there, or is there not a difference?

The Blessed Lord replied: No, Mahamati, my Womb of Tathagatahood is not the same as the Divine Atman as taught by the philosophers. What i teach is Tathagatahod in the sense of Dharmakaya, Ultimate Oneness, Nirvana, emptiness, unbornness, unqualifiedness, devoid of will-effort. The reason why I teach the doctrine of Tathagatahood is to cause the ignorant and simple-minded to lay aside their fears as they listen to the teaching of egolessness and come to understand the state of non-discrimination and imagelessness. The religious teaching of the Tathagatas are just like a potter making various vessels by his own skill of hand with the aid of rob, water and thread, out of the one mass of clay, so the Tathagatas by their command of skillful means issuing from Noble Wisdom, by various terms, expressions, and symbols, preach the twofold egolessness in order to remove the last trace of discrimination that is preventing disciples from attaining a self-realisation of Noble Wisdom. The doctrine of the Tathagata-womb is disclosed in order to awaken philosphers from their clinging to the notion of a Divine Atman as a transcendental personality, so that their minds that have become attached to the imaginary notion of a "soul" as being something self-existing, may be quickly awakened to a state of perfect enlightement. All such notions as causation, succesion, atoms, primary elements, that make up personality, personal soul, Supreme Spirit, Sovereing God, Creator, are all figments of the imagination and manifestations of mind. No, Mahamati, the Tathagata's doctrine of the Womb of Tathagatahood is not the same as the philosopher's Atman.

The Bodhisattva is said to have well grasped the teaching of the Tathagatas when, all alone in a lonely place, by means of his Transcendental Intelligence, he walks the path leading to Nirvana. Thereon his mind will unfold by percieving, thinking, meditating, and, abiding in the practise of concentration until he attains the "turning-about" at the source of habit-energy, he will thereafter lead a life of excellent deeds. His mind concentrated on the state of Buddhahood, he will become thoroughly conversant with the noble truth of self-realisation; he will become perfect master of his own mind; he will be like a gem radiating many colors; he will be able to assume bodies of transformation; he will be able to enter into the minds of all to help them; and; finally, by gradually ascending the stages he will become established in the perfect Transcendental Intelligence of the Tathagatas.

Nevertheless, Transcendental Intelligence (Arya-jnana) is not Noble Wisdom (Arya-prajna) itself; only an intuitive awareness of it. Noble Wisdom is a perfect state of imagelessness; it is the Womb of "Suchness"; it is the all-conserving Divine Mind (Alaya-vijnana) which in its pure Essence forever abides in perfect patience and undisturbed tranquility.

Chapter VII: Self Realisation

Then said Mahamati: Pray tell us, Blessed Lord, what is the nature of Self-realisation by reason of which we shall be able to attain Transcendental Intelligence?

The Blessed Lord Replied: Transcendental Intelligence rises when the intellectual-mind reaches its limit and, if things are to be realised in their true and essence nature, its processes of mentation, which are based on particularised ideas, discriminations and judgements, must be transcended by an appeal to some higher faculty of cognition, if there be such a higher faculty. There is such a faculty in the intuitive-mind (Manas), which as we have seen is the link between the intellectual-mind and Universal Mind. While it is not an individualised organ like the intellectual-mind, it has that which is much better,- direct dependence upon Universal Mind. While intuition does not give information that can be analysed and discriminated, it gives that which is far superior,- self-realisation through indentification.

Mahamati then asked the Blessed Lord, saying: Pray tell us, Blessed Lord, what clear understandings an earnest disciple should have if he is to be successful in the discipline that leads to self-realisation?

The Blessed Lord replied: There are four things by the fulfilling of which an earnest disciple may gain self-realisation of Noble Wisdom and become and Bodhisattva-Mahasattva: First, he must have a clear understanding that all things are only manifestations of mind itself; second, he must discard the notion of birth, abiding and disappearance; third, he must clearly understand the egolessnes of both things and persons; and fourth, he must have a true conception of what constitutes self-realisation of Noble Wisdom. Provided with these four understandings, earnest disciples may become Bodhisattvas and attain Transcendental Intelligence.

As to the first; he must recognise and be fully convinced that this triple world is nothing but a complex manifestation of one's mental activities; that is devoid of selfness and its belongings; that there are no striving, no commings, no goings. He must recognise and accept the fact that this trple world is manifested and imagined as real only under the influence of habit-energy that has been accumulated since beginningless past by reason of memory, false-imagination, false-reasoning, and attachments to the multiplicities of objects and reactions in close relationship and in conformity to ideas of body-property-and-abode.

As the to second; hemust recognise and be convinced that all things are to be regarded as forms seen in a vision and a dream, empty of substance, un-born and without self-nature; that all things exist only by reason of a complicated network of causation which owes its rise to the discrimination and attachment and which eventuates in the rise of the mind-system and its belongings and evolvements.

As to the third; he must recognise and patiently accept the fact that his own mind and personality is also mind-constructed, that it is empty of substance, unborn and egoless. With these three things clearly in mind, the Bodhisattva will be able to enter into the truth of imagelessness.

As to the fourth; he must have a true conception of what constitutes self-realisation of Noble Wisdom. First, it is not comparable to the perceptions attained by the sense-mind, and neither is comparable to the cognition of the discriminating and intellectual-mind. Both of these presuppose a difference between self and not-self and the knowledge so attained is characterised by individuality and generality. Self-realisation is based on identity and oneness; there is nothing to be discriminated nor predicated concerning it. But to enter into it the Bodhisattva must be free from all presuppositions and attachments to things, ideas and selfness.

Then said Mahamati to the Blessed Lord: Prey tell us, Blessed Lord, concerning the characteristics of deep attachments to existence and as to how we may become detached from existence?

The Blessed Lord replied: When one tries to understand the significance of things by means of words and discriminations, there follow immeasurably deep-seated attachments to existence. For instance: there are the deep-seated attachments to signs of individuality, to causation, to the notion of being and non-being, to the discrimination of birth and death, of doing and of not-doing, to the habit of discrimination itself upon which philosophers are so dependent.

There are three attachments that are especially deep-seated in the minds of all: greed, anger and infatuation, which are based on lust, fear and pride. Back to these lies discrimination and desire which is procreative and is accompanied with excitement and avariciousness and love of comfort and desire for eternal life; and, following, is a succesion of rebirths on the five paths of existence and a continuation of attachments. But if these attachments are broken off, no signs of attachment nor of detachment will remain because they are based on things that are non-existent; when this truth is clearly understood the net of attachment is cleared away.

But depending upon and attaching itself to to the triple combination which works in unision there is the rising and the continuation of the mind-system incessantly fuctioning, and because of it there is the deep-felt and continuous assertion of the will-to-live. When the triple combination that causes the fuctioning of the mind-system ceases to exist, there is the triple emancipation and there is no further rising of any combination. When the existence and the non-existence of the external world are recognised as rising from the mind itself, then the Bodhisattva is prepared to enter into the state of imagelessness and therein to see into the emptiness which characterises all discrimination and all the deep-seated attachments resulting therefrom. Therein he will see no signs of deep-rooted attachment nor detachment; therein he will see no one in bondage and no one in emancipation, expect those who themselves cherish bondange and emancipation, because in all things there is no "substance" to be taken hold of.

But so long as these discriminations are cherished by the ignorant and simple-minded they go on attaching themselves to them and, like the silkworms, go on spinning their thread of discrimination and enwrapping themselves and others, and are charmed with their poison. But to the wise there are no signs of attachment nor of detachment; all things are seen as abiding in solitude where there is no evolving of discrimination. Mahamati, when you and other Bodhisattvas understand well the distinction between attachment and detachment, you will be in possesion of skillful means for avoiding becoming attached to words according to which one proceeds to grasp meanings. Free from the domination of words you will be able to establish yourselves where there will be a "turning-about" in the deepst seat of consciousness by means of which you will attain self-realisation of Noble Wisdom and be able to enter into all the Buddha-lands and assemblies. There you will be stamped with the stamp of powers, self-command, the psychic faculties, and will be endowed with the wisdom and the power of the ten inexhaustible vows, and will become radiant with the variegated rays of the Transformation Bodies. Therewith you will shine without effort like the moon, the sun, the magic wishing-jewel, and at every stage will view things as being of perfect oneness with yourself, uncontaminated by any self-consciousness. Seeing that all things are like a dream, you will be able to enter into the stage of the Tathagatas and be able to deliver discourses on the Dharma to the world of beings in accordance with their needs and be able to free them from all dualistic notions and false discriminations.

Mahamati, there are two ways of considering self-realisation: namely, the teachings about it, and the realisation itself. The teachings as variously given in the nine divisions of the doctrinal works, for the instructions of those who are inclined toward it, by making use of skillful means and expedients, are intended to awaken in all beings a true perception of the Dharma. The teachings are designed to keep one away from all dualistic notions of being and non-being and oneness and otherness.

Realisation itself is within the inner consciousness. It is an inner experience that has no connection with the lower mind-system and its discriminations of words, ideas and philosophical speculations. It shines out with its own clear light to reveal the error and foolishness of mind-constructed teachings, to render impotent evil influences from without, and to guide one unerringly to the realm of the good non-outflowings. Mahamati, when the earnest diciple and Bodhisattva is provided with these requirements, the way is open to his perfect attainment of self-realisation of Noble Wisdom, and to the full enjoyment of the fruits that arise therefrom.

Then Mahamati asked the Blessed Lord, saying: Pray tell us, Blessed Lord, about the One Vehicle which the Blessed Lord has said characterises the attainment of the inner self-realisation of Noble Wisdom?

The Blessed Lord replied: In order to discard some easily discriminations and erroneous reasonings, the Bodhisattva should retire by himself to a quiet, secluded place where he may reflect within himself without relying on anyone else, and there let him exert himself to make successive advances advances along the stages; this solitude is the characteristic feature of the inner attainment of self-realisation of Noble Wisdom.

I call this the One Vehicle, not because it is the One Vehicle, but because it is onlyin solitude that one is able to recognise and realise the path of the One Vehicle. So long as the mind is distracted and is making conscious effort, there can be no culmination as regards the various vehicles; it is only when the mind is alone and quiet that it is able to forsake the discriminations of the external world and seek realisation of an inner realm where there is neither vehicle nor one who rides in it. I speak of the three vehicles in order to carry the ignorant. I do not speak much about the One Vehicle because there is no way by which earnest disciples and masters can realise Nirvana, unaided. According to the discourses of the Tathagatas earnest disciples should be segregated and disciplined and trained in meditation and dhyana whereby they are aided by many devices and expedients to realise emancipation. It is because earnest disciples and masters have not fully destroyed the habit-energy of karma and the hindrances of discriminative knowledge and human passion that they are often unable to accept the twofold egolessness and the inconceivable transformation death, that I preach the triple vehicle and not the One Vehicle. When earnest disciples have gottan rid of all their evil habit-energy and been able to realise the twofold egolessness, then they will not be intoxicated by the bliss of the Samadhis and will be awakened into the super-realm of the good non-outflowings. Being awakened into the realm of the good non-outflowings, they will be able to gather up all the requisities for the attainment of Noble Wisdom which is beyond conception and is of sovereing power. Bu really, Mahamati, there are no vehicles, and so i speak of the One Vehicle. Mahamati, the full recognition of the One Vehicle has never been attained by either earnest disciples, masters, or even by the great Brahma; it has been attained only by the Tathagatas themselves. That is the reason that it is known as the One Vehicle. I do not speak much about it because there is no way by which earnest disciples can realise Nirvana unaided.

Then Mahamati asked the Blessed Lord, saying: What are the steps that will lead an awakened disciple toward the self-realisation of Noble Wisdom?

The Blessed Lord replied: The beginning lies in the recognition that the external world is only a manifestation of the activities of the mind itself, and that the mind grasps it as an external world simply because of its habit of discrimination and false-reasoning. The disciple musy get into the habit of looking at things truthfully. He must recognise the fact that the world has no self nature, that it is un-born, that it is like a passing cloud, like an imaginary wheel made by a revolving firebrand, like the castle of the Gandharvas, like the moon reflected in the ocean, like a vision, a mirage, a dream. He must come to understand that mind in its essence-nature has nothing to do with discrimination nor causation; he must not listen to discourses based on the imaginary terms and qualifications; he must understand that Universal Mind in its pure essence is a state of imagelessness, that it is only because of the accumulated defilments on its face that body-property-and-abode appear to be its manifestations, that in its own pure nature it is unaffected and unaffecting by such changes as rising, abiding and destruction; he must fully understand that all these things come with the awakening of the notion of an ego-soul and its conscious mind. Therefore, Mahamati, let those disciples who wish to realise Noble Wisdom by following the Tathagata Vehicle desist from all discrimination and erroneous reasoning about personality and its sense-world or about such ideas as causation, rising, abiding and destruction, and exercise themselves in the discipline of dhyana that leads to the realisation of Noble Wisdom.

To practice dhyana, the earnest disciple should retire to a quiet and solitary place, remembering that life-long habits of discriminative thinking cannot be broken off easily nor quickly. There are four kinds of concentrative meditation (dhyana): The dhyana practiced by the ignorant; the dhyana devoted to the examination of meaning; the dhyana with "suchness" (tathata) for its object; and the dhyana of the Tathagatas.

The dhyana practiced by the ignorant is the one resorted to by those who are following the example of the disciples and masters but who do not understand its purpose and, therefore, it becomes "still-sitting" with vacant minds. This dhyana is practiced, also, by those who, despising the body, see it as a shadow and a skeleton full of suffering and impurity, and yet who cling to the notion of an ego, seek to attain emancipation by the mere cessation of thought.

The dhyana devoted to the examination of meaning, is the one practised by those who, perceiving the untenability of such ideas as self, other and both, which are held by the philosophers, and who have passed beyond the twofold-egolessness, devote dhyana to an examnitation of the significance of egolessness and the differentiations of the Bodhisattvas stages.

The dhyana with Tathata, or "Suchness", or Oneness, or Divine Name, for its object is practised by those earnest disciples and masters who, while fully recognising the twofold egolessness and the imagelessness of Tathata, yet cling to the notion of ultimate Tathata.

The dhyana of the Tathagatas is the dhyana of those who are entering upon the stage of Tathagatahood and who, abiding in the triple bliss which characterises the self-realisation of Noble Wisdom, are devoting themselves for the sake of all beings to the accomplishment of incomprehensible works for their emancipation. This is the pure dhyana of the Tathagatas. Whe all lesser things and ideas are transcended and forgotten, and there remains only a perfect state of imagelessness where Tathagata and Tathata are merged into perfect Oneness, then the Buddhas will come together from all their Buddha-lands and with shining hands resting on his forhead will welcome a new Tathagata.

Chapter VIII: Attaining Self Realisation

Then said Mahamati to the Blessed Lord: Pray tell us more as to what constitutes the state of self-realisation?

The Blessed Lord replied: In the life of an earnest disciple there are two aspects that are to be distinguished: namely, the state of attachment to the self-natures arising from discrimination of himself and his field of consciousness to which he is related; and second, the excellent and exalted state of self-realisation of Noble Wisdom. The state of attachment to the discriminations of the self-natures of things, ideas and selfhood is accompanied by emotions of pleasure or aversion according to experience or as laid down in books of logic. Conforming himself to the egolessness of things and holding back wrong views as to his egoness, he should abandon these thoughts and hold himself firmly to the continuously ascending journey of the stages.

The exalted state of self-realisation as it relates to an earnest disciple is a state of mental concentration in which he seeks to indentify himself with Noble Wisdom. In that effort he must seek to annihilate all vagrant thoughts and notions belonging to the externality of things, and all ideas of individuality and generality, of suffering and impermanence, and cultivate the noblest ideas of egolessness and emptiness and imagelessness; thus will he attain a realisation of truth that is free from passion and is ever serene. When this active effort at mental concentration is succesful it is followed by a more passive, receptive state of Samadhi in which the earnest disciple will enter into the blissful abode of Noble Wisdom and experience its consumations in the transformations of Samapatti. This is an earnest disciple's first experience of the exalted state of realisation, but as yet there is no discarding of habit-energy nor escaping from the transformation of death.

Having attained this exalted and blissful state of realisation as far as it can be attained by disciples, the Bodhisattva must not give himself up to the enjoyment of its bliss, for that would mean cessation, but should think compassionately of other beings and keep ever fresh his original vows; he should never let himself rest nor exert himself in the bliss of the Samadhis.

But, Mahamati, as earnest disciples go on trying to advance on the path that leads to full realisation. There is one danger against which they must be on their guard. Disciples may not appreciate that the mind-system, because of its accumulated habit-energy, goes on fuctioning, more or less unconsciously, as long as they live. They may sometimes think that they can expedite the attainment of their goal of tranquilisation by entirely supressing the activities of the mind-system. This is a mistake, for even if the activities of the mind are supressed, the mind will still go on fuctioning because the seeds of habit-energy will still remain in it. What they think is extinction of mind, is really the non-fuctioning of the mind's external world to which they are no longer attached. That is, the goal if tranquilisation is to be reached not by supressing all mind activity but by getting rid of discriminations and attachments.

Then there are others who, afraid of the suffering incident to the discriminations of life and death, unwisely seek Nirvana. They have come to see that all things subject to discrimination have no reality and so imagine that Nirvana must consist in the annihilation of the senses and their fields of sensation; they do not appreciate that birth-and-death and Nirvana are not separate one from the other. They do not know that Nirvana is Universal Mind in its purity. Therefore, these stupid ones who cling to the notion that Nirvana is a world by itself that us outside what is seen of the mind, ignoring all the teachings of the Tathagatas concerning the external world, go on rolling themselves along the wheel of birth-and-death. But when they experiment the "turning-about" in their deepest consciousness which will bring with it the perfect self-realisation of Noble Wisdom, then they will understand.

The true functioning of the mind is very subtle and difficult to be understood by young disciples, even masters with all their powers of right-knowledge and Samadhis often find it baffling. It is only the Tathagatas and the Bodhisattvas who are firmly established on the seventh stage who can fully understand its workings. Those earnest disciples and masters who wish to fully understand all the aspects of the different stages of Bodhisattvahood by the aid of their right-knowledge must do so by becoming thoroughly conviced that objects of discrimination are only seen to be so by the mind and, thus, by keeping themselves away from all discriminations and false reasonings which are also of the mind itself, by ever seeking to see things truly (yathabhutam), and by planting roots of goodness in Buddha-lands that know no limits made by differentiations.

To do all this the Bodhisattva must keep himself away from all turmoil, social excitements and sleepiness; let him keep away from the treasies and writtings of worldly philosophers, and from the ritual and ceremonies of professional priestcraft. Let him retire to a secluded place in the forest and there devote himself to the practice of the various spiritual disciplines, because it is only by so doing that he will become capable of attaining in this world of multiplicities a true insight into the workings of Universal Mind in its Essence. There surrounded by his good friends the Buddhas, earnest disciples will become capable of understanding the significance of the mind-system and its place as a mediating agent between the external world and Universal Mind and he will become capable of crossing the ocean of birth-and-death which rises from ignorance, desire and deed.

Having gained a thorough understanding of the mind-system, the three self-natures, the twofold egolessness, and established himself in the measure of self-realisation that goes with that attainment, all of which may be gained by his right-knowledge, the way will be clear to the Bodhisattva's further advance along the stages of Bodhisattvahood. The disciple should then abandon the understanding of mind which he has gained by right-knowledge, which in comparison with Noble Wisdom is like a lame donkey, and entering on the eight stage of Bodhisattvahood, he should then disciple himself in Noble Wisdom according to its three aspects.

These aspects are: First, imagelessness which come forth when all things belonging to dicipleship, mastership, and philosophy are thoroughly mastered. Second, the power added by all the Buddhas by reason of their original vows including the identification of their lives and the sharing of their lives and the sharing of their merit with all sentient lives. Third, the perfect self-realisation that thus far has only been realised in a measure. As the Bodhisattva succeeds in detaching himself from viewing all things, including his own imagined egoness, in their phenomenality, and realises the states of Samadhi and Samapatti whereby he surveys the world as a vision and a dream, and being sustained by all the Buddhas, he will be able to pass on to the full attainment of the Tathagata stage, which is Noble Wisdom itself. This is the triplicity of the noble life and being furnished with this triplicity the perfect self-realisation of Noble Wisdom has been attained.

Then Mahamati asked the Blessed Lord, saying: Blessed Lord, is the purification of the evil out-flowings of the mind which come from clinging to the notions of an objective world and an empirical soul, gradual or instantaneous?

The Blessed Lord replied: There are three characteristic out-flows of the mind, namely, the evil out-flowings that rise from thirst, grasping and attachment; the evil out-flowings that arise from the illusions of the mind and the infatuations of egoism; and the good non-outflowings that arise from Noble Wisdom.

The evil out-flowings that take place from recognising an external world, which in truth is only a manifestation of mind, and from becoming attached to it, are gradually purified and not instantaneously. Good behavior can only come by the path of restraint and effort. It is like a potter making pots that is done gradually and with attention and effort. It is like the mastery of comedy, dancing, singing, lute-playing, writing, and any other art; it must be acquired gradually and laboriously. Its reward will be a clearing insight into the emptiness and transciensy of all things.

The evil out-flowings that arise from the illusions of the mind and the infatuations of egoism, concerns the mental life more directly and are such things as fear, anger, hatred and pride; these are purified by study and meditation and that, too, must be attained gradually and not instantaneously. It is like the amra fruit that ripens slowly; it is like grass, shrubs, herbs and trees that grow up from the earth gradually. Each must follow the path of study and meditation by himself gradually and with effort, but because of the original vows of the Bodhisattvas and all the Tathagatas who have devoted their merits and identified their lives with all animate life that all may be emancipated, they are not without aid and encouragement; but even with the aid of the Tathagatas, the purification of the evil out-flowings of the mind are at best slow and gradual, requiring both zeal and patience. Its reward is the gradual understanding of the twofold egolessness and its patience acceptance, and the feet well set on the stages of Bodhisattvahood.

But the good non-outflowings that come with the self-realisation of Noble Wisdom, is a purification that comes instantaneously by the grace of the Tathagatas. It is like a mirror reflecting all forms and images instantaneously and without discrimination; it is like the sun or moon revealing all forms instantaneously and illuminating them dispassionately with its light. In the same way the Tathagatas lead earnest disciples to a state of imagelessness; all the accumulations of habit-energy and karma that had been collecting since beginningless time because of attachment to erroneous views which have been entertained regarding an ego-soul and its external world, are cleansed away, revealing instantaneously the realm of Transcendental Intelligence that belongs to Buddhahood. Just as Universal Mind defiled by accumulations of habit-energy and karma reveals multiplicities of ego-souls and their external worlds of false-imagination, so Universal Mind cleared of its defilments through the gradual purifications of the evil out-flowings that come by effort, study and meditation, and by the gradual self-realisation of Noble Wisdom, at the long last, like the Dharmata Buddha shining forth spontaneously with the rays that issue from its pure Self-nature, shines forth instantaneously. By it the mentality of all Bodhisattvas is matured instantaneously: they find themselves in the palatial abodes of the Akanistha heavens, themselves spontaneously radiating the various treasures of its spiritual abundance.

Chapter IX: The Fruits of Self Realisation

Mahamati asked the Blessed Lord: Prey tell us, Blessed Lord, what is the fruitage that comes with the self-realisation of Noble Wisdom?

The Blessed Lord replied: First, there will come a clearing insight into the meaning and significance of things and following that will come an unfolding insight into the significance of spiritual ideals (Paramitas) by reason of which the Bodhisattva will be able to enter more deeply into the abode of imagelessness and be able to experience the higher Samadhis and gradually to pass through the higher stages of Bodhisattvahood.

After experiencing the "turning-about" in the deepest seat of consciousness, they will experience other Samadhis even to the highest, the Vajravimbopama, which belongs to the Tathagatas and their transformations. They will be able to enter into the realm of consciousness that lies beyond the consciousness of the mind-system, even the consciousness of Tathagatahood. They will become endowed with all the powers, psychic faculties, self-mastery, loving compassion, skillful means, and ability to enter into other Buddha-lands. Before they had attained self-realisation of Noble Wisdom they had been influenced by the self-interests of egoism, but after they attain self-realisation they will find themselves reacting spontaneously to the impulses of a great and compassionate heart endowed with skillful and boundless means and sincerely and wholly devoted to the emancipation of all beings.

Mahamati said: Blessed Lord, tell us about the sustaining power of the Tathagatas by which the Bodhisattvas are aided to attain self-realisation of Noble Wisdom?

The Blessed Lord replied: There are two kinds of sustaining power, which issue from the Tathagatas and are at the service of the Bodhisattvas, sustained by which the Bodhisattvas should prostrate themselves before them and show their appreciation by asking questions. The first kind of sustaining power is the Bodhisattva's own adoration and faith in the Buddhas by reason of which the Buddhas are able to manifest themselves and render their aid and to ordain them with their own hands. The second kind of sustaining power is the power radiating from the Tathagatas that enables the Bodhisattvas to attain and to pass through the various Samadhis and Samapattis without becoming intoxicated by their bliss.

Being sustained by the power of the Buddhas, the Bodhisattva even at the first stage will be able to attain the Samadhi known as the Light of Mahayana. In that Samadhi Bodhisattvas will become conscious of the presence of the Tathagatas comming from all their different abodes in the ten quarters to impart to the Bodhisattvas their sustaining power in various ways. As the Bodhisattva Vajragarbha was sustained in his Samadhis and as many other Bodhisattvas of like degree and virtue have been sustained, so all earnest disciples and masters and Bodhisattvas may experience this sustaining power of the Buddhas in their Samadhis and Samapattis. The disciple's faith and the Tathagata's merit are two aspects of the same sustaining power and by it alone are the Bodhisattvas enabled to become one with the company of the Buddhas.

Whatever Samadhis, psychic faculties and teachings are realised by the Bodhisattvas, they are made possible only by the sustaining power of the Buddhas; if it were otherwise, the ignorant and the simple-minded might attain the same fruitage. Wherever the Tathagatas enter with their sustaining power there will be music, not only music made by human lips and played by human hands on various instruments, but there will be music among the grass and shrubs and trees, and in the mountains and towns and palaces and hovels; much more will there be music in the heart of those endowed with sentiency. The deaf, dumb and blind will be cured of their deficiencies and will rejoice in their emancipation. Such is the extraordinary virtue of the sustaining power imparted by the Tathagatas.

By the bestowal of this sutaining power, the Bodhisattvas are enabled to avoid the evils of passion, hatred and enslaving karma; they are enabled to transcend the dhyana of the beginners and to advance beyond the experience and truth already attained; they are enabled to demostrate the Paramitas; and finally, to attain the stage of Tathagatahood. Mahamati, if it were not for this sustaining power, they would relapse into the ways and thoughts of the philosophers, easy-going disciples and the evil-minded, and would thus fall short of the highest attainement. For these reasons, earnest disciples and sincere Bodhisattvas are sustained by the power of all the Tathagatas.

Then said Mahamati: It has been said by the Blessed Lord that by fulfilling the six Paramitasm Buddhahood is realised. Pray tell us what the Paramitas are, and how they are to be fulfilled?

The Blessed Lord replied: The Paramitas are ideals of spiritual perfection that are to be the guide of the Bodhisattvas on the path to self-realisation. There are six of them but they are to be considered in three different ways according to the progress of the Bodhisattva on the stages. At first they are to be considered as ideals for the worldly life; next as ideals for the mental life; and, lastly, as ideals of the spiritual and unitive life.

In the worldly life where one is still holding tenaciously to the notions of an ego-soul and what concerns it and holding fast to the discriminations of dualism, if only for worldly benefits, one should cherish ideals of charity, good behavior, patience, zeal, thoughtfulness and wisdom. Even in the worldly life the practice of these virtues will bring rewards of happiness and success.

Much more in the mind-world of earnest disciples and masters will their practice bring joys of emancipation, enlightenment and peace of mind, because the Paramitas are grounded on right-knowledge and lead to thoughts of Nirvana, even if the Nirvana of their thoughts is for themselves. In the mind-world the Paramitas become more ideal and more sympathetic; charity can no longer be expressed in the giving of impersonal gifts but will call for the more costly gifts of sympathy and understanding; good behavior will call for something more than outward conformity to the five precepts because in the light of the Paramitas they must practise humilty, simplicity, restraint and self-giving. Patience will call for something more than forbearance with external circumstances and the temperaments of other people: it will now call for patience with one's self. Zeal will call for something more than industry and outward show of earnestness: it will call for more self-control in the task of following the Noble Path and in manifesting the Dharma in one's own life. Thoughtfulness will give way to mindfulness wherein discriminated meanings and logical deductions and rationalisations will give way to intuitions of significance and spirit. The Paramita of Wisdom (Prajna) will no longer be concerned with pragmatic wisdom and erudition, but will reveal itself in its true perfectness of All-inclusive Truth which is Love.

The third aspect of the Paramitas as seen in the ideal perfection of the Tathagatas can only be fully understood by the Bodhisattva-Mahasattvas who are devoted to the highest spiritual disciple and have fully understood that there is nothing to be seen in the world but that which issues from the mind itself; in whose minds the discrimination of dualities has ceased to fuction; and seizing and clinging has become non-existent. Thus free from all attachements to individual objects and ideas, their minds are free to consider ways of benefiting and giving happiness to others, even to all sentient beings. To the Bodhisattva-Mahasattvas the ideal of charity is shown in the self-yielding of the Tathagata's hope of Nirvana that all may enjoy it together. While having relations with an objective world there is no rising in the minds of the Tathagatas of discriminations between the interests of self and the interests of others, between good and evil,- there is just the spontaneity and effortless actuality of perfect behavior. To practise patience with full knowledge of this and that, of grasp and grasping, but with no thought of discrimination nor of attachment,- that is the Tathagatas Paramita of Patience. To exert oneself with energy from the first part of the night to its end in conformity with the disciplinary measures with no rising of discrimination as to comfort or discomfort,- that is the Tathagata's Paramita of Zeal. Not to discriminate between self and others in thoughts of Nirvana, but to keep the mind fixed on Nirvana,- that is the Paramita of Mindfulness. As to the Prajna-Paramita, which is Noble Wisdom, who can predicate it? When in Samadhi the mind ceases to discriminate and there is only perfect and love-filled imagelessness, then an inscrutable "turning-about" will take place in the inmost consciousness and one will have attained self-realisation of Noble Wisdom,- that is the highest Prajna-Paramita.

Then Mahamati said to the Blessed Lord: You have spoken of an astral-body, a "mind-vision-body" (manomayakaya) which the Bodhisattvas are able to assume, as being one of the fruits of self-realisation of Noble Wisdom: pray tell us, Blessed Lord, what is meant by such transcendental body?

The Blessed Lord replied: There are three kinds of such transcendental bodies: First, there is one in which the Bodhisattva attains enjoyment of the Samadhis and Samapattis. Second, there is the one which is assumed by the Tathagatas according to the class of beings to be sustained, and which achieves and perfects spontaneously with no attachment and no effort. Third, there is the one in which the Tathagatas receive their intuition of Dharmakaya.

The transcendental personality that enters into the enjoyment of the Samadhis comes with the third, fourth and fifth stages as the mentations of the mind-system become quieted and waves of consciouness are no more stirred on the face of Universal Mind. In this state, the conscious-mind is still aware, in a measure, of the bliss being experienced by this cessation of the mind's activities.

The second kind of transcendental personality is the kind assumed by Bodhisattvas and Tathagatas as bodies of transformation by which they demostrate their original vows in the work of achieving and perfecting; it comes with the eighth stage of Bodhisattvahood. When the Bodhisattva has a thorough-going penetration into the maya-like nature of things and understands the dharma of imagelessness, he will experience the "turning-about" in his deepest consciousness and will become able to experience the higher Samadhis even to the highest. By entering into these exalted Samadhis he attains a personality that transcends the conscious-mind, by reason of which he obtains supernatural powers of self-mastery and activities because of which he is able to move as he wishes, as quickly as a dream changes as quickly as an image changes in a mirror.

This transcendental body is not a product of the elements and yet there is something in it that is analogous to what is so produced; it is furnished with all the differences appertaining to the world of form but without their limitations; possessed of this "mind-vision-body" he is able to be present in all the assemblages in all the Buddha-lands. Just as his thoughts move instantly and without hindrance over walls and rivers and trees and mountains, and just as in memory he recalls and visits the scenes of his past experiences, so, while his mind keeps fuctioning in the body, his thoughts may be a hundred thousand yojanas away. In the same fashion the trasncendental personality that experiences the Samadhi Vajravimbopama will be endowed with supernatural powers and psychic faculties and self-mastery by reason of which he will be able to follow the noble paths that lead to the assemblages of the Buddhas, moving about as freely as he may wish. But his wishes will no longer be self-centered nor tainted by discrimination and attachment, for this transcendental personality is not his old body, but is the transcendental embodiment of his original vows of self-yielding in order to bring all beings to maturity.

The third kind of transcendental personality is so ineffable that it is able to attain intuitions of the Dharmakaya, that is, it attains intuitions of the boundless and inscrutable cognition of Universal Mind. As Bodhisattva-Mahasattvas attain the highest of the stages and become conversant with all the treasures to be realised in Noble Wisdom, they will attain this inconceivable transformation-body which is the true nature of all the Tathagatas past, present and future, and will participate in the blissful peace which pervades the Dharma of all the Buddhas.

Chapter X: Discipleship - Lineage of the Arhats

Then Mahamati asked the Blessed Lord: Prey tell us how many kinds of disciples there are?

The Blessed Lord replied: There are as many kinds of disciples as there are individuals, but for convenience they may be divided into two groups: disciples of the lineage of the Arhats, and disciples known as Bodhisattvas. Disciples of the lineage of the Arhats may be considered under two aspects: First, according to the number of times they will return to this life of birth-and-death; and second, according to their spiritual progress. Under the first aspect, they may be subdivided into three groups: The "Stream-entered," the "Once-returning," and the "Never-returning."

The Stream-entered are those disciples, who having freed themselves from the attachments to the lower discriminations and who have cleansed themselves from the twofold hindrances and who clearly understand the meaning of the twofold egolessness, yet who still cling to the notion of individuality and generality and to their own egoness. They will advance along the stages to the sixth only to succumb to the entrancing bliss of the Samadhis. They will be reborn seven times, or five times, or three times, before they will be able to pass the sixth stage. The Once-returning are the Arhats, and the Never-returning are the Bodhisattvas who have reached the seventh stage.

The reasons for these graduations is because of their attachment to the three degrees of false-imagination: namely, faith in moral practices, doubt, and the view of their individual personality. When this three hindrances are overcome, they will be able to attain the higher stages. As to moral practices: the ignorant, simple-minded disciples obey the rules of morality, piety and penance, because they desire thereby to gain worldly advancement and happiness, with the added hope of being reborn in more favorable conditions. The Stream-entered ones do not cling to moral practices for any hope of reward for their minds are fixed on the exalted state of self-realisation; the reason they devote themselves to the details of morality is that they wish to master such truths as are in conformity with the undefiled out-flowings.

As regards the hindrance of doubt in the Buddha's teaching, that will continue so long as any of the notions of discrimination are cherished and will disappear when they disappear. Attachment to the view of individual personality will be gotten rid of as the disciple gains a more thorough understanding of the notions of being and non-being, self-nature and egolessness, thereby getting rid of the attachments to his own selfness that goes with those discriminations. By breaking up and clearing away these three hindrances the Stream-entered one will be able to discard all greed, anger and folly.

As for the Once-returning Arhats; there was once in them the discrimination of form, signs, and appearances, but as they gradually learned by right-knowledge not to view individual objects under the aspect of quality and qualifying, and as they became acquainted with what marks the attainment of the practice of dhyana, they have reached the stage of enlightenment where in one more rebirth they will be able to put an end to the clinging to their own self-interests. Free from this burden of error and its attachments, the passions will no more assert themselves and the hindrances will be cleared away forever.

Under the second aspect disciples may be grouped according to the spiritual progress they have attained, into four classes, namely, disciples (sravaka), masters (pratyekabuddha), Arhats, and Bodhisattvas.

The first class of disciples mean well but they find it difficult to understand unfamiliar ideas. Their minds are joyful when studying about and practising the things belonging to appearances that can be discriminated, but they become confused by the notion of an uninterrupted chain of causation, and they become fearful when they consider the aggregates that make up personality and its object world as being maya-like, empty and egoless. They were able to advance to the fifth or sixth stage where they are able to do away with the rising of passions, but not with the notions that give rise to passion and, therefore, they are unable to get rid of the clinging to an ego-soul and its accompanying attachments, habits and habit-energy. In this same class the disciples are the earnest disciples of other faiths, who clinging to the notions of such things as, the soul as an external entity, Supreme Atman, Personal God, seek a that is in harmony with them. There are others, more materialistic in their ideas, who think that all things exist in dependance upon causation and, therefore, that Nirvana must be in like dependence. But none of these, earnest though they be, have gained an insight into the truth of the twofold egolessness and are, therefore, of limited spiritual insights as regards deliverance and non-deliverance; for them there is no emancipation. They have great self-confidence but they can never gain a true knowledge of Nirvana until they have learned to disciple themselves in the patient acceptance of the twofold egolessness.

The second class of masters are those who have gained a high degree of intellectual understanding of the truths concerning the aggregates that make up personality and its external world but who are filled with fear when they face the significance and consequences of these truths, and the demands which their learning makes upon them, that is, not to become attached to the external world and its manifold forms making for comfort and power, and to keep away from the entanglements of its social relations. They are attracted by the possibilities that are attainable by so doing, namely, the possesion of miraculous powers such as dividing the personality and appearning in different places at the same time, or manifesting bodies of transformation. To gain these powers they even resort to the solitary life, but this class of master never gets beyond the seductions of their learning and egoism, and their discourses are always in conformity with that characteristic and limitation.

Among them are many earnest disciples who show a degree of spiritual insight that is characterised by sincerity and undismayed willingness to meet all the demands that the stages make upon them. When they see that all that nakes up the objective world is only a manifestation of mind, that it is without self-nature, un-born and egoless, they accept it without fear, and when they see their own ego-soul is also empty, un-born and egoless, they are untroubled and undismayed, with earnest purpose they seek to adjust their lives to the full demands of these truths, but they cannot forget the notions that lie back of these facts, especially the notion of their own conscious ego-self and its relation to Nirvana. They are of the Stream-entered class.

The class known as Arhats are those earnest masters who belong to the returning class. But their spiritual insight they have reached the sixth and seventh stages. They have thoroughly understood the truth of the twofold egolessness and the imagelessness of Reality; with them there is no more discrimination, nor passions, nor pride of egoism; they have gained an exalted insight and seen into the immensity of the Buddha-lands. By attaining an inner perception of the true nature of Universal Mind they are steadily purifying their habit-energy. The Arhats has attained emancipation, enlightenment, the Dhyanas, the Samadhis, and his whole attention is given to the attainment of Nirvana, but the idea of Nirvana causes mental perturbations because he has the wrong idea of Nirvana. The notions of Nirvana in his mind is divided: he discriminated Nirvana from self, and self from others. He has attained some of the fruits of self-realisation but he still thinks and discourses on the Dhyanas, subjects for meditation, the Samadhis, the fruits. He pridefully says: "There are fetters, but I am disengaged from them." His is a double fault: he both denounces the vices of the ego, and still cling to its fetters. So long as he continues to discriminate notions of dhyana, dhyana practice, subjects fro dhyana, right-knowledge and truth, there is a bewildered state of mind,- he has not attained perfect emancipation. Emancipation comes with the acceptance of imagelessness.

He is master of the Dhyanas and enters into the Samadhis, but to reach the higher stages one must pass beyond the Dhyanas, the immeasurables, the world of no-form, and the bliss of the Samadhis into the Samapattis leading to the cessation of thought itself. The dhyana-practicer, dhyana, the subject of dhyana, the cessation of thought, once-returning, never-returning, all these are divided and bewildering states of mind. Not until all discrimination is abandoned is there perfect emancipation. Thus the Arhats, master of the dhyanas, participating in the Samadhis, but unsupported by the Buddhas yields to the entrancing bliss of the Samadhis – and passes to his Nirvana.

Disciples and masters and Arhats may ascend the stages up to the sixth. They perceive that the triple world is no more than mind itself; they perceive that there is no becoming attached to the multiciplicites of external objects except through the discriminations and activities of the mind itself; they perceive that there is no ego-soul; and, therefore, they attain a measure of tranquilisation. But their tranqulisation is not perfect every minute of their lives, for with them there is something effect-producing, some grasped and grasping, some lingering trace of dualism and egoism. Though disengaged from the habit-energy of passion and, becoming intoxicated with the wine of the Samadhis, they will have their abode in the realm of the out-flowings. Perfect tranqulisation is possible only with the seventh stage. So long as their minds are in confusion, they cannot attain to a clear conviction as to the cessation of all multiplicity and the actuality of the perfect oneness of all things. In their minds the self-nature of things is still discriminated as good and bad, therefore, their minds are in confusion and they cannot pass beyond the sixth stage. But at the sixth stage all discrimination ceases as they become engrossed in the bliss of the Samadhis wherein they cherish the thought of Nirvana and, as Nirvana is possible at the sixth stage, they pass into their Nirvana, but it is not the Nirvana of the Buddhas.

Chapter XI: The Stages of Bodhisattvahood

Then said Mahamati to the Blessed Lord: Will you tell us now about the disciples who are Bodhisattvas?

The Blessed Lord replied: The Bodhisattvas are those earnest disciples who are enlightened by reason of their efforts to attain self-realisation of Noble Wisdom and who have taken upon themselves the task of enlightening others. They have gained a clear understanding of the truth that all things are empty, un-born, and of a maya-like nature; they have ceased from viewing things discriminatively and from considering them in their relations; they thoroughly understand the truth of twofold egolessness and have adjusted themselves to it with patient acceptance; they have attained a definite realisation of imagelessness; and they are abiding in the perfect-knowledge that they have gained by self-realisation of Noble Wisdom.

Well stamped by the seal of "Suchness" they entered upon the first of the Bodhisattva stages. The first stage is called the stage of Joy (Pranudita). Entering this stage is like passing out of the glare of the shadows into a realm of "no-shadows"; it is like passing out of the noise and tumult of the crowded city into the quietness of solitude. The Bodhisattva feels within himself the awakening of a great heart of compassion and he utters his ten original vows: To honor and serve all Buddhas; to spread the knowledge and practice of the Dharma; to welcome all comming Buddhas; to practice the six Paramitas; to persuade all beings to embrace the Dharma; to attain a perfect understanding of the universe; to attain a perfect understanding of the mutuality of all beings; to attain perfect self-realisation of the oneness of all the Buddhas and Tathagatas in self-nature, purpose and resources; to become acquainted with all skillful means for the carrying out of these vows for the emancipation of all beings; to realise supreme enlightenment through the perfect self-realisation of Noble Wisdom, ascending the stages and entering Tathagatahood.

In the spirit of these vows the Bodhisattva gradually ascends the stages to the sixth. All earnest disciples, masters and Arhats have ascended thus far, but being enchanted by the bliss of the Samadhis and not being supported by the power of the Buddhas, they pass to their Nirvana. The same fate would befall the Bodhisattvas except for their sustaining power of the Buddhas, by that they are enabled to refuse to enter Nirvana until all beings can enter Nirvana with them. The Tathagatas point out to them the virtues of Buddhahood which are beyond the conception of the intellectual-mind, and they encourage and strengthen the Bodhisattvas not to give in to the enchantment of the bliss of the Samadhis, but to press on to further advancement along the stages. If the Bodhisattvas had entered Nirvana at this stage, and they would have done so without the sustaining power of the Buddhas, there would have been the cessation of all things and the familiy of the Tathagatas would have become extinct.

Strengthened by the new strength that comes to them from the Buddhas and with more perfect insight that is theirs by reason of their advance in self-realisation of Noble Wisdom, they re-examine the nature of the mind-system, the egolessness of personality, and the part that grasping and attachment and habit-energy play in the unfolding drama of life; they re-examine the illusions of the fourfold logical analysis, and the various elements that enter into enlightenment and self-realisation, and, in the thrill of their new powers of self-mastery, the Bodhisattvas enter upon the seventh stage of Far-going (Durangama).

Supported by the sustaining power of the Buddhas, the Bodhisattvas at this stage enter into the bliss of the Samadhi of perfect tranquilisation. Owing to their original vows they are transported by emotions of love and compassion as they become aware of the part they are to perform in the carrying out of their vows for emancipation of all beings. Thus they do not enter into Nirvana, but, in truth, they too are already in Nirvana because because in their emotions of love and compassion there is no rising of discrimination; henceforth, with them, discrimination no more takes place. Because of Transcendental Intelligence only one conception is present – the promotion of the realisation og Noble Wisdom. This is called the Bodhisattva's Nirvana – the losing oneself in the bliss of perfect self-yielding. This is the seventh stage, the stage of Far-going.

The eighth stage, is the stage of No-recession (Acala). Up to this stage, because of the defilments upon the face of Universal Mind caused by the accumulation of habit-energy since beginningless time, the mind-system and all that pertains to it has been evolved and sustained. The mind-system fuctioned by the discriminations of an external and objective world to which it became attached and by which it was perpetuated. But with the Bodhisattva's attainment of the eighth stage there come a "turning-about" within his deepest seat of consciousness from self-centered egoism to universal compassion for all beings, by which he attains perfect self-realisation of Noble Wisdom. There is an instant of cessation of the delusive activities of the whole mind-system; the dancing of the waves of habit-energy on the face of Universal Mind are forever stilled, revealing its own inherent quietness and solitude, the inconceivable Oneness of the Womb of Tathagatahood.

Henceforth there is no more looking outward upon an external world by senses and sense-minds, nor a discrimination of particularised concepts and ideas and propositions by an intellectual-mind, no more grasping, nor attachment, nor pride of egoism, nor habit-energy. Henceforth there is only the inner experience of Noble Wisdom which has been attained by entering into its perfect Oneness.

Thus establishing himself at the eighth stage of No-recession, the Bodhisattva enters into the bliss of the ten Samadhis, but avoiding the path of the disciples and masters who yielded themselves up to their entrancing bliss and who passed to their Nirvanas, and supported by his vows and the Transcendental Intelligence which now is his and being sustained by the power of the Buddhas, he enters upon the higher paths that lead to Tathagatahood. He passes through the bliss of the Samadhis to assume the transformation body of a Tathagata that through him all beings may be emancipated. Mahamati, If there had been no Tathagata-womb and no Divine Mind then there would have been no rising and disappearance of the aggregates that make up personality and its external world, no rising and disappearance of ignorant people nor holy people, and no task for Bodhisattvas; therefore, while walking in the path of self-realisation and entering into the enjoyments of the Samadhis, you must never abandon working hard for the emancipation of all beings and your self-yielding love will never be in vain. To philosophers the conception of Tathagata-womb seems devoid of purity and soiled by these external manifestations, but it is not so understood by the Tathagatas,- to them it is not a proposition of philosophy but an intuitive experience as real as though it was an amalaka fruit held in the palm of the hand.

With the cessation of the mind-system and all its evolving discriminations, there is cessation of all strain and effort. It is like a man in a dream who imagines he is crossing a river and who exerts himself to the utmost to do so, who is suddenly awakened. Being awake, he thinks: "Is this real or is it unreal?" Being now enlightened he knows that it is neither real nor unreal. Thus even when the Bodhisattva arrives at the eighth stage, he is able to see all things truthfully and, more than that, he is able to thoroughly understand the significance of all dream-like things of his life as to how they came to pass and as to how they pass away. Ever since beginningless time the mind-system has perceived multiplicities of forms and conditions and ideas which the thinking-mind has discriminated and the empirical-mind has experienced and grasped and clung to. From this has risen habit-energy that by its accumulation has conditioned the illusions of existence and non-existence, individuality and generality, and has thus perpetuated the dream-state of false-imagination. But now, to the

Bodhisattvas of the eighth stage, life is past and is remembered as it truly was – a passing dream.

As long as the Bodhisattva had not passed the seventh stage, even though he had attained an intuitive understanding of the true meaning of life and its maya-like nature, and as to how the mind carried on its discriminations and attachments yet, nevertheless, the cherishing of the notions of these things had continued and, although he no longer experienced within himself any ardent desire for things nor any impulse to grasp them yet, nevertheless, the notions concerning them persisted and perfumed his efforts to practise the teachings of the Buddhas and to labor for the emancipation of all beings. Now, in the eighth stage, even the notions have passed away, and all effort and striving is seen to be unnecessary. The Bodhisattva's Nirvana is perfect tranquilisation, but it is not extinction nor inertness; while there is an entire absence of discrimination and purpose, there is the freedom and spontaneity of potentiality that has come with the attainment and patience acceptance of the truths of egolessness and imagelessness. Here is perfect solitude, undisturbed by any gradation or continuous succesion, but radiant with the potency and freedom of its self-nature which is the self-nature of Noble Wisdom, blissfully peaceful with the serenity of Perfect Love.

Entering upon the eighth stage, with the "turning-about" at the deepest seat of consciousness, the Bodhisattva will become conscious that he has received the second kind of Transcendental-body (Manomayakaya). The transition from mortal-body to Transcendental-body has nothing to do with mortal death, for the old body continues to fuction and the old mind serves the needs of the old body, but now it is free from the control of mortal mind. There has been an inconceivable transformation-death (accintya-parinama-cyuti) by which the false-imagination of his particularised individual personality has been transcended by a realisation of his oneness with the universalised mind of Tathagatahood, from which realisation there will be no recession. With that realisation he finds himself amply endowed with all the Tathagata's powers, psychic faculties, and self-mastery, and, just as the good earth is the support of all beings in the world of desire (karmadathu), so the Tathatagatas become the support of all beings in the Transcendental World of No-form.

The first seven of the Bodhisattva stages were in the realm of mind and the eighth, while transcending mind, was still in touch with it; but in the ninth stage of Transcendental Intelligence (Sadhumati), by reason of his perfect intelligence and insight into the imagelessness of Divine Mind which he had attained by self-realisation of Noble Wisdom, he is in the realm of Tathagatahood. Gradually the Bodhisattva will realise his Tathagata-nature and the possesion of all its powers and psychic faculties, self-mastery, loving compassion, and skillful means, and by means of them will enter into all the Buddha-lands. Making use of these new powers, the Bodhisattva will assume various transformation-bodies and personalities for the sake of benefiting others. Just as in the former mental life, imagination had risen from relative-knowledge, so now skillful means rise spontaneously from Transcendental Intelligence. It is like the magical gem that reflects instantaneously appropiate responses to one's wishes. The Bodhisattva passes over to all the assemblages of the Buddhas and listens to them as they discourse on the dream-like nature of all things and concerning the truths that transcend all notions of being and non-being, that have no relation to birth and death, nor to eternality nor extinction. Thus facing the Tathagatas as they discourse on Noble Wisdom that is far beyond the mental capacity of disciples and masters, he will attain a hundred thousand Samadhis, indeed, a hundred thousand nyutas of kotis of Samadhis, and in the spirit of these Samadhis he will instantly pass from one Buddha-land to another, paying homage to all the Buddhas, being born into all the celestial mansions, manifesting Buddha-bodies, and himself discoursing on the Triple Treasure to lesser Bodhisattvas that they too may partake of the fruits of self-realisation of Noble Wisdom.

Thus passing beyond the last stage of Bodhisattvahood, he becomes a Tathagata himself endowed with all the freedom of the Dharmakaya. The tenth stage belongs to the Tathagatas. Here the Bodhisattva will find himself seated upon a lotus-like throne in a splendid jewel-adorned palace and surrounded by Bodhisattvas of equal rank. Buddhas from all Buddha-lands will gather about him and with their pure and fragant hands resting on his forehead will give him ordination and recognition as one of themselves. Then they will assign him a Buddha-land that he may posses and perfect as his own.

The tenth stage is called the Great Truth Cloud (Dharmamegha), inconceivable, inscrutable. Only the Tathagatas can realise perfect Imagelessness and Oneness and Solitude. It is Mahesvara, the Radiant Land, the Pure Land, the Land of Far-distances; surrounding and surpassing the lesser worlds of form and desire (karmadathu), in which the the Bodhisattva will find himself at-one-moment. Its rays of Noble Wisdom which is the self-nature of the Tathagatas, many-colored, entrancing, auspicious, are transforming the triple world as other worlds have been transformed in the past, and still other worlds will be transformed in the future. But in the Perfect Oneness of Noble Wisdom there is no gradation nor succesionnor effort. The tenth stage is the first, the first is the eighth, the eighth is the fifth, the fifth the seventh: what gradation can there be where perfect Imagelessness and Oneness prevail? And what is the reality of Noble Wisdom? It is the ineffable potency of the Dharmakaya; it has no bounds nor limits; it surpasses all the Buddha-lands, and pervades the Akanistha and the heavenly masions of the Tushita.

Chapter XII: Tathagatahood and Noble Wisdom

Then said Mahamati to the Blessed Lord: It has been taught in the canonical books that the Buddhas are subject to neither birth nor destruction, and you have said that "the Un-born" is one of the names of the Tathagatas; does that mean that the Tathagata is a non-entity?

The Blessed Lord replied: The Tathagata is not a non-entity nor is he to be conceived as other things are as neither born nor disappearing, nor is he subject to causation, not is he without significance; yet I refer to him as "The Un-born." There is yet another name for the Tathagata. "The Mind-appearing One" (Manomayakaya) which his Essence-body assumes at will in the transformations incident to his work of emancipation. This is beyond the understanding of common disciples and masters and even beyond the full comprehension of those Bodhisattvas who remain in the seventh stage. Yes, Mahamati, "The Un-born" is synonymous with Tathagata.

Then Mahamati said: If the Tathagatas are un-born, there does not seem to be anything to take hold of – no entity – or is there something that bears another name than entity? And what can that "something" be?

The Blessed Lord replied: Objects are frequently known by different names according to different aspects that they present, -- the god Indra is sometimes known as Shakra, and sometimes as Purandara. These different names are sometimes used interchangeably and sometimes they are discriminated, but different objects are not to be imagined because of the different names, nor are they without individuation. The same can be said of myself as I appear in this world of patience before ignorant people and where I am known by uncounted trillions of names. They address me by different names not realizing that they are all names of the one Tathagata. Some recognize me as Sun, as Moon; some as a reincarnation of the ancient sages; some as one of "ten powers"; some as Rama, some as Indra, and some as Varuna. Still there are others who speak of me as The Un-born, as Emptiness, as "Suchness," as Truth, as Reality, as Ultimate Principle; still there are others who see me as Dharmakaya, as Nirvana, as the Eternal; some speak of me as sameness, as non-duality, as un-dying, as formless; some think of me as the doctrine of Buddha-causation, or of Emancipation, or of the Noble Path; and some think of me as Divine Mind and Noble Wisdom.

Thus in this world and in other worlds am I known by these uncounted names, but they all see me as the moon is seen in the water. Though they all honor, praise and esteem me, they do not fully understand the meaning and significance of the words they use; not having their own self-realization of Truth they cling to the words of their canonical books, or to what has been told to them, or to what they have imagined, and fail to see that the name they are using is only one of the many names of the Tathagata. In their studies they follow the mere words of the text vainly trying to gain the true meaning, instead of having confidence in the one "text" where self-confirming Truth is revealed, that is, having confidence in the self-realization of noble Wisdom.

Then said Mahamati: Pray tell us, Blessed Lord, about the self-nature of the Tathagatas?

The Blessed Lord replied: If the Tathagata is to be described by such expressions as made or un-made, effect or cause, we would have to describe him as neither made, nor un-made, nor effect, nor cause; but if we so described him we would be guilty of dualistic discrimination. If the Tathagata is something made, he would be impermanent; if he is impermanent anything made would be a Tathagata. If he is something un-made, then all effort to realize Tathagatahood would be useless. That which is neither an effect or cause, is neither a being nor a non-being, and that which is neither a being nor non-being is outside the four propositions. The four propositions belong to worldly usage ; that which is outside them is no more than a word, like a barren-woman's child; so are all the terms concerning the Tathagata to be understood.

When it is said that all things are egoless, it means that all things are devoid of self-hood. Each thing may have its own individuality—the being of a horse is not of cow nature—it is such as it is of its own nature and is thus discriminated by the ignorant, but, nevertheless, its own nature is of the nature of a dream or vision. That is why the ignorant and the simpleminded, who are in the habit of discriminating appearances, fail to understand the significance of egolessness. It is not until discrimination is gotten rid of that the fact that all things are empty, un-born and without self-nature can be appreciated.

Mahamati, all these expressions as applied to the Tathagatas are without meaning, for that which is none of these is something removed from all measurement, and that which is removed from all measurement turns into a meaningless word; that which is a mere word is something un-born; that which is un-born is not subject to destruction; that which is not subject to destruction is like space and space is neither effect nor cause; that which is neither effect nor cause is something unconditioned; that which is unconditioned is beyond all reasoning; that which is beyond all reasoning, -- that is the Tathagata. The self-nature of Tathagatahood is far removed from all predicates and measurements; the self-nature of Tathagatahood is Noble Wisdom.

Then Mahamati said to the Blessed Lord: Are the Tathagatas permanent or impermanent?

The Blessed Lord replied: The Tathagatas are neither permanent nor impermanent; if either is asserted there is error connected with the creating agencies for, according to the philosophers, the creating agencies are something uncreated and permanent. But the Tathagatas are not connected with the so-called creating agencies and in that sense he is impermanent. If he is said to be impermanent then he is connected with things that are created for they also are impermanent. For these reasons the Tathagatas are neither permanent nor impermanent.

Neither can the Tathagatas be said to be permanent in the sense that space is said to be permanent, or that the horns of a hare can be said to be permanent for, being unreal, they exclude all ideas of permanency or impermanency. This does not apply to the Tathagatas because they come fourth from the habit-energy of ignorance which is connected with the mind-system and the elements that make up personality. The triple world originates from the discrimination of unrealities and where discrimination takes place there is duality and the notion of permanency and impermanency, but the Tathagatas do not rise from the discrimination of unrealities. Thus, as long as there is discrimination there will be the notion of permanency and impermanency; when discrimination is done away with, Noble Wisdom, which is based on the significance of solitude, will be established.

However, there is another sense in which the Tathagatas may be said to be permanent. Transcendental Intelligence rising with the attainment of enlightenment is of a permanent nature. This Truth-essence which is discoverable in the enlightenment of all who are enlightened, is realizable as the regulative and sustaining principle of Reality, which forever abides. The Transcendental Intelligence attained intuitively by the Tathagatas by their self-realization of Noble Wisdom, is a realization of their own self-nature, -- in this sense the Tathagatas are permanent. The eternal-unthinkable of the Tathagatas is the "suchness" of noble Wisdom realized within themselves. It is both eternal and beyond thought. It conforms to the idea of a cause and yet is beyond existence and non-existence. Because it is the exalted state of Noble-Wisdom, it has its own character. Because it is the cause of highest Reality, it is its own causation. Its eternality is not derived from reasonings based on external notions of being and non-being, nor of eternality nor non-eternality. Being classed under the same head as space, cessation, Nirvana, it is eternal. Because it has nothing to do with existence and non- existence, it is no creator; because it has nothing to do with creation, nor with being and non-being, but is only revealed in the exalted state of noble Wisdom, it is truly eternal.

When the twofold passions are destroyed, and the twofold hindrances are cleared away, and the twofold egolessness is fully understood, and the inconceivable transformation death of the Bodhisattva is attained – that which remains is the self-nature of the Tathagatas. When the teachings of the Dharma are fully understood and are perfectly realized by the disciples and masters, that which is realized in their deepest consciousness is their own Buddha-nature revealed as Tathagata.

In a true sense there are four kinds of sameness relating to Buddha-nature: there is sameness of letters, sameness of words, sameness of meaning, and sameness of Essence. The name of the Buddha is spelt: B-U-D-D-H-A; the letters are the same when used for any Buddha or Tathagata. When the Brahmans teach they use various words, and when the Tathagatas teach they use the very same words; in respect to the words there is a sameness between us. In the teachings of all the Tathagatas there is a sameness in meaning. Among all the Buddhas there is a sameness of meaning. They all have the thirty-two marks of excellence and the eighty minor signs of bodily perfection; there is no distinction among them except as they manifest various transformations according to the different dispositions of beings who are to be disciplined and emancipated by various means. In the Ultimate Essence which is Dharmakaya, all the Buddhas of the past, present and future, are of one sameness.

Then said Mahamati to the Blessed Lord: It has been said by the Blessed Lord that from the night of Enlightenment to the night of the Parinirvana, the Tathagata has uttered no word nor ever will utter a word. In what deep meaning is this true?

The Blessed Lord replied: By two reasons of deepest meaning is it true: In the light of Truth self-realized by Noble Wisdom; and in the Truth of an eternally-abiding Reality. The self-realization of Noble Wisdom by all Tathagatas is the same as my own self-realization of Noble Wisdom; there is no more, no less, no difference, and all the Tathagatas bear witness that the state of self-realization is free from words and discriminations and has nothing to do with the dualistic way of speaking, that is, all beings receive the teachings of the Tathagatas through self-realization of Noble Wisdom, not though words of discrimination.

Again Mahamati, there has always been an eternally-abiding Reality. The "substance" of Truth (dharmadhatu) abides forever whether a Tathagata appears in the world or not. So does the Reason of all things (dharmata) eternally abide; so does Reality (paramartha) abide and keep its order. What has been realized by my myself and all other Tathagatas is this Reality (Dharmakaya), the eternally-abiding self-orderliness of Reality; the "suchness" (tathata) of all things; the realness of things (bhutata); Noble Wisdom which is Truth itself. The sun radiates its splendor spontaneously on all alike and with no words of explanation; in like manner do the Tathagatas radiate the Truth of Noble Wisdom with no recourse to words and to all alike. For these reasons is it stated by me that from the night of enlightenment to the night of the Tathagata's Parinirvana, he has not uttered, nor will he utter, one word. And the same is true of all the Buddhas.

Then said Mahamati: Blessed Lord, you speak of the sameness of all Buddhas, but in other places you have spoken of Dharmata-Buddha, Nishyanda-Buddha and Nirmana-Buddha as though they were different from each other; how can they be the same and yet different?

The Blessed Lord replied: I speak of the different Buddhas as opposed to the views of the philosophers who base their teachings on the reality of an external world of from and who cherish discrimination and attachments arising therefrom; against the teachings of these philosophers I disclose the Nirmana-Buddha, the Buddha of Transformations. In the many transformations of the Tathagata stage, the Nirmana-Buddha establishes such matters as charity, morality, patience, thoughtfulness, and tranquillization: by right-knowledge he teaches the true understanding of maya-like nature of the elements that make up personality and its external world; he teaches the true nature of the mind-system as a whole and in the distinctions of its forms, functions and ways of performance. In a deeper sense, the Nirmana-Buddha symbolizes the principles of differentiation and integration by reason of which all component things are distributed, all complexities simplified, all thoughts analyzed; at the same time it symbolizes the harmonizing, unifying power of sympathy and compassion; it removes all obstacles, it harmonizes all differences, it brings into perfect Oneness the discordant many. For the emancipation of all beings the

Bodhisattvas and Tathagatas assume bodies of transformation and employ many skilful devices,-- this is the work of the Nirmana-Buddha.

For the enlightenment of the Bodhisattvas and their sustaining along the stages, the Inconceivable is made realizable. The Nishyanda-Buddha, the "Out-flowing-Buddha," though Transcendental Intelligence, reveals the true meaning and significance of appearances, discrimination, attachment; and of the power of habit-energy which is accumulated by them and conditions them; and of the un-bornness, the emptiness, the egolessness of all things. Because of Transcendental Intelligence and the purification of evil out-flowings of life, all dualistic self-realization of Noble Wisdom the true

Imagelessness of Reality is made manifest. The inconceivable glory of Buddhahood is made manifest in rays of Noble Wisdom; Noble Wisdom is the self-nature of the Tathagatas. This is the work of the Nishyanda-Buddha. In a deeper sense, the Nishyanda-Buddha symbolizes the emergence of the principles of intellection and compassion but as yet undifferentiated and in perfect balance, potential but unmanifest. Looked at from the in-going side of the Bodhisattva, Nishyanda-Buddha is seen in the glorified bodies of the Tathagatas; looked at from the fourth-going side of Buddhahood, Nishyanda-Buddha is seen in the radiant personalities of the Tathagatas ready and eager to manifest the inherent Love and Wisdom of the Dharmakaya.

Dharmata-Buddha is Buddhahood in its self-nature of perfect oneness in whom absolute Tranquility prevails. As noble Wisdom, Dharmata-Buddha transcends all differentiated knowledge, is the goal of intuitive self-realization, and is the self-nature of the Tathagatas. As Noble Wisdom, Dharmata-Buddha is the ultimate Principle of Reality from which all things derive their being and truthfulness, but which in itself transcends all predicates. Dharmata-Buddha is the central sun which holds all, illumines all. Its inconceivable Essence is made manifest in the "out-flowing" glory of Nishyanda-Buddha and in the transformations of the Nirmana-Buddha.

Then said Mahamati: Pray tell us, Blessed Lord, more about the Dharmakaya?

The Blessed Lord replied: We have been speaking of it in terms of Buddhahood, but it is inscrutable and beyond predicate we may just as well speak of it as the Truth-body, or the Truth-principle of ultimate Reality (Paramartha). This Ultimate Principle of Reality may be considered as it is manifested under seven aspects: First, as Citta-gocara, it is the world of spiritual experience and the abode of the Tathagatas on their outgoing mission of emancipation. It is Noble Wisdom manifested as the principle of irradiancy and individuation. Second, as Jnana, it is the mind-world and its principle of the intellection and consciousness. Third as Dristi, it is the realm of dualism which is the physical world of birth and death wherein are manifested all the differentiation, desire, attachment and suffering.

Fourth, because of the greed, anger, infatuation, suffering and need of the physical world incident to discrimination and attachment, it reveals a world beyond the realm of dualism wherein it appears as the integrating principle of charity and sympathy. Fifth, in a realm still higher, which is the abode of the Bodhisattva stages, and is analogous to the mind-world, where the interests of hear transcend those of the mind, it appears as the principle of compassion and self-giving, Sixth, in the spiritual realm where the Bodhisattvas attain Buddhahood, it appears as the principle of perfect Love (Karuna). Here the last clinging to an ego-self is abandoned and the Bodhisattva enters into his realization of noble Wisdom which is the bliss of the Tathagata's perfect enjoyment of his inmost nature. Seventh as Prajna it is the active aspect of the Ultimate Principle wherein both the forth-going and the in-coming principles are alike implicit and potential, and wherein both Wisdom and Love are in perfect balance, harmony and the Oneness.

These are the seven aspects of the ultimate Principle of the Dharmakaya, by reason of which all things are made manifest and perfected and then reintegrated, and all remaining within its inscrutable Oneness, with no signs of individuation, nor beginning, nor succession, nor ending, We speak of it as Dharmakaya, as Ultimate Principle, as Buddhahood, as Nirvana; what matters it? They are only other names for Noble-Wisdom.

Mahamati, you and all Bodhisattva-Mahasattvas should avoid the erroneous reasoning of the philosophers and seek for self-realization of Noble Wisdom.

Chapter XIII: Nirvana

Then said Mahamati to the Blessed Lord: Pray tell us about Nirvana?

The Blessed Lord replied: the term, Nirvana, is used with many different meanings, by different people, but these people may be divided into four groups: There are people who are suffering, or who are afraid of suffering, and who think of Nirvana; there are philosophers who try to discriminate Nirvana; there are the class of disciples who think of Nirvana in relation to themselves; and finally there is the Nirvana of the Buddhas. Those who are suffering or who fear suffering, think of Nirvana as an escape and recompense. They imagine that Nirvana consists in the future annihilation of the senses and the sense-minds; they are not aware that this life-and-death world and Nirvana are not to be separated. These ignorant ones, instead of meditating on the imageless of Nirvana, talk of different ways of emancipation. Being ignorant of, or not understanding, the teachings of the Tathagatas, they cling to the notion of Nirvana that is outside what is seen of the mind and, thus, go on rolling themselves along with the wheel of life and death.

As to the Nirvana discriminated by the philosophers: there really are none. Some philosophers conceive Nirvana to be found where the mind-system no more operates owing to the cessation of the elements that make up personality and its world; or is found where there is utter indifference to the objective world and its impermanency. Some conceive Nirvana to be a state where there is no recollection of the past or present, just as when a lamp is extinguished, or when a seed is burnt, or when a fire goes out; because then there is the cessation of all the substrata, which is explained by the philosophers as the non-rising of discrimination. But this is not Nirvana, because Nirvana does not consist in simple annihilation and vacuity.

Again, some philosophers explain deliverance as though it was the mere stopping of discrimination, as when the wind stops blowing, or as when one by self-effort gets rid of the dualistic view of knower and known, or gets rid of the notions of permanency and impermanency; or gets rid of the notions of good and evil; or overcomes passion by means of knowledge-to them Nirvana is deliverance. Some, seeing in "form" the bearer of pain alarmed by the notion of "form" and look for happiness in a world of "no-form." Some conceive that in consideration of individuality and generality recognizable in all things inner and outer, that there is no destruction and that all beings maintain their being forever and, in this eternality, see Nirvana.

Others see the eternally of things in the conception of Nirvana as the absorption of the finite-soul in the supreme Atman; or who see all things as a manifestation of the vital-force of some Supreme Sprit to which all return; and some, who are especially silly, declare that there are two primary things, a primary substance and a primary soul, that react differently upon each other and thus produce all things from the transformations of qualities; some think that the world is born of action and interaction and that no other cause is necessary; others think that Ishvara is free creator of all things; clinging to these foolish notions, there is no awakening, and they consider Nirvana to consist in the fact that there is no awakening. Some imagine that Nirvana is where self-nature exists in its own right, unhampered by other self-natures, as the variegated feathers of a peacock, or various crystals, or the pointedness of a thorn. Some conceive being to be Nirvana, some non-being, while others conceive that all things and Nirvana are not to be distinguished from one another.

Some, thinking that time is the creator and that as the rise of the world depends on time, they conceive that Nirvana consists in the recognition of time as Nirvana. Some think that there will be Nirvana when the "twenty-five" truths are generally accepted, or when the king observes the six virtues, and some religionists think that Nirvana is the attainment of paradise. These views severally advanced by the philosophers with their various seasonings are not in accord with logic nor are they acceptable to the wise. They all conceive Nirvana dualistically and in some causal connection; by these discriminations philosophers imagine Nirvana, but where there is no rising and no disappearing, how can there be discrimination?

Each philosopher relying on his own textbook from which he draws his understanding, sins against the truth, because truth is not where he imagines it to be. The only result is that it sets his mind to wandering about and becoming more confused as Nirvana is not to be found by mental searching, the more his mind becomes confused the more he confuses other people. As to the notion of Nirvana as held by disciples and masters who still cling to the notion of an ego-self, and who try to find it by going off by themselves into solitude: their notion of Nirvana is an eternity of bliss like the bliss of the Samadhis-for themselves. They recognize that the world is only a manifestation of mind and that all discriminations are of the mind, and so they forsake social relations and practice various spiritual disciplines and in solitude seek self-realization of

Noble Wisdom by self-effort. They fallow the stages to the sixth and attain the bliss of the Samadhis, but as they are still clinging to egoism they do not attain the "turning-about" at the deepest seat of consciousness and, therefore, they are not free from the thinking-mind and the accumulation of its habit-energy. Clinging to the bliss of the Samadhis, they pass to their Nirvana, but it is not the Nirvana of the Tathagatas. They are of those who have "entered the stream"; they must return to this world of life and death.

Then said Mahamati to the Blessed Lord: When the Bodhisattvas yield up their stock of merit for the emancipation of all beings, they become spiritually one with all animate life; they themselves may be purified, but in others there yet remain unexhausted evil and unmatured karma. Pray tell us, Blessed Lord, how the Bodhisattvas given assurance of Nirvana? And what is the Nirvana of the Bodhisattvas?

The Blessed Lord replied: Mahamati, this assurance is not an assurance of numbers nor logic; it is not the mind that is to be assured but the heart. The Bodhisattva's assurance comes with the unfolding insight that fallows passion hindrances cleared away, knowledge hindrance purified, and egolessness clearly perceived and patiently accepted. As the mortal-mind ceases to discriminate, there is no more thirst for life, no more sex-lust, no more thirst for learning, no more thirst for eternal life; with the disappearance of these fourfold thirsts, there is no more accumulation of habit-energy; with no more accumulation of habit-energy the defilements on the face of the Universal Mind clear away, and the Bodhisattva attains self-realization of Noble Wisdom that is the heart's assurance of Nirvana.

There are Bodhisattvas here and in other Buddha-lands, who are sincerely devoted to the Bodhisattva's mission and yet who cannot wholly forget the bliss of the Samadhis and the peace of Nirvana-for themselves. The teaching of Nirvana in which there is no substrate left behind, is revealed according to a hidden meaning for the sake of these disciples who still cling to thoughts of Nirvana for themselves, that they may be inspired to exert themselves in the Bodhisattva's mission of emancipation for all beings. The Transformation-Buddhas teach a doctrine of Nirvana to meet conditions as they find them, and to give encouragement to the timid and selfish. In order to turn their thoughts away from themselves and to encourage them to a deeper compassion and more earnest zeal for others, they are given assurance as to the future by the sustaining power of the Buddhas of Transformation, but not by the Dharmata-Buddha.

The Dharma which establishes the Truth of Noble Wisdom belongs to the realm of the Dharmata-Buddha. To the Bodhisattvas to the seventh and eighth stages, Transcendental Intelligence is revealed by the Dharmata-Buddha and the Path is pointed out to them which they are to follow. In the perfect self-realization of Noble Wisdom that fallows the inconceivable transformation death of the Bodhisattva's individualized will-control, he no longer lives unto himself, but the life that he lives thereafter is the Tathagata's universalized life as manifested in its transformations. In this perfect self-realization of Noble Wisdom the Bodhisattva realizes that for the Buddhas there is no Nirvana. The death of a Buddha, the great Parinirvana, is neither destruction nor death, else would it be birth and continuation. If it were destruction, it would be an effect-producing deed, which is not. Neither is it a vanishing nor an abandonment, neither is it attainment, nor is it of no attainment; neither is it of one significance nor of no significance, for there is no Nirvana for the Buddhas.

The Tathagata's Nirvana is where it is recognized that there is nothing but what is seen of the mind itself; is where, recognizing the nature of the self-mind, one no longer cherishes the dualisms of discrimination; is where there is no more thirst nor grasping; is where there is no more attachment to external things. Nirvana is where the thinking-mind with all its discriminations, attachments, aversions and egoism is forever put away; is where logical measures, as they are seen to be inert, are no longer seized upon; is where even the notion of truth is treated with indifference because of its causing bewilderment; is where, getting rid of the four propositions, there is insight into the abode of Reality. Nirvana is where the twofold passions have subsided and the twofold hindrances are cleared away and the twofold egolessness is patiently accepted; is where, by the attainment of the "turning-about" in the deepest seat of consciousness, self-realization of Noble Wisdom is fully entered into,--that is the Nirvana of the Tathagatas.Nirvana is where the Bodhisattva stages are passed one after another; is where the sustaining power of the Buddhas upholds the Bodhisattvas in the bliss of the Samadhis; is where compassion for others transcends all thoughts of self; is where the Tathagata stage is finally realized.

Nirvana is the realm of the Dharmata-Buddha; it is where the manifestation of Noble Wisdom that is Buddhahood expresses itself in Perfect Love for all; it is where the manifestation of Perfect Love that is Tathagatahood expresses itself in Noble Wisdom for the enlightenment of all -there, indeed, is Nirvana! There are two classes of those who may not enter the Nirvana of the Tathagatas: there are those who have abandoned the Bodhisattva ideals, saying, they are not in conformity with the sutras, the codes of morality, nor with emancipation. Then there are the true

Bodhisattvas who, on account of their original vows made for the sake of all beings, saying, "So long as they do not attain Nirvana, I will not attain it for myself," voluntarily keep themselves out of Nirvana. But no beings are left outside by the will of the Tathagatas; some day each and every one will be influenced by the wisdom and love of the Tathagatas of Transformation to lay up stock of merit and ascend the stages. But, if they only realized it, they are already in the Tathagata's Nirvana for, in Noble Wisdom, all things are in Nirvana from the beginning.

Master Xuyun's Essentials of Ch'an Practice

Introduction

Xu Yun, translated into English, means "Empty Cloud". This translation often confuses people. We all know what a cloud is, but what, we wonder, is meant by "empty"?

In Chan or Zen literature the term "empty" appears so often and with so many variations of definition, that I will begin by trying to clarify its meaning.

To be empty means to be empty of ego, to be without any thought of self, not in the sense that one functions as a vegetable or a wild animal - living things which merely process water, food and sunlight in order to grow and reproduce - but in the sense that one ceases to gauge the events, the persons, the places, and the things of one's environment in terms of "I" or "me" or "mine". A person who is "empty of self" seldom has occasion even to use these pronouns.

A person who is truly empty possesses nothing, not even a consciousness of self. His interests lie not with his own needs and desires, for indeed, he is unaware of any such considerations, but only with the welfare of others. He does not evaluate people as being likable or unlikable, worthy or unworthy, or as useful or useless. He neither appreciates nor depreciates anyone. He simply understands that the Great Buddha Amitabha, the Buddha of Infinite Light and Goodness, dwells within every human being, and it is in the interest of this Buddha Self that he invests himself.

Attaining such emptiness is never easy. An old Chan story illustrates this:

A Chan Master once undertook the instruction of a novice who was having great difficulty in detaching himself from the persons of his former, secular life. "You cannot serve the Dharma until you sever these bonds," said the Master. "You must destroy these possessive relationships! Kill them! Regard them as if they no longer existed!"

The novice asked, "But my parents? Must I slay them, too?"

And the Master replied, "Who are they to be spared?"

"And you, Master," said the novice, "must I kill you, too?"

And the Master smiled and said, "Don't worry. There is not enough of me left for you to get your hands on."

Such a master was Xu Yun. There was not enough of him left for anyone to grasp. When he was an old man of ninety-three, cadres of thugs beat him repeatedly; but although they broke his bones and did succeed in killing younger, stronger priests, they could not get their hands on him, either. There was not enough of him left for anyone to grasp. How can the Buddha Self be killed? Xu Yun would not die until he was ready to die, until he accomplished the tasks which he had set for himself.

The Prerequisites and Understanding Necessary to Begin Ch'an Practise

1. The Objective of Ch'an Practice:

The objective of Ch'an practice is to illuminate the mind by eradicating its impurities and seeing into one's true self-nature. The mind's impurities are wrong thoughts and attachments. Self-nature is the wisdom and virtue of the Tathagata. The wisdom and virtue of Buddhas and sentient beings are not different from one another. To experience this wisdom and virtue, leave, leave behind duality, discrimination, wrong thinking and attachment. This is Buddhahood. If one cannot do this, then one remains an ordinary sentient being.

It is because you and I are defiled that we have been wandering lost and confused through samsara for limitless kalpas; and that we cannot immediately cast off wrong thinking and see our original nature. For this reason we must practice Ch'an.

The prerequisite for Ch'an practice is to eradicate wrong thinking. Shakyamuni Buddha taught much on this subject. His simplest and most direct teaching is the word "stop" from the expression "stopping is Bodhi." From the time when Bodhidharma transmitted Ch'an teachings to today, the winds of Ch'an have blown far and wide, shaking and illuminating the world. Among the many things that Bodhidharma and the Sixth Patriarch taught to those who came to study with them, none is more valuable than the saying, "Put-down all entangling conditions, let not one thought arise."

This expression is truly the prerequisite for the practice of Ch'an. If you cannot fulfill this requirement, then not only will you fail to attain the ultimate goal of Ch'an practice, but you will not even be able to enter the door of Ch'an. How can you talk of practicing Ch'an if you are entangled by worldly phenomena with thought after thought arising and passing away?

2. Put Down All entangling conditions

"Put down all entangling conditions, let not one thought arise" is a prerequisite for the practice of Ch'an. Now that we know this, how do we accomplish it? The best practitioner, one of superior abilities, can stop all thoughts forever, arrive directly at the condition of non-arising, and instantly experience Bodhi. such a person is not entangled by anything.

The next best kind of practitioner users principle to cut off phenomena and realizes that self-nature is originally pure. Vexation and bodhi , Samsara and Nirvana -- all are false names which have nothing to do with one's self-nature. All things are dreams and illusions, like bubbles or reflections.

Within self-nature, my body, made up of the four great earth itself are like bubbles in the sea, arising and disappearing, yet never obstructing the original surface. Do not bed captivated by the arising, abiding, changing and passing away of illusory phenomena, which give rise to pleasure and aversion, grasping and rejecting. Give up your whole body, as if you were dead, and the six sense organs, the six sense objecting. and the six sense organs, the six sense objects and the six sense consciousness will naturally disperse. Greed, hatred, ignorance and love will be destroyed. All the sensations of pain, suffering and pleasure which attend the body --- hunger, cold, satiation, warmth, glory, insult, birth and death, calamity, prosperity, good and bad luck, praise, blame, gain and loss, safety and danger--- will no longer be your concern. Only this can be considered true renunciation --- when you put everything down forever. This is what is meant by renouncing all phenomena.

When all phenomena are renounced , wrong thoughts disappear, discrimination does not arise, and attachment is left behind. When thoughts no longer arise, the brightness of self-nature manifests itself completely. At this time you will have fulfilled the necessary conditions for Ch'an practice. Then, further hard work and sincere practice will enable you to illuminate the mind and see into your true nature.

3. Everyone Can Instantly Become a Buddha:

Many Ch'an practitioners ask questions about the Dharma. The Dharma that is spoken is not the true Dharma. As soon as you try to explain things, the true meaning is lost. When you realize that "one mind" is the Buddha, from that point on there is nothing more to do. Everything is already complete. All talk about practice or attainment is demonic deception.

Bodhidharma's "direct pointing at the mind, seeing into one's nature and attaining Buddhahood" clearly instructs that all sentient beings are Buddhas. Once pure self-nature is recognized, one can harmonize with the environment yet remain undefiled. The mind will remain unified throughout the day, whether walking, standing, sitting or lying down. This is to already be a Buddha. At this point there is no need to put forth effort and be diligent. Any action is superfluous. No need to bother with the slightest thought or word. Therefore, to become a Buddha is the easiest, most unobstructed task. Do it by your-self. do not seek outside yourself for it.

All sentient beings --- who wish to avoid rebirth for eternal kalpas in the four forms of birth and the six paths of existence; who eternally sink in the sea of suffering; and who vow to attain Buddhahood and the four virtues of Nirvana (eternity, joy, self, purity) ----- can immediately attain Buddhahood if they wholly believe in the sincere words of the Buddha and the patriarchs, renounce everything, and think neither of beings, made by all the Buddhas, Bodhisattvas and patriarchs, is not a boast nor is it a baseless, empty vow.

The Dharma is exactly that. It has been elucidated again and again by the Buddha and the patriarchs. They have exhorted us with the truth. They do not deceive us. Unfortunately, sentient beings are confused and for limitless kalpas they have experienced birth and death in the sea of suffering, appearing and disappearing, endlessly taking on new forms of life. dazed and confused, entangled in the worldly dust of the six senses with their backs to enlightenment, they are like pure gold in a cesspool. Because of the severity of the problem, Buddha compassionately taught 84,000 Dharma doors to accord with the varying karmic roots of sentient beings, so that sentient beings may use the methods to cure them-selves of 84,000 habits and faults, which include greed, hatred, ignorance and desire.

4. Investigating Ch'an and Contemplating Mind:

Our sect focuses on investigating Ch'an. The purpose of practicing Ch'an is to "Illuminate the mind and see into one's true nature." This investigation is also called " Clearly realizing one's self-mind and completely perceiving one's original nature."

Since the time when Buddha held up a flower and Bodhidharma came to the East, the methods for entry into this Dharma door have continually evolved. Most Ch'an practitioners, before the Tang and Sung dynasties, became enlightened after hearing a word or half a sentence of the Dharma. The transmission from master to disciple was the sealing of Mind with Mind. There was no fixed Dharma. Everyday questions and answers only untied the bonds. It was nothing more than prescribing the right medicine for the right illness.

After the Sung Dynasty, however, people did not have such good karmic roots as their predecessors. They could not carry out what had been said, For example, practitioners were taught to "Put down everything" and " Not think about good and evil, "but they could not do it. They could not put down everything, and if they weren't thinking about good, they were thinking about evil. Under these circumstances, the patriarchs had no choice but to use poison to fight poison, so they taught the method of investigating gong an [and hua to].

When one begins looking into a hua to, one must grasp it tightly, never letting go. It is like a mouse trying to chew its way out of a coffin. It concentrates on one point. It doesn't try different places and it doesn't stop until it gets through. Thus, in terms of hua to, the objective is to use one thought to eradicate innumerable other thoughts. This method is a last resort, just as if someone had been pierced by a poison arrow. drastic measures must be taken to cure the patient.

The ancients used gong ans, but later on practitioners started using hua tos. Some hua tos are: "Who is dragging this corpse around?" "Before you were born what was your original face?' and, "Who is reciting Buddha's name?'

In fact, all hua tos are the same. There is nothing uncommon, strange, or special about them. If you wanted to, you could say: "Who is reciting the sutras?" "Who is reciting the mantras? "Who is prostrating to the Buddha? " Who is eating?" "Who is wearing these clothes?" "Who's walking?" "Who's sleeping?" They're all the same. The answer to the question "who" is derived from one's Mind. Mind is the origin of all words. Thoughts come out of Mind ; Mind is the origin of all thoughts. Innumerable dharmas generate from the Mind ; Mind is the origin of all dharmas. In fact, hua to is a thought. Before a thought arises, there is the origin of words. Hence, looking into a hua to is contemplating Mind. There was Mind before your parents gave birth to you, so looking into your original face before you were born is contemplating Mind.

Self-nature is Mind. When one turns inward to hear one's self-nature, one is Turning inward to contemplate Mind. In the phrase, "Perfectly illuminating pure awareness," pure awareness is Mind and illumination is contemplation. Mind is Buddha. When one recites Buddha's name one contemplates Buddha. Contemplating Buddha is contemplating Mind.

Investigating hua to or "looking into who is reciting Buddha's name" is contemplating Mind. Hence, contemplating Mind is illuminating pure awareness. It is also illuminating the Buddha-nature within oneself. Mind is nature, pure awareness, Buddha. Mind has no form, no characters, no directions; it cannot be found in any particular place. It cannot be grasped. Originally, Mind is purity, universally embracing all Dharma realms. No inn or out, no coming or going. Originally, Mind is pure Dharmakaya.

When investigating hua to , the practitioner should first close down all six sense organs and seek where thoughts arise. Practitioners should concentrate on the hua to until they see the pure original mind which is apart from thoughts. If one does this without interruption, the mind becomes fine, quiet tranquil, silently illuminating. At that moment the five skandhas are empty, body and mind are extinguished, nothing remains. From that point, walking, standing, sitting and lying down are all done motionlessly. In time the practice will deepen, and eventually practitioners will see their self-nature and become Buddhas and suffering will cease.

A past patriarch named Gaofeng(1238-1295) once said: "You must contemplate hua to like a falling roof tile sinking endlessly down into a pond ten thousand feet deep. If in seven days you are not enlightened, I will give you permission to chop off my head. "These are the words of an experienced person. He did not speak lightly. His words are true.

Although many modem day practitioners use hua tos, few get enlightened. This is because compared to practitioners of the past, practitioners today have inferior karmic roots and less merit. Also, practitioners today are not clear about the purpose and path of hua to. Some practitioners search from east to west and north to south until they die, but still do not penetrate even one hua to. They never understand or correctly approach the hua to. They only grasp the form and the words. They use their intellect and attach only to the tail of the words.

hua to is One Mind. This mind is not inside, outside, or in the middle. On the other hand, it is inside, outside, and in the middle. It is like the stillness of empty space prevailing every where.

hua to should not be picked up. Neither should it be pressed down. If you pick it up, your mind will waver and become unstable. If you press it down you will become drowsy. These approaches are contrary to the nature of the original mind and are not in accordance with the Middle Path.

Practitioners are distressed by wandering thoughts. They think it is difficult to tame them. Don't be afraid of wandering thoughts. Do not waste your energy trying to repress them. All you have to do is recognize them. Do not attach to wandering thoughts, do not follow them, and do not try to get rid of them. As long as you don't string thoughts together, wandering thoughts will depart by themselves.

Lectures on the Methods of Practise in the Ch'an Hall

1. Introduction:

Many people come to ask me for guidance. This makes me feel ashamed. Everyone works so hard --- splitting firewood, hoeing the fields, carrying soil, moving bricks --- and yet from morning to night not putting down the thought of practicing the Path. Such determination for the Path is touching. I, Xuyun, repent my inadequacy on the Path and my lack of virtue. I am unable to instruct you and can use only a few saying from the ancients in response to your questions. There are four prerequisites concerning methods of practice: (1) Deep faith in the law of cause and consequence; (2) Strict observance of precepts; (3) Immovable faith (4) Choosing a Dharma door method of practice.

2. Essentials of Ch'an Practice:

Our everyday activities are executed within the Path itself. Is there anywhere that is not a place for practicing the Path? A Ch'an Hall should not even be necessary. Furthermore, Ch'an practice is not just sitting meditation. The Ch'an Hall and Ch'an sitting meditation are for sentient beings with deep karmic obstructions and shallow wisdom.

When one sits in meditation, one must first know how to regulate the body and mind. If they are not well regulated, then a small harm will turn into an illness and a great harm will lead to demonic entanglements. This would be most pitiable. Walking and sitting meditation in the Ch'an Hall are for the regulation of body and mind. There are other ways to regulate the body and mind, but I will talk about these two fundamental methods.

When you sit in the lotus position, you should sit naturally straight. Do not push the waist forward purposely. Doing so will raise your inner heat, which later on could result in having sand in the corner of your eyes, bad breath, uneasy breathing, loss of appetite, and in the worst case, vomiting blood. If dullness or sleepiness occur, open your eyes wide, straighten your back and gently move your buttocks from side to side. dullness will naturally vanish. If you practice with an anxious attitude, you will have a sense of annoyance. At that time you should put everything down, including your efforts to practice. Rest for a few minutes. Gradually, after you recuperate, continue to practice. If you don't do this, as time goes on you will develop a hot-tempered character, or, in the worst case, you could go insane or fall into demonic entanglements.

There are many experiences you will encounter when sitting Ch'an, too many to speak of. However, if you do not attach to them, they will not interfere with you. This is why the proverb says: "See the extraordinary yet do not think of it as being extraordinary, and the extraordinary will retreat." If you encounter or perceive an unpleasant experience, take no notice of it and have no fear. If you experience something pleasant, take no notice of it and don't give rise to fondness. The Surangama Sutra says: " If one does not think he has attained a supra mundane experience, then this is good. On the other hand, if one thinks he has attained something supra mundane, then he will attract demons."

3. How to Start the Practice: Distinction Between Host and Guest:

How should one begin to practice? In the Surangama assembly, Kaundinya the Honored One mentioned the two words "guest" and "dust." This is where beginners should begin their practice. He said, "A traveler who stops at an inn may stay overnight or get something to eat. When he is finished or rested, he packs and continues his journey, for he does not have time to stay longer. If he were the host, he would have no place to go. Thus I reason : he who does not stay is called a guest because not staying is the essence of being a guest. He who stays is called a host. Again, on a clear day, when the sun rises and the sunlight enters a dark room through an opening, one can see dust in empty space. The dust is moving but the space is still. That which is clear and still is called space; that which is moving is called dust because moving is the essence of being dust." Guest and dust refer to illusory thoughts, whereas host and space refer to self-nature. That the permanent host does not follow the guest in his comings and goings illustrates that permanent self-nature does not follow illusory thoughts in their fleeting rise and fall. therefore it was said, "It was said, "If one is unaffected by all things, then there will be no obstructions even when one is constantly surrounded by things." The moving dust does not block the clear, still empty space; illusory thoughts which rise and fall by themselves do not hinder the self-nature of Suchness. Thus it was said, "If my mind does not arise, all things are blameless." In such a state of mind, even the guest does not drift with illusory thoughts. If he understands space and dust, illusory thoughts will no longer be hindrances. It is said that when one recognizes an enemy, there will be no more enemy in your mind. If one can investigate and understand all this before starting to practice, it is unlikely that one will make serious mistakes.

4. Hua tos and doubt

The ancient patriarchs pointed directly at Mind. When one sees self-nature, one attains Buddhahood. This was the case when Bodhidharma helped his disciple to calm his mind and when the sixth Patriarch spoke only about seeing self-nature. All that was necessary was the direct understanding and acceptance of Mind and nothing else. There was no such thing as investigating hua to. More recent patriarchs, however, saw that practitioners could not throw themselves into practice with total dedication and could not instantaneously see their self-nature. Instead, these people played games and imitated words of wisdom, showing off other people's treasure and imagining it was theirs. For this reason, later patriarchs were compelled to set up schools and devise specific ways to help practitioners, hence the method of investigating hua to.

There are many hua tos, such as "all dharmas return to one, where does this one return to?" What was my original face before I was born?" and so on. The most common one, however, is "who is reciting the Buddha's name?"

What is meant by hua to? Hua means the spoken word; to means the head or beginning, so hua to means that which is before the spoken word. for example, reciting Amitabha Buddha is a hua, and hua to is that which precedes one's reciting the Buddha's name. The hua to is that moment before the thought arises. Once the thought arises, it is already the tail of the hua. The moment before the thought has arisen is called non-arising. When one's mind is not distracted, is not dull, is not attached to quiescence, or has not fallen into a state of nothingness, it is called non-perishing. Single-mindedly and uninterruptedly, turning inward and illuminating the state of non-arising and non-perishing is called investigating the hua to, to taking care of the hua to.

To investigate the hua-t', one must first generate doubt. doubt is like a walking cane for the method of investigating hua to. what is meant by doubt? For example, one may ask, :who is reciting the Buddha's name?" Everyone knows that it is he himself who is reciting the name, but is he using his mouth or mind? If it is his mouth, then after the person dies and the mouth still exists, how come the dead person is unable to recite Buddha's name? If it is the mind, then what is the mind like? It cannot be known. Thus there is something one does not understand, and this gives rise to a slight doubt regarding the question of " who."

This doubt should never be coarse. The finer it is the better. At all times and in all places, one should single-mindedly watch and keep this doubt, and keep it going like a fine stream of water. Do not get distracted by any other thought. When the doubt is there, do not disturb it. When the doubt is no longer there, gently give rise to it again. Beginners will find that it is more effective to use this method when stationary rather than when moving; but you should not have a discriminating attitude. Regardless of whether your practice is effective or not or whether you are stationary or moving, just single-mindedly use the method and practice.

In the hua to, "Who is reciting the Buddha's name?" The emphases should be on the word "who." The other words serve to provide a general idea, just like in asking, "Who is dressing?" "Who is eating?" "Who in moving their bowels?" "Who is urinating?" "Who is ignorantly fighting for an ego?" "Who is being aware?" "Regardless of whether one is walking, standing, sitting, or reclining, the word "who" is direct and immediate. Not having to rely on repetitive thinking, conjecture, or attention, it is easy to give rise to a sense of doubt.

Hence, hua to's involving the word "who " are wonderful methods for methods for practicing Ch'an. But the idea is not to repeat, " Who is reciting Buddha's name?" like one might repeat the Buddha's name itself; nor is it right to use reasoning to come up with an answer to the question, thinking that this is what is meant by having doubt. There are people who uninterruptedly repeat the phrase, "Who is reciting the Buddha's name?" They would accumulate more merit and virtue if they repeatedly recited Amitabha Buddha's name instead. There are others who let their minds wander, thinking that is the meaning of having doubt, and they end up more involved in illusory thoughts. This is like trying to ascend but descending instead. Be aware of this.

The doubt that is generated by a beginning practitioner tends to be coarse, intermittent and irregular. This does not truly qualify as a state of doubt. It can only be called thoughts. Gradually, after the wild thoughts settle and one has more control, the process can be called can (pronounced ts'an which means to investigate or look into). As one's cultivation gets smoother, the doubt naturally arises without one's actively inducing it to. At this point one is not aware of where one is sitting. One is not aware of the existence of a body or mind or environment. Only the doubt is there. This is a true state of doubt.

Realistically speaking, the initial stage cannot be considered cultivation. One is merely engaging in illusory thoughts. Only when true doubt arises by itself can it be called true cultivation. This moment is a crucial juncture, and it is easy for the practitioner to deviate from the right path:

(1) At this moment it is clear and pure and there is an unlimited sense of lightness and peace. However if one fails to fully maintain one's awareness and illumination (awareness is wisdom, not delusion; illumination is samadhi, not disorder), one will fall into a light state of mental dullness. If there is an open-eyed person around, he will be able to tell right away that the practitioner is in this mental state and hit him with the incense stick, dispersing all clouds and fog. Many people become enlightened this way.

(2) At this moment it is clear and pure, empty and vacuous. If it isn't, then the doubt is lost. Then it is "no content," meaning one is not making an effort to practice anymore. This is what is meant by "the cliff with dry wood" or "the rock soaking in cold water. " In this situation the practitioner has to " bring up." "Bring up" means to develop awareness and illumination. It is different from earlier times when the doubt was coarse. Now it has to be extremely fine --- one thought, uninterrupted and extremely subtle. With utter clarity, it is illuminating and quiescent, unmoving yet fully aware. Like the smoke from a fire that is about to go out, it is a narrow stream without interruption. When one's practice reaches this point, it is necessary to have a diamond eye in the sense that one should not try to "bring up" anymore. To "bring up" at this point would be like putting a head on top of one's head.

Once a monk asked Ch'an master Zhaozhou, "What should one do when not one thing comes?" Zhaozhou replied, "Put it down." The monk asked, "If not one thing comes, what does one put down?" Zhaozhou replied, "If it cannot be put down, take it up." This dialogue refers precisely to this kind of situation. The true flavor of this state cannot be described. Like someone drinking water, only he knows how cool or warm it is. If a person reaches this state, he will naturally understand. If he is not at this state, no explanation will be adequate. To a sword master you should offer a sword; do not bother showing your poetry to someone who is not a poet.

5. Taking Care of hua to and Turning Inward to Hear One's Self-nature:

Someone might ask, "How is Bodhisattva Avalokitesvara's method of turning inward to hear self-nature considered investigating Ch'an?" I have previously explained that taking care of hua to is being, moment after moment, with only one thought, single-mindedly shining the light inward on "that which is not born and not destroyed." Inward illumination is reflection. Self-nature is that which is not born and not destroyed. When "hearing" and "illuminating" follow sound and form in the worldly stream, hearing does not go beyond sound and seeing does not go beyond form. However, when one turns inward and contemplates self-nature against the worldly stream, and does not pursue sound and form then he becomes pure and transparent. At that time "hearing" and "illuminating" are not two different things.

Thus we should know that taking care of the hua to and turning inward to hear self-nature does not mean using our eyes to see and our ears to hear. If we use our ears to hear or our eyes to see, then we are chasing sound and form. As a result we will be affected by them. This is called submission to the worldly stream. If one practices with one thought only, single-mindedly abiding in that which is not born and not destroyed, not chasing after sound and form, with no wandering thoughts, then one is going against the stream. This is also called taking care of the hua to or turning inward to hear one's self-nature. This is not to say you should close your eyes tightly or cover your ears. Just do not generate a mind of seeking after sound and form.

6. Determined to Leave samsara and Generating a Persevering Mind:

In Ch'an training the most important thing is to have an earnestness to leave birth and death and to generate a persevering mind. If there is no earnestness to leave birth and death, then one cannot generate the "great doubt" and practice will not be effective. If there is no perseverance in one's mind, the result will be laziness, like a man who practices for one day and rests for ten. The practice will be incomplete and when great doubt arises, vexations will come to an end by themselves. When the time comes, the melon will naturally depart from the vine.

I will tell you a story. During the Ching dynasty in the year of Geng Ze (1900) when the eight world powers sent their armies to Peking, the Emperor Guang Xu fled westward from Peking to Shanxi province. Everyday he walked tens of miles. for several days he had no food to eat. On the road, a peasant offered him sweet potato stems. after he ate them, he asked the peasant what they were because they tasted so good. Think about the emperor's usual awe-inspiring demeanor and his arrogance! How long do you think he could continue to maintain his imperial attitude after so long a journey on foot? do you think he had ever gone hungry? Do you think he ever had to eat sweet potato stems? At that time he gave up all of his airs. After all, he had walked quite a distance and had eaten stems to keep from starving. Why was he able to put down everything at that time? Because the allied armies wanted his life and his only thought was to save himself. But when peace prevailed and he returned to Peking, once again he became proud and arrogant. He didn't have to run anymore. He no longer had longer had to eat any food that might displease him. Why was he unable to put down everything at that time? Because the allied armies no longer wanted his life. If the emperor always had an attitude of running for his life and if he could turn such an attitude toward the path of practice, there would be nothing he could not accomplish. It's a pity he did not have a persevering mind. When favorable circumstances returned, so did his former habits.

Fellow practitioners! Time is passing, never to return. It is constantly looking for our lives. It is more frightening than the allied armies. Time will never compromise or make peace with us. Let us generate a mind of perseverance immediately in order to escape from birth and death! Master Gaofeng (1238-1295) once said, "concerning the practice, one should act like a stone dropping into the deepest part of the pool --- ten thousand feet deep --- continuously and persistently dropping without interruption toward the bottom. If one can practice like this without stopping, continuously for seven days and still be unable to cut off one's wandering, illusory thoughts and vexations, I, Gaofeng, will have my tongue pulled out for cows to plow on forever. "He continued by saying, "When one practices Ch'an, one should set out a certain time for success, like a man who has fallen into a pit a thousand feet deep. All his tens of thousands of thoughts are reduced to one --- escape from the pit. If one can really practice from morning to dusk and from night to day without a second thought, and if he does not attain complete enlightenment within three, five, or seven days, I shall be committing a great lie for which I shall have my tongue pulled out for cows to plow on forever." This old master had great compassion. Knowing that we would probably be unable to generate such a persevering mind, he made two great vows to guarantee our success.

7. Enlightenment and Practice

The patriarch, Hanshan (1546-1623), once said (in this document), "There are practitioners who get enlightened first and then start their cultivation, and those who practice first and then get enlightened. However, there are two kinds of enlightenment: insight through reason and insight through experience. If a person realizes Mind by following the teachings of the Buddha and the patriarchs, it is considered insight through reason. One with such an experience will only have a conceptual understanding. In all circumstances he will still be powerless. The mind of the practitioner and the environment are separate and do not reach totality. Therefore, his experience is an obstruction. It is called simulated Prajna and is not real practice.

"On the other hand, those who become enlightened through practice stick to their methods in a straightforward manner until they force themselves into a corner. suddenly their last conceptual thought disappears and they completely realize Mind. It is like seeing your father at a cross road there is no doubt. It is like drinking water: only the person drinking knows if it is warm or cold. There is no way to express it. This is real practice and enlightenment. Afterward, the practitioner will still have t deal with different mental states that arise in accordance with his experience. He will still have to get rid of strong karmic obstructions and wandering and emotional thoughts, leaving only pure Mind. This is enlightenment by experience.

"concerning true enlightenment experiences, there are deep and shallow ones. If one puts effort in following the fundamental principle, destroys the nest of the eighth consciousness and overturns the dark caves of ignorance, then one head directly for enlightenment. There is no other way. Those who achieve this have extremely sharp karmic roots and experience deep enlightenment.

"Those who practice gradually experience shallow enlightenment. The worst case is when someone attains little and is satisfied. One should not take illusions, like shadows created by light, for enlightenment. Why? Because they do not chop down the root of the eighth consciousness. The experiences these people have are manifestations of their own consciousness. Believing such an experience to be real is like mistaking a thief for your son. an ancient said, 'Because cultivators believe that the activities of their consciousness are real, they do not recognize what is real. This is the reason for their transmigration through innumerable kalpas of birth and death. Ignorant people take consciousness for their true selves. 'Therefore, you must pass through this gate.

"On the other hand, there are those who experience sudden enlightenment and cultivate gradually. Although these people have experience deep enlightenment, they still have habitual tendencies that they cannot eliminate immediately. At this point , progress depends on circumstance. It all depends on the clarity of their practice in different situations. They have to use their enlightened principle to illuminate these situations. while passing through them they can check their minds. If they can melt away one percent of the external appearances, then they will have gained one percent of their Dharmakaya. By eliminating one percent of their wandering thoughts, one percent of their original wisdom will manifest. This is how one can strengthen one's experience."

Listening to Hanshan's words, we can see that it is not important whether someone is enlightened or not. Those who understand enlightenment either through reason or experience have to continue their practice and follow it through. The difference is that those who are enlightened first and then cultivate are like old horses who are familiar with the road. They will not go the wrong way. It is much easier than cultivating first and then getting enlightened.

Those who are enlightened are rooted and are not like those who understand enlightenment through reason. People with the latter understanding are shaky. Their experience is superficial. those who are enlightened through experience are more likely to derive benefit form their practice. Even at the age of eighty, the elder master Zhaozhou (778-897) still traveled. For forty years, the master used his mind without any wanderings; he only investigated the word "nothingness." He is a great model. Do you doubt that the master was enlightened? He truly reminds us not to be satisfied when we have little and not to praise ourselves highly.

There are those who, after reading a few sutras or collections of talks of Ch'an masters, say things like, "The mind is the Buddha," and , "It is throughout the three periods and ten directions." Their words have nothing to do with the fundamental principle. They firmly believe that they are ancient Buddhas who have come back again. When they meet people, they praise themselves and say that they have attained complete enlightenment. Blind followers will even brag for them. It is like mistaking fish eyes for pearls. They do not know the difference between the real and the false. They mix things up. It not only makes people lose faith; it also gives rise to criticism. The reason the Ch'an sect is not flourishing is mainly because of the faults of these crazy people. I hope you can be diligent in your practice. Do not start something false. Do not speak about Ch'an with empty words. You must investigate seriously and attain real enlightenment. In the future you can propagate the Dharma and be a great master, like a dragon or an elephant in the animal kingdom, and help Ch'an Buddhism to flourish.

8. Investigating Ch'an and Reciting Buddha's Name

Those who recite Buddha's name usually criticize those who investigate Ch'an and those who investigate Ch'an usually slander those who recite Buddha's name. They seem to oppose each other like enemies. Some of them even wish that the others would die. This is a terrible thing to have happen in Buddhism. There is a saying which goes something like this: "A family in harmony will succeed in everything, whereas a family in decline is sure to argue. "With all of this fighting among brothers, it is no wonder that others laugh at us and look down at us.

Investigating Ch'an, reciting Buddha's name, and other methods are all teachings of Shakyamuni Buddha. The original Path is not separate from these methods. It is only because of the different karmic roots and mentalities of sentient beings that different methods are taught. It is like giving different antidotes for different poisons. Later on, patriarchs divided Buddha's teaching into different sects corresponding to different theories. Because the needs of people differ at different times, patriarchs propagated the Dharma in different ways.

If an individual practices a method that fits his character, then regardless of which Dharma door he uses., he can penetrate the Path. Actually, there are no superior and inferior Dharma doors. Furthermore, Dharma doors are interconnected. all are perfect and without obstruction. For example, when one recites the Buddha's name to the point of one-mindedness, is this not investigating Ch'an? When one investigates Ch'an to the point of no separation between the investigator and that which is being investigated, is this not reciting the real characteristic of the Buddha? Ch'an is not other than the Ch'an within the Pure Land and Pure Land is not other than the Pure Land within Ch'an. Ch'an and pure Land are mutually enriching, and they function together.

However, there are people who favor one view over another, and from these distinctions arise different ideas and opinions, which can unfortunately lead to praising oneself while slandering others. Such people are like fire and water. They cannot exist together. they have misunderstood the intention of the patriarchs who started the different sects. These people are unintentionally responsible for damaging, slandering and endangering Buddhism. Is this not sad and pitiable?

I hope that all of us , no matter which dharma door we practice, understand the Buddha's principle of not discriminating and not arguing.

We should have the mind of helping one another so that we may save this ship which floats amidst dangerous and violent waves.

9. The Two Kinds of difficulty and Ease which Practitioners experience

There are two kinds of difficulty and ease practitioners face on the Path, and which they experience depends primarily on the shallowness or depth of their practice. The first kind of difficulty and ease is associated with beginners, while the second kind corresponds to advanced practitioners.

The symptoms of the common beginner's disease are: incapability of putting down wandering thoughts, habitual tendencies, ignorance, arrogance, jealousy, greed, anger, stupidity, desire, laziness, gluttony, and discrimination between self and other. All these fill big bellies. How can this be in accordance with the Path?

There are other kinds of people who are born into wealthy and noble families. Never forgetting their habitual tendencies and bad influences, they cannot endure one bit of difficulty or withstand any hardship. How can these people practice the Path? They do not consider the status of our original teacher, Shakyamuni Buddha, when he decided to become a monk.

There are other people who know a few words but do not understand that the ancients were actually tests to evaluate practitioners' levels of understanding. These people think they are smart. Every day they scrutinize the recorded sayings and writings, talk about Mind and Buddha, explain and interpret the teachings of the ancients. Talking about food but not eating it, counting the treasure of others and not owning it themselves, they think they are extraordinary people. They become incredibly arrogant. But when these people become seriously ill, they will cry out for help; and at the end of their lives they will panic and become bewildered. At that time, what they have learned and understood will be useless, and it will be too late to regret.

There are other people who misunderstand the saying, " Originally we are Buddhas." These people say that the original self is complete and that there is no need for rectification. All day long they loaf about with nothing to do, following their emotions, wasting their time. These people praise themselves as eminent people and conform to causes and conditions. In the future these people will suffer greatly.

Then there are people who have determined minds to practice, but who do not know where to begin their endeavors, or who are afraid of wandering thoughts. Unable to get rid of their thoughts, they abide inn vexation all day long, thinking about and mourning their heavy karmic obstructions. Because of this their determined minds backslide.

There are also those people who want to battle till death with their wandering thoughts. Furiously, they tense up their fists and push out their chests and eyes. It seems like they are involved in something big. Ready to die in battle against their wandering thoughts, they do not realize that wandering thoughts cannot be defeated. These people end up vomiting blood or going insane.

There are people who fear falling into emptiness. Little do they know that demons have arisen in their minds. They can neither empty their minds nor get enlightened. And there are those who strongly seek enlightenment, not understanding that seeking enlightenment and wanting to attain Buddhahood are all grave wandering thoughts. One cannot cook sand hoping to eat rice. They can seek until the year of the donkey and they still won't get enlightened. sometimes people become elated when occasionally they sit through a couple of peaceful sittings. These situations are like a blind turtle whose head happens to pass through a small hole in a piece of wood floating in the middle of the ocean. It is not the result of real practice. In their elation these people have served to add another obstruction.

There are those who dwell in false purity during meditation and enjoy themselves. Since they cannot maintain a peaceful mind within activity , they avoid noisy places and spend their days soaking in stale water. There are numerous examples of this. for beginners, it is very difficult to find entrance to the Path. If there is illumination without awareness, then it's like sitting in stale water waiting to die.

Even though this practice is hard, once you find entrance to the path, it becomes easier. What is the easiest way for beginners? There is nothing special other than being able to "put it down." put what down? Put down all vexations arising from ignorance. Fellow practitioners, once this body of ours stops breathing, it becomes a corpse. The main reason we cannot put it down is because we place too much importance on it. Because of this, we give rise to the idea of self and other, right and wrong, love and hate, gain and loss. If we can have a firm belief that this body of ours is like a corpse, not to cherish it or look upon it as being ourselves, then what is there that we cannot put down? we must learn to put it down anywhere, anytime, whether walking, standing, sitting or sleeping, whether in motion or still, whether resting or active. we have to hold onto the doubt of the hua to internally, and externally, and externally ignore everything. Continuously keep this up, calmly and peacefully, without a moment of extraneous thought, like a long sword extending into the sky. If anything comes in contact with the sharp edge, it will be extinguished without a trace or sound. If one could do this, would he still be afraid of wandering thoughts? What could harm him? Who is it that would be distinguishing between movement and stillness? Who is it that would be attached to existence or emptiness?

If there are fears of wandering thoughts, then you have already added another wandering thought. If you feel you are pure, then you are already defiled. If you are afraid of falling into emptiness, then you are already dwelling in existence. If you want to become a Buddha, then you have to know is the entrance to the Path. afterward, carrying water and gathering firewood are not separate from the wonderful Path. Hoeing and planting fields are all Ch'an opportunities (Ch'an ji). Practicing the Path is not limited to sitting cross-legged throughout the day.

What difficulties are encountered by advanced practitioners? Although some have practiced until the emergence of genuine doubt and possess both awareness and illumination, they are still bound by birth and death. Those who have neither awareness nor illumination fall into false emptiness. To arrive at either of these situations is truly hard. After reaching this point , many people cannot detach themselves further. They stand at the top of a ten thousand foot pole unable to advance. Some people, having progressed to this stage and being skilled in practice, and having sidestepped situations they cannot solve, think that they have already eradicated ignorance. They believe that their practice has reached home. Actually, these people are living in the wave of ignorance and do not even know it. When these people encounter a situation that they cannot solve --- where they must be their own master --- they just give up. This is a pity.

There are others who reach real doubt, gain a little wisdom from the experience of emptiness, and understand a few ancient gong ans; and then they give up the great doubt because they think they are completely enlightened. These people compose poems and gathas, act arrogantly and call themselves virtuous men of the Path. Not only do they fool themselves, they also mislead others. They are creating bad karma. In other cases there are those who mistake the words of Bodhidharma, "To isolate from external conditions, internally the mind becomes still, like a wall, and one can enter the Path, " or the Sixth Patriarch's, "Not thinking of good or evil, at this time what is your original face, venerable Ming?" They think that meditating by rotten wood or by large boulders is the ultimate principle. These people take the illusory city as their treasured palace. They take the temporally guest house as their home. This i s what the gong an of the old woman who burned down the hut to reprimand one such living corpse refers to.

What is the easy way for these advanced practitioners? Do not be proud and do not quit in the middle of cultivation. In the midst of well-meshed continuous practice, you have to be even finer. While practicing in a cautious and attentive manner, you have to be more careful. When the time comes, the bottom of the barrel will naturally drop off. If you cannot do this, then find a virtuous teacher to pry off the nails of the barrel and pull out the joints.

Master cold Mountain once chanted: "On the peak of the highest mountain, the four directions expand to infinity. Sitting in silence, no one knows. The solitary moon shines on the cold spring. Here inn the spring there is no moon. is high in the sky. Though I'm humming this song, in the song there is no Ch'an. "The first two lines of this song reveal that the appearance of real nature does not belong to anything. The whole world is filled with bright and pure light without any obstructions. The third line speaks of the real body of Suchness. Surely, ordinary people cannot know this. Even the Buddhas of the three periods do not know where I abide. Therefore, no one can know the path. The three lines beginning with, "The solitary moon shines on the cold spring," is an expedient example of the level of Master Cold Mountain's practice. The last two lines are mentioned because he is afraid that we will "mistake the finger for the moon." He especially warns us that words and language are not Ch'an.

10. Conclusion:

I have said too much and have interrupted your practice. It is like pulling vines. The more one pulls, the more they tangle together. whenever there are words, there is no real meaning. when the ancient virtuous masters guided their students, either they used sticks or shouted. There were not so many words. However, the present cannot be compared with the past. One has no choice but to point a finger at the moon. After all, which is the finger? Which is the moon? Investigate!

The Writings of Dogen Zenji

Introduction

Dōgen envisioned the primacy of zazen as Shikantaza (Sheer Seated Meditation): Shikan means "utmost" or "fervently" or "simply"; da means "hitting" in the sense of "throwing oneself"; za means "sitting." Shikantaza basically means "to throw oneself to and fervently do zazen."Dōgen interpreted zazen not as a separate means to reach the goal of Enlightenment, but as a manifestation of Enlightenment itself. Seated mediation is often interpreted as a practical method to reach the state of the Enlightenment.

Dōgen developed the idea of the oneness of practice and embodiment; becoming and being; doing and attainment. Based upon this concept of the unity of being and doing, he presented authentic zazen as the presence and the working of Buddha nature. Buddha nature is also conceived not only as a static essence but also as a dynamic working principle.

Dōgen explicated the temporality of being. His concept of Shikantaza is rooted in his ontology. For Dōgen, the fact of to-be or existence is a temporal event or process where eternal truth is manifested. Existence is an event where eternity and the moment, permanence and change, meet and cross over. Existence is possible only when eternal truth manifests itself in time.

Dōgen comprehended truth not as some kind of object one can possess or lose, but as that which make all phenomena possible. All phenomena can take place as the work of truth. For example, a flower can blossom by virtue of the work of truth. Thus, the entire world and phenomena are nothing but the manifestation of or the work of truth.

Knowing the truth is therefore not a matter of "having" or "finding" truth as an object. One already exists in truth. When one drops all one's conscious acts, truth discloses itself. Dōgen's epistemology is not separate from his ontology, and knowing and being are intricately fused within the context of practice.

Enlightenment is the realization of the fact that all being, including the self, exists in truth. The pre-condition for realizing Enlightenment is the elimination of all conscious acts and disturbances in the mind, including conscious acts of attempting to find truth. If one prepares oneself, truth discloses itself. Dōgen explains the relationship between the self and truth by an analogy of water and moon:

Enlightenment is like a reflection of the Moon on water: The Moon does not get wet and the water is not disturbed.

This explains the relationship between mind and truth. If one reaches an absolutely tranquil state of mind like still water, the truth that is working in the entire cosmos can be reflected in one's mind. Enlightenment is the state where the truth is naturally reflected in the mind just like the Moon is reflected on still and calm water without distortion. The truth discloses itself without one's preconception ("The Moon does not get wet.") and mind also becomes like a mirror that reflects truth as it discloses itself ("the water is not disturbed.").

It is an irony of the mechanism of consciousness that the more one tries to calm the consciousness and reach tranquility, the more it is disturbed. Dōgen warns not to attempt to find truth but to prepare oneself so that one can be opened up to truth in the way that truth shows itself.

One is enlightened by and opened up to truth with the advent of truth. Enlightenment is also an experiential or existential realization that the truth is at work in existence, including the existence of the self.

A General Recommended Way of Sitting Meditation

The Way is fundamentally complete and perfect, all-pervasive, how could it depend upon cultivation and realization?

The vehicle of the source is free; why expend effort? The whole being is utterly beyond defiling dust; who would believe in a method of wiping it clean? The great whole is not apart from here; why go someplace to practice? Nevertheless, the slightest discrepancy is as the distance between sky and earth: as soon as aversion and attraction arise, you lose your mind in confusion. Even though you may boast of comprehension and wallow in understanding, having gotten a glimpse of insight, and though you find the Way and understand the mind, though you may roam freely within the bounds of initial entry, you are still somewhat lacking in a living road of emancipation.

Even Gautama Buddha, who had innate knowledge, at upright for six years; this is a noteworthy example. When referring to the transmission of the mind seal at Shaolin, the fame of nine years facing a wall is still mentioned. Since the ancients did so, why should people today not do so? Therefore you should stop the intellectual activity of pursuing words and chasing sayings, and should learn the stepping back of turning the light around and looking back. Body and mind will naturally be shed, and the original countenance will become manifest. If you want to attain something, you should set right about working on it. For intensive Zen meditation, a quirt room is appropriate. Food and drink are to be moderate. Letting go of all mental objects, taking a respite from all concerns, not thinking of good or evil, not being concerned with right or wrong, halt the operations of mind, intellect, and consciousness, stop assessment by thought, imagination, and view. Do not aim to become a Buddha; and how could it be limited to sitting or reclining? Spread a thick sitting mat where you usually sit, and use a cushion on top of this. You may sit in the full-lotus posture, or in the half-lotus posture. For the full-lotus posture, first place the right foot on the left thigh, then the left foot on the right thigh. For the half-lotus posture, just place the left foot on the right thigh. Wear loose clothing, and keep it orderly. Next place the right hand on the left leg, and the left hand on the right hand, with palms facing upward. The two thumbs face each other and hold each other up. Now sit upright, with your body straight. Do not lean to the left or tilt to the right, bend forward or lean backward. Align the ears with the shoulders, and the nose with the navel. The tongue should rest on the upper palate, the teeth and lips should be closed. The eyes should always be open. The breathing passes subtly through the nose. Once the physical form is in order, exhale fully through the mouth once, sway left and right, then settle into sitting perfectly still. Think of what does not think. How do you think of what does not think? It is not thinking. This is the essential art of sitting Zen meditation. What I call sitting Zen meditation is not practice of dhyana. It is just a method of comfort, a practical way of experiencing thoroughgoing investigation of enlightenment: objective reality becomes manifest, beyond any trap. If you can get the meaning of this, you will be like dragons taking to the water, like tigers in the mountains. You will know that the truth has spontaneously become evident, while oblivion and distraction will already have been overcome. When you are going to rise from sitting, move your body gradually, getting up gently. Do not be hasty or careless.

We have seen stories of transcending the ordinary and going beyond the holy, shedding the mortal coil while sitting or passing away while standing upright: all of these depend on the power in this.

And how about the transformations of state upon the lifting of a finger, a pole, a needle, a hammer? How about the realizations of accord on the raising of a whisk, a fist, a cane, a shout? They have never been susceptible to understanding but thought and conceptualizations; how could they be known by cultivated realization of supernatural powers? It could be called dignified behavior beyond sound and form; is it not a guiding example prior to knowledge and views? Being such, it is not an issue whether one has more or less intelligence, making no distinction between the quick and the slow. Focused, unified concentration is what constitutes work on the Way. The practice and realizations are spontaneously undefiled; the process of heading for the aim, furthermore, is being normal. Whatever they are, one's own world and the realms of others; West and East, they equally hold the seal of Buddha, based as one on the way of the source. Just work on sitting, remaining in an immobile state. Even though it seems there are myriad differences and a thousand distinctions, just attend to intensive meditation to master the Way. Why abandon a seat in your own house to idly roam in the dusty realms of alien countries? Take a single misstep, and you blunder past what's right in front of you. Having gotten the key to the human body, do not pass time uselessly: preserve and uphold the essential potential of the Buddha Way. Who has the folly to look forward to what lasts but a moment? Add to this consideration the fact that the physical body is like a dewdrop on the grass, a lifetime is like a lightning flash: all of a sudden they are void, in an instant they are gone. May those high-minded people who participate in this study and have long learned to feel an elephant by hand not be suspicious of a real dragon. Proceed energetically on the straightforward path of direct pointing, and honor people who have transcended learning and gone beyond effort. Join in the enlightenment of the Buddhas, inherit the state of mind of the Zen founders.

Having long been thus, we should be thus. The treasury opens of itself, to be used at will.

Bendowa

The various Buddhas and Tathagatas have a most enlightened way of realizing superior wisdom and transmitting the supreme law. When transmitted from Buddha to Buddha, its mark is self-joyous meditation. To enter this meditation naturally, right sitting is the true gate. Though each man has Buddha-nature in abundance, he cannot make it appear without practice or live it without enlightenment. If you let it go, it fills your hand; it transcends the one and many. If you talk about it, it fills your mouth; it is beyond measurement by height and width. All Buddhas eternally have their abode here without becoming attached to one-sided recognition. All beings are working here without attachment to sides in each recognition. The devices and training that I teach now manifest all things in original enlightenment and express unity in action. And when you thoroughly understand, why cling to such trifles as these?

On awakening of the desire to seek the way, I visited Buddhist masters in all parts of the country. Finally I met Zenko (Myozen, disciple of Eisai) at Kennin temple. The nine years that If served as his follower passed quickly. From him I heard about the Rinzai style. Zenko, as the leading disciple of Eisai, truly transmitted the highest Buddhism. Other disciples could not compare with him. I also went to China, visited Zen masters of both Cheh-chiang (Chekiang, formerly divided into east and west), and heard about the styles of the five schools. Finally I studied with Zen master Ju-sting (Nyojo) on Ta-p'ein (Taihaku) peak. In this was I completed the valuable training for my life. After that at the beginning of the Shotei period (1227), I returned to Japan. Because I had the idea of spreading the Law and saving all beings, I was like a man carrying a heavy burden. Then I thought of abandoning this idea of spreading the Law and wait for a more propitious time. I wandered here and there for some time sincerely trying to teach the style of the former Zen master. There are true trainees who deliberately shun fame and profit and concentrate on the search for the way. But unfortunately they are misled by false masters, so real understanding is veiled and the trainees uselessly become drunk with self- madness and drown for long years in the world of delusion. How can the right seed of wisdom sprout and the chance for enlightenment be grasped? I am now wandering here and there like a cloud or water grass - what mountain or river shall I visit? Because I sympathize with such seekers, I went to China, saw the form and style of the monasteries, and received the essence of the Zen teaching. Gathering and recording all this, I am leaving it for the trainees so that they may be helped toward knowing the essence of Buddhism. Isn't this the core of Zen? Buddha Sakyamuni transmitted the right law to Mahakasyapa on Grdhrakuta Mountain, and a long line of patriarchs handed it down to Bodhidharma. And Bodhidharma went to China and transmitted the right law to Hui-k'o (Eka).

This started the transmission of Zen Buddhism to the East. Transmitted thus in its essential purity, it came down by a natural route to the Sixth Patriarch, Hui-neng. At this time true Buddhism was transmitted to China, and it expressed a meaning free from trivialities. The Sixth Patriarch had two outstanding disciples- Nan-yueh Huai-jang and Ch'ing-yuan Hsing-ssu. Together they transmitted the Buddha seal; they were leaders of man and heaven. These two schools spread, and five styles of Zen appeared. They were the schools of Fa-yen, Wei-yang, Ts'ao-tung, Yun-men, and Lin-chi. In present-day China only the Lin-chi (Rinzai) school is flourishing. Although the five schools differ, they are all based on the single seal of the Buddha Mind. From the later Han period to the present in China, the scriptures of the other teachings were propagated, but it was impossible to determine which was best. With the coming of Bodhidharma from India the root of the conflict was abruptly cut, and pure Buddhism spread. We must also try to do the same in our country. All the Buddhas and patriarchs who transmitted Buddhism considered sitting and practicing self-joyous meditation the true way of enlightenment. The enlightened ones in both the East and West followed this style. This is because the masters and their disciples correctly transmitted this superior method from person to person and received the uncorrupted truth.

1. Q: I have heard of the superior merits of zazen. But an ordinary person will have doubts and say there are many gates in Buddhism. Why do you urge only zazen?

A: Because it is the right gate to Buddhism - this is my answer to him.

2. Q: Why is it the only right gate?

A: The great teacher Sakyamuni handed down this unexcelled method of enlightenment. And the Tathagatas of the past, present, and future were similarly enlightened by zazen. They, too, transmitted it as the right gate. The patriarchs in India and China were also enlightened by zazen. For this reason, I now indicate the right gate for human beings and heaven.

3 Q: Such reasons as correct transmission by the unexcelled method of the Tathagatas and following in the footsteps of the patriarchs are beyond common sense. To ordinary people, reading the sutra and

saying the Nembutsu are the natural means to enlightenment. You just sit cross-legged and do nothing. How is this a means to enlightenment?

A: You look on the meditation of the Buddhas and the supreme law as just sitting and doing nothing. You disparage Mahayana Buddhism. Your delusion is deep; you are like someone in the middle of the ocean crying out for water. Fortunately we are already sitting at ease in the self-joyous meditation of the Buddhas. Isn't this a great boon? What a pity that your true-eye remains shut-that your mind remains drunk. The world of the Buddhas eludes ordinary thinking and consciousness. It cannot be known by disbelief and inferior knowledge. To enter one must have right belief. The disbeliever, even if taught, has trouble grasping it. For example, when the Buddha was preaching at Grdhrakuta, the disbelieves were allowed to go away. To bring out the right belief in your mind you must train and study. If you cannot do this, you should quit for awhile, regretting that you lack the influence of the law from a former beneficial relation. What good are such actions as reading the sutras and saying the Nembutsu. How futile to think that Buddhist merits accrue from merely moving the tongue and raising the voice. If you think this covers Buddhism, you are far from the truth. Your only purpose in reading the sutras should be to learn thoroughly that the Buddha taught the rules of gradual and sudden training and that by practicing his teachings you can obtain enlightenment. You should not read the sutras merely to pretend to wisdom through vain intellections. To strive for the goal of Buddhism by reading many sutras is like pointing the hill to the north and heading south. It is like putting a square peg in a round hole. While you look at words and phrases, the path of your training remains dark. This is as worthless as a doctor who forgets his prescription. Constant repetition of the Nembutsu is also worthless-like a frog in a spring field croaking night and day. Those deluded by fame and fortune, find it especially difficult to abandon the nembutsu. Bound by deep roots to a profit-seeking mind, they existed in ages past, and they exist today. They are to be pitied. Understand only this: if enlightened Zen masters and their earnest disciples correctly transmit the supreme law of the seven Buddhas, its essence emerges, and it can be experienced. Those who merely study the letters of the sutras cannot know this. So put a stop to this doubt and delusion. Follow the teachings of a real master and, by zazen; attain to the self-joyous samadhi of the Buddhas.

4. Q: The Tendai school and Kegon teachings have both came across to this country; they represent the cream of Buddhism. In the Shingon school-transmitted directly from Vairocana Tathagata to Vajrasattva - there is no stain between master and disciple. This school maintains that "this mind is the Buddha", and that "this mind becomes the

Buddha"; it does not advocate long step-by-step training. It teaches the simultaneous enlightenment of the five Buddhas. It is unexcelled in Buddhism. In view of all this what superiority does zazen have that you recommend it alone and exclude the other teachings?

A: You must understand that in Buddhism the stress falls on the truth or falsity of the training-not on the excellence or mediocrity of the teaching or the depth or shallowness of the principle. In times past, men were drawn to Buddhism by grass, flowers, mountains, and water. Some received the Buddha seal by grasping dirt, stones, sand, and pebbles. The dimensionless letters overflow all forms, and we can hear the sermon now in a speck of dust. "This mind is the Buddha" - these words are like a moon reflected in water; and the meaning of the words: "sitting cross-legged is itself Buddhism"? Like a figure in the mirror. Do not be victimized by clever manipulation of words. When I recommend the training of immediate enlightenment, I want to make you a true human being by indicating the superior path transmitted by the Buddhas and patriarchs. To transmit the Buddha law you should always make the enlightened person your Zen master. Don't follow a scholar who counts the letters of the scripture. This would be like the blind leading the blind. In the teachings directly transmitted from the Buddhas and patriarchs, the Buddha law is sustained by respect for the enlightened person. When the Gods of darkness and light reject the Zen masters and when the enlightened Arhats ask the path, they provide the means of opening the Buddha Mind. In the other teachings we could not endure it. The followers of Buddhism only have to study the Buddha law. You must understand that we do not lack the highest wisdom. Though we enjoy it eternally, we do not always harmonize with it. This is because we meet setbacks on the Great Way through clinging to individual opinion and chasing after material things. Through individual opinions various phantoms arise. For example, there are countless views on the 12 chains of transmigration, the 25 worlds, the three vehicles, the five vehicles, the Buddha, and the non-Buddha. Training in the true path does not require learning these opinions. So when we sit cross-legged, depending on the Buddha sign and abandoning all things, we can enjoy great wisdom. We enter at once the superior field beyond delusion and enlightenment - a field without distinction between sage and commoner. How can one who clings to verbal tools rise up to this?

5. Q: Samadhi dwells in the three training, and dhyanaparamita (means of meditation) in the six means of enlightenment. All Bodhisattvas study them from the beginning. They train without discriminating cleverness and stupidity. Even this zazen may be a part of them. Why do you say that the true law is gathered in zazen?

A: This question comes from giving the name "Zen sect" to the treasury of the essence of the true law, and to the unexcelled doctrine-the most important teachings of the Buddha. You must understand that the name "Zen sect" emerged from China and the East; it was not heard in India. When Bodhidharma stayed at Shao-Lin ssu in Sung-shan, gazing at the wall for nine years, the priests and laymen did not understand the true law of the Buddha; they called him a Brahmana who emphasized sitting cross-legged. Afterward every patriarch devoted himself to sitting cross-legged. Unenlightened laymen who saw them carelessly referred to them as the zazen sect without understanding the truth. Today the "Za" has been dropped, and the followers of this practice are known as members of the Zen sect. This is clear in the manuscripts of the patriarchs. You must not equate zazen with the meditation in the six means and the three training. The spirit of transmission in Buddhism is clear in the career of the Buddha. To Mahakasyapa alone on Grdhrakuta Mountain the Buddha transmitted the eye and treasury of the true law, the superior mind of enlightenment and supreme doctrine, and some gods in heaven saw it. Don't doubt this. The gods of heaven protect Buddhism eternally. This is still a living fact. You must understand that zazen is the full way of Buddhism. It is incomparable.

6. Q: Why does Buddhism advocate meditation and enlightenment through cross-legged sitting alone (of the four actions)?

A: I do not analyze the way of training and enlightenment followed by the various Buddhas. If you ask why, I say simply that it is the way used in Buddhism. You should not seek no further. But the patriarchs praised cross-legged sitting, calling it the comfortable way. I know this sitting is the most comfortable of the four actions. It is not only the training of one Buddha or two Buddhas but of all Buddhas and patriarchs.

7. Q: Those who do not know Buddhism have to attain enlightenment by zazen and training. What use is zazen to those who have clearly obtained enlightenment?

A: Though I do not talk about last night's dream and cannot give a paddle to a woodcutter, I have something to teach you. The view that training and enlightenment are not one is heretical. In Buddhism these two are the same. Because this is training enfolding enlightenment, the training even at the outset is all of original enlightenment. So the Zen master, when giving advice to his disciples, tells them not to seek enlightenment without training because training itself points directly to original enlightenment. Because it is already enlightenment of training, there is no end to enlightenment. Because it is training of enlightenment, there is no beginning to training. Sakyamuni Tathagata and Mahakasyapa, therefore, were both used by training based on enlightenment. Training, based on enlightenment similarly moved both Bodhidharma and Hui-neng. This is typical of all traces of transmission in Buddhism. Already there is training that is inseparable from enlightenment. Because training even at the outset transmits a part of superior training, we fortunately gain a part of original enlightenment in this natural way. You must understand that the Buddhas and patriarchs emphasized the need for intensive training so as not to stain the enlightenment that is self-identical with training. If you throw away superior training, original enlightenment fills your hand. If you abandon original enlightenment, superior training permeates your body. In China I saw Zen monasteries in many districts, each with a meditation hall where 500 to 1,200 monks lived and practiced zazen day and night. When I asked the Zen masters who have been entrusted with the Buddha seal, "What is the essence of Buddhism?" they answered: "Training and enlightenment are not two but one." So they urged disciples to follow the footsteps of the Zen masters in accordance with the teachings of the Buddhas and patriarchs. They recommended zazen not only to their disciples, but to all those who seek the true way, to those who yearn for true Buddhism, regardless of whether one is a beginner or an advanced student, a commoner or a sage. As a patriarch (Nangaku) has said:

"It is not true that there is no training and enlightenment, but do not stain them by clinging to them." Another patriarch has said: "He who sees the way trains the way." You must, therefore, train within enlightenment.

8. Q: Why did Japanese patriarchs of the past, who went to China and returned to propagate Buddhism, transmit other teachings besides this Zen?

A: The patriarchs of the past did not transmit this Zen because the time was not ripe.

9. Q: Did the patriarchs of the past understand this Zen?

A: If they had understood, they would have propagated it.

10. Q: Someone has said, "Don't throw away delusion (birth and death). There is an easy shortcut to freedom from birth and death. This is because the spirit is eternal." The meaning here is that even if this body is born, it will eventually come to nothing, but this spirit does not perish. If

this Spirit that is not subject to rising and ceasing resides in my body, this is the original spirit. Because of this, the body takes temporal form and remains unfixed, for it dies here and arises there. This spirit is eternal and does not change in past, present, and future. To know this is to free oneself from birth and death. For those who know this, the birth and death they have known up to now disappear, and they enter into an ocean of the spirit. When you embrace this ocean, superior virtue will be complete like the Buddhas. Even if you know this, because this body is the result of former delusive actions, you differ from the sages. Those who do not know this transmigrate eternally. So know only the eternity of the spirit. If you sit in vain and waste your whole life, what can you possibly hope for? Does this view conform to the way of the Buddhas and patriarchs?

A: Your view is not Buddhism. It is the Srenika heresy. This heretical view says: "In our body there is a spiritual knowledge. Through the knowledge we recognize like and dislike, right and wrong, pain and titillation, and suffering and pleasure. This spiritual knowledge, when the body deteriorates, is released here and is born anew elsewhere. Therefore, though it seems to die here, it is born there. It never dies; it continues eternally." This is the heretical view. If you absorb this and think it is Buddhism, it is more foolish than holding roof tiles and pebbles and thinking they are the golden treasures. This foolish delusion is shameful. It is beyond serious consideration. National master Hui-Chung of the Tang dynasty issued a sharp warning against this view. Those who hold this delusive view think that the mind is eternal and that appearance is transitory and equate this with the superior training of the Buddhas; they create the cause of transmigration and think that they have broken free from transmigration. Isn't this false? In deed, it is pathetic. This is nothing but delusive heresy. Don't listen to it. Although I hesitate to say it, I will correct your delusion with sympathy. In Buddhism you have to know this: the body and mind are one; essence and form are one. Make no mistake-this is known also in India and China. In a teaching that talks about eternity, all things become eternal. Don't separate body and mind. In a teaching that talks about cessation, all things are ceasing. Don't separate essence and form. Why do you say that the body ceases while the mind is eternal? Isn't this against the right law? You must realize that life-death itself is nirvana. We cannot talk about nirvana without life-death. You think erroneously that this is the Buddha wisdom free from life and death. Your mind, which understands and perceives, arises and perishes; it is not eternal. Understands this thoroughly: the unity of body and mind is always upheld in Buddhism. In the light of this, why is the mind only released from the body to become free from arising and perishing while the body arises and perishes? If you assert that body and mind are one now and that they are not one at another time, you becloud the Buddha's teachings. To think that birth and death are things to be avoided is a sin against Buddhism. They are truly the tools of Buddhism. In Buddhism, especially in the Awakening of Faith in the Mahayana, the great teaching of the Tathagata-garba embraces the Dharma-dhatu. It does not divide suchness and appearance, nor discuss arising and perishing. Even enlightenment and nirvana are nothing but the Tathagata-garba. It is self-identical with all things and appearances and contains them. These various teachings are all based on One Mind. There is no mistake about this. This is understanding of the Mind of Buddhism. How can you divide this into body and mind and delusion and nirvana. You are already the son of Buddha. Do not listen to madmen who preach heretical views.

11. Q: Does one who seriously practices zazen have to observe the precepts strictly and purify his body and mind?

A: Observing the precepts and living purely are rules of Zen Buddhism and practices handed down by the Buddhas and patriarchs. Those who have not received the precepts should receive them; those who violate the precepts should repent. They shall then absorb the Buddha's wisdom.

12. Q: Is there any objection to a serious student of zazen practicing the mantra of the Shingon sect and the Samathavipa'syana (calm and insight) of the Tendai sect together?

A: When I was in China and heard the gist of Buddhism from the Zen masters, they said they had never heard of any patriarchs who truly transmitted the Buddha seal, now and in the past, undertaking such simultaneous training. Unless we earnestly concentrate on one thing, we cannot gain one wisdom.

13: Q: Can a layman practice this zazen or is it limited to priests?

A: The patriarchs have said that to understand Buddhism there should be no distinction between man and woman and between rich and poor.

14. Q: The priests are free from myriad relations; for them there is no obstruction to zazen training. How can the busy layman attain enlightenment by earnest training?

A: Through their boundless love the Buddhas and patriarchs have flung the vast gates of compassion for all beings- whether Human beings or Deva. We many examples in past and present: Tan-tsung and Sung-tsung, though very busy with state affairs practiced zazen and understood the great way of the Buddhas and patriarchs. Prime ministers Li and Fang were close advisers to the emperors, and they too practiced zazen and were enlightened in the great way of the Buddhas and patriarchs. It simply depends on the will. It has nothing to do with being either a priest or a lay man. Those who can discern excellence and inferiority will believe Buddhism naturally. Those who think that worldly tasks hinder Buddhism know only that there is no Buddhism in the world; they do not know that there is nothing that can be set apart as worldly tasks in Buddhism. In the great Sung dynasty a Prime Minister named P'ing mastered the way of the patriarchs and wrote a poem about himself: "Away from state affairs I practiced zazen, hardly ever laying on my side in bed and sleeping; although I am the prime minister, my fame as a Zen master spread throughout the world." Official business kept P'ing busy, but because he had the will to train earnestly, he gained enlightenment. Consider yourself through these cases (persons); look at the present through the past. At this moment, in the great Sung dynasty, emperors, ministers, soldiers and commoners, and men and women take interest in the way of the patriarchs. Warriors and intellectuals have the will to train, and many of them will eventually experience enlightenment. All this tells us that worldly tasks do not hinder Buddhism. If true Buddhism spreads in the state, the Buddhas and heavenly beings always protect that state, and the world becomes peaceful. If the world becomes peaceful, Buddhism acquires strength. In the age of the Buddha, even misguided criminals were enlightened through his teachings. Under the patriarchs, even hunters and woodcutters were enlightened. And others will gain enlightenment. All you have to do is to receive instructions from a real teacher.

15. Q: Can one gain enlightenment by this zazen, even if one trains in this degenerate age and evil world?

A: Other teachings argue about the name and form of the doctrines. The true teaching does not differentiate the three periods of Sho, Zo and Matsu. Anybody who trains will inevitably gain enlightenment. In the correctly transmitted right law, you can always enjoy the rare treasure of your own house. Those who train know whether enlightenment has been obtained, just as one who drinks water knows personally whether it is cold or warm.

16. Q: Some people say that to know Buddhism you only have to understand the meaning of "this mind itself is the Buddha"; you do not have to chant the sutras or train the body in Buddhism. Understand only that Buddhism is inherent in your self - this is full enlightenment. There is no need for seeking anything from others. So is there any use going to the trouble of practicing zazen?

A: That is a most grievous error. If what you say is true - even though the sages teach this ("this mind itself is the Buddha") - you cannot understand it. To study Buddhism you have to transcend the viewpoint of self and others. If you become enlightened by knowing that the self itself is the Buddha, Sakyamuni long ago would not have tried so hard to teach the way. This is evident in the high standards of the ancient Zen masters. Long ago there was a monk named Tse-kung Chien-yuan under Zen master Fa-yen. Fa-yen asked him: "Tse-kung, how long have you been in this monastery?" Tse-kung answered: "I have been here three years." Fa-yen: "You are younger than me. Why don't you ever ask me about Buddhism?" Tse-kung: "I will not lie. While studying under Zen master Ch'ing-feng, I understood the serenity of Buddhism." Fa-yen: "By what words did you gain this understanding?" Tse-kung: "I asked Ch'ing-feng, What is the real self of the trainee? He answered, The God of Fire calls for fire." Fa-yen: "That's a fine expression. But you probably did not understand it." Tse-kung: "The God of Fire belongs to fire. Fire needs fire. It is like saying that the self needs the self. This is how I understood it." Fa-yen: "I see clearly that you did not understand. If Buddhism is like that, it would not have continued until now." This disturbed Tse-kung deeply, and he left there. On the way home he thought: "Fa-yen is an excellent Zen master and the leader of 500 disciples. He has pointed out my fault. There must be a valuable point in his words." Tse-kung then returned to Fa-yen's monastery. Repenting and giving his salutation, he asked: "What is the real self of the trainee?" Fa-yen answered: "The God of Fire calls for fire." On hearing this, Tse-kung was fully enlightened about Buddhism. Obviously one does not know Buddhism by merely understanding that this self is the Buddha. If this is Buddhism, Fa-yen could not have guided Tse-kung in the manner described above, nor would he have given the advice he did. On first visiting a Zen master, you should ask for the rules of training. Only practice zazen earnestly and avoid cluttering your mind with superficial knowledge. The unexcelled method of Buddhism will then bear fruit.

17. Q: In India and China-from ancient times to now-some Zen masters were enlightened by the sound of a stone striking bamboo, and others had their minds cleared by seeing the color of plum blossoms. Even the great teacher Sakyamuni was enlightened by seeing the morning star.

The venerable Ananda saw the truth in a stick falling. In addition after the sixth patriarch many Zen masters of the five schools were enlightened by a single word. Did all of these persons practice zazen?

A: From ancient times until now all those who have been enlightened by seeing color or hearing sound practiced zazen without zazen and immediately became unexcelled.

18. Q: In India and China men had inner integrity, and because culture was widespread, trainees were able to understand Buddhism when it was taught to them. In our country, from ancient times, many people have lacked superior intellect; it has been difficult to store the right seeds of wisdom. This comes from the barbaric current. It is very regrettable. Again the priests in this country are inferior to laymen in other countries. Everybody in Japan is foolish and narrow-minded. People cling tightly to worldly merit and hunger for the superficial good. Can such people quickly attain enlightenment about Buddhism even if they practice zazen?

A: It is as you say. The people in this country have neither knowledge nor integrity. Even if they are shown the true law, they change its sweet taste to poison. They tend to seek fame and profit and find it difficult to free themselves from attachments. But to become enlightened about Buddhism, we cannot rely on the worldly knowledge of human beings and heaven. Even during the time of the Buddha, those who enlightened the four results (includes the Arhats) by handball and those who enlightened the great path by the kesa were foolish and crazy. But they found the way to free themselves from delusion by the help of right faith. Again a woman trainee who waited with a prepared meal was enlightened by seeing the silent sitting of a foolish old priest. None of these cases depend on knowledge. They do not rely on scholarship, words, or speech. They all underline help through right faith. In the some 2,000 years since the birth of Buddhism, it spread to various countries. Its appeal was not limited to highly cultured nations or to people who were clever and wealthy. The true law of the Buddha, with its indeterminate power for good, will spread throughout the world when the right chance comes. All who train with right faith will be enlightened equally with no gap between the wise and foolish. Don't imagine that because Japan is not a highly cultured country and because its people lack knowledge, it is not ready for Buddhism. You must realize that all human beings have the seed of wisdom in abundance. Only there is little recognition of this fact. People do not train with right faith because they do not adequately recognize the essence of Buddhism and lack experience in practical application.

These questions and answers seem unwarranted. But I have tried to help those with poor eyesight to see a flower where nothing appeared before. For in this country the gist of zazen training has not been transmitted, and those who want to know about it are made sorrowful. Therefore, gathering what I saw and heard in China and recording the essence of the Zen masters, I would like to guide those who seek training. I would also like to teach the rules of the Zen monasteries and the rituals of the temples, but I have no time. These things cannot be described simply. Though our country is east of the sea and far from India, the Buddhism of the west was transmitted here about the time of the emperors Kinmei and Yomei. This was our good fortune. But because names, forms, things, and relations become tangled, we lose direction in training.

Now I will take my simple robe and bowl and make my abode among the reed-wrapped rocks of blue and white. Here, while I sit and train true Zen Buddhism - Buddhism transcending the Buddha manifests itself, and with this the object of training it fulfilled. This is the teaching of the Buddha and the style left behind by Mahakasyapa. The rules for this zazen depends on Fukanzazengi, which was transcribed during the Karoku period. To spread Buddhism within a country one must get the permission of the king. But in the light of the Buddha's transmission at Grdhrakuta there emerged kings and nobles and ministers and generals, who appeared in various countries, who gratefully received the guidance of the Buddha, and who did not forget the original spirit that preserved the Buddhism of former ages. All places where the teaching has spread are the Buddha's land. So to spread the way of the Buddhas and patriarchs there is no point in selecting the place or awaiting good conditions. Do not think that today is the beginning. I have, therefore, gathered this record and left it for the superior seeker of Buddhism and for serious trainees who wander here and there in search for the way.

Time-Mid-autumn, 1231

Dogen, Transmitter of the Law

From China

Guidelines for Studying the Way

1

You should arouse the thought of enlightenment.

The thought of enlightenment has many names but they all refer to one and the same mind.

Ancestor Nagarjuna said, "The mind that fully sees into the uncertain world of birth and death is called the thought of enlightenment."

Thus if we maintain this mind, this mind can become the thought of enlightenment.

Indeed, when you understand the discontinuity the notion of self does not come into being, ideas of name and gain to not arise. Fearing the swift passage of the sunlight, practice the way as though saving your head from fire. Reflecting on this ephemeral life, make endeavor in the manner of Buddha raising his foot.

When you hear a song of praise sung by a kinnara god or a kalavinka bird, let it be as the evening breeze brushing against your ears. If you see the beautiful face of Maoqiang or Xishi, let it be like the morning dewdrops coming into your sight. Freedom from the ties of sound and form naturally accords with the essence of the way-seeking mind.

If in the past or present, you hear about students of small learning or meet people with limited views, often they have fallen into the pit of fame and profit and have forever missed the buddha way in their life. What a pity! How regrettable! You should not ignore this.

Even if you read the sutras of the expedient or complete teaching, or transmit the scriptures of the exoteric or esoteric schools, without throwing away name and gain it cannot be called arousing the thought of enlightenment.

Some of these people say, "The thought of enlightenment is the mind of supreme, perfect enlightenment. Do not be concerned with the cultivation of fame or profit."

Some of them say, "The thought of enlightenment is the insight that each thought contains three thousand realms."

Some of them say, "The thought of enlightenment is the mind of entering the buddha realm."

Such people do not yet know and mistakenly slander the thought of enlightenment. They are remote from the buddha way.

Try to reflect on the mind concerned only with your own gain. Does this one thought blend with the nature and attributes of the three thousand realms? Does this one thought realize the dharma gate of being unborn? There is only the deluded thought of greed for name and love of gain. There is nothing which could be taken as the thought of enlightenment.

From ancient times sages have attained the way and realized dharma. Although as an expedient teaching they lived ordinary lives, still they had no distorted thought of fame or profit. Not even attached to dharma, how could they have worldly attachment?

The thought of enlightenment, as was mentioned, is the mind which sees into impermanence. This is most fundamental, and not at all the same as the mind pointed to by confused people. The understanding that each thought is unborn or the insight that each thought contains three thousand realms is excellent practice after arousing the thought of enlightenment. This should not be mistaken.

Just forget yourself for now and practice inwardly—this is one with the thought of enlightenment. We see that the sixty-two views are based on self. So when a notion of self arises, sit quietly and contemplate it. Is there a real basis inside or outside your body now? Your body with hair and skin is just inherited from your father and mother. From beginning to end a drop of blood or lymph is empty. So none of these are the self. What about mind, thought, awareness, and knowledge? Or the breath going in and out, which ties a lifetime together: what is it after all? None of these are the self either. How could you be attached to any of them? Deluded people are attached to them. Enlightened people are free of them.

You figure there is self where there is no self. You attache to birth where there is no birth. You do not practice the buddha way, which should be practiced. You do not cut off the worldly mind, which should be cut off. Avoiding the true teaching and pursuing the groundless teaching, how could you not be mistaken?

2

Once you see or hear the true teaching, you should practice it without fail.

One phrase offered by a loyal servant can have the power to alter the course of the nation. One word given by a buddha ancestor cannot fail to turn people's minds. The unwise ruler does not adopt the servant's advice. One who does not step forward cannot accept the buddha's teaching. If you are unbending, you cannot stop floating along in birth and death. If appropriate advice is not heeded, governing with virtue cannot be realized.

3

In the buddha way, you should always enter enlightenment through practice.

A worldly teacher says, "Through study one can gain wealth." Buddha says, "Within practice there is enlightenment."

It is unheard-of that without studying someone should earn wealth or that without practicing someone should attain enlightenment. Though practice varies—initiated by faith or dharma knowledge, with emphasis on sudden or gradual enlightenment—you always depend on practice to go beyond enlightenment. Though study can be superficial or profound, and students can be sharp or dull, accumulated studying earns wealth. This does not necessarily depend on the king's excellence or inability, nor should it depend on one's having good or bad luck. If someone were to get wealth without studying, how could he transmit the way in which ancient kings, in times of either order or disorder, ruled the country? If you were to gain realization without practice, how could you comprehend the Tathagata's teaching of delusion and enlightenment.

You should know that arousing practice in the midst of delusion, you attain realization before you recognize it. At this time you first know that the raft of discourse is like yesterday's dream, and you finally cut off your old understanding bound up in the vines and serpents of words. This is not made to happen by Buddha, but is accomplished by your all-encompassing effort.

Moreover, what practice calls forth is enlightenment; your treasure house does not come from outside. How enlightenment functions is through practice; how could actions of mind-ground go astray? So if you turn the eye of enlightenment and reflect back on the realm of practice, nothing in particular hits the eye, and you just see white clouds for ten thousand miles. If you arouse practice as thought climbing the steps of enlightenment, not even a speck of dust will support your feet; you will be as far from true practice as heaven is from earth. Now step back and leap beyond the buddha land.

This portion was written on the night day, third month, second year of Tempuku [1234].

4

You should not practice Buddha's teaching with the idea of gain.

The practice of Buddha's teaching is always done by receiving the essential instructions of a master, not by following your own ideas. In fact, Buddha's teaching cannot be attained by having ideas or not having ideas. Only when the mind of pure practice coincides with the way will body and mind be calm. If body and mind are not yet calm, they will not be at ease. When body and mind are not at ease, thorns grow on the path of realization.

So that pure practice and the way coincide, how should we proceed? Proceed with the mind which neither grasps nor rejects, the mind unconcerned with name or gain. Do not practice buddha-dharma with the thought that it is to benefit others.

People in the present world, even those practicing the buddha-dharma, have a mind which is far apart from the way. They practice what others praise and admire, even though they know it does not accord with the way. They reject and do not practice what others fail to honor and praise, even though they know it is the true way. How painful! You should try to quiet your mind and investigate whether these attitudes are buddha-dharma or not. You may be completely ashamed. The eye of the sage illuminates this.

Clearly, buddha-dharma is not practiced for one's own sake, and even less for the sake of fame and profit. Just for the sake of buddha-dharma you should practice it.

All buddhas' compassion and sympathy for sentient beings are neither for their own sake nor for others. It is just the nature of buddha-dharma. Isn't it apparent that insects and animals nurture their offspring, exhausting themselves with painful labors, yet in the end have no reward when their offspring are grown? In this way the compassion of small creatures for their offspring naturally resembles the thought of all buddhas for sentient beings.

The inconceivable dharma of all buddhas is not compassion alone, but compassion is the basis of the various teachings that appear universally. Already we are children of the buddhas. Why not follow their lead?

Students! Do not practice buddha-dharma for your own sake. Do not practice buddha-dharma for name and gain. Do not practice buddha-dharma to attain miraculous effects. Practice buddha-dharma solely for the sake of buddha-dharma. This is the way.

5

You should seek a true teacher to practice Zen and study the way.

A teacher of old said, "If the beginning is not right, myriad practices will be useless.

How true these words are! Practice of the way depends on whether the guiding master is a true teacher or not.

The disciple is like wood, and the teacher resembles a craftsman. Even if the wood is good, without a skilled craftsman its extraordinary beauty is not revealed. Even if the wood is bent, placed in skilled hands its splendid merits immediately appear. By this you should know that realization is genuine or false depending on whether the teacher is true or incompetent.

But in our country from ancient times, there have not been many true teachers. How do we know this is so? We can guess by studying their sayings, just as we can scoop up stream water and find out about its source. In our country from ancient times, various teachers have written books and instructed their disciples, offering their teaching to human and heavenly beings. Their words are immature, their discourse has not yet ripened. They have not yet reached the peak of study; how could they have come close to the state of realization? They only transmitted words and phrases or taught the changing of Buddha's name. They count other people's treasure day and night, not having half a penny themselves.

Previous teachers are responsible for this. They taught people to seek enlightenment outside mind, or to seek rebirth in another land. Confusion starts from this. Mistaken ideas come from this.

Though you give good medicine, if you do not teach a method of controlling its use it will make one sicker than taking poison. In our country since ancient times it seems as though no one has given good medicine. There are as yet no masters who can control the poisonous effects of medicine. Because of this, it is difficult to penetrate birth and death. How can old age and death be overcome.

All this is the teacher's fault, not at all the fault of the disciples. The reason is that those who are teachers let people neglect the root and go out on the limbs. Before they establish true understanding, they are absorbed only in their own thinking, and they unwittingly cause others to enter a realm of confusion. What a pity! Those who are teachers do not yet understand this confusion. How could students realize what is right and wrong?

How sad! In this small, remote nation buddha-dharma has not yet spread widely. True masters have not yet appeared here. If you wish to study the unsurpassed buddha way, you have to travel a great distance to call on the masters in Song China, and you have to reflect deeply n the vital road outside thought. Until you have a true teacher, it is better not to study.

Regardless of his age or experience, a true teacher is simply one who has apprehended the true teaching and attained the authentic teacher's seal of realization. He does not put texts first or understanding first, but his capacity is outside any framework and his spirit freely penetrates the nodes in bamboo. He is not concerned with self-views and does not stagnate in emotional feelings. Thus, practice and understanding are in mutual accord.

ABOUT THE AUTHOR

I am not important; only the words are important.

Once there is a deep understanding of what the words point to, the words likewise become unimportant in much the same way that the address is unimportant once there is arrival at the destination.

Printed in Great Britain
by Amazon